W9-BEY-303

"I was enthralled by this fine book. . . . Garrity has written a heartfelt elegy to his parents and brother framing his emotions and reflections amid the rugged and inspiring links of Carne. A sense of loss shadows the book but also self-discovery, hope, and redemptive love. . . . There's much to relish in this book and you don't have to have played Carne or Irish links or even been to Ireland to appreciate it. . . . Garrity has taken it all in and the reader goes along for a wonderful, insightful ride.

—Terry Moore, *Michigan Golfer*

"[*Ancestral Links* is] part memoir—the recollections of both his father and brother, both recently dead of cancer, are poignant and revealing—part golfer's travelogue, and part search for roots. . . . Garrity's humility and ingratiating style soften the inevitable envy problem (Why him and not me?) that often makes reading golf travelogues a mixed blessing."

—*Booklist*

"Part family memoir, part travelogue, Garrity offers some wry insights into the sport of golf and the often profound reasons why hitting a small ball into a hole means so much to so many people—and why they would travel to the ends of the earth (or at least to Scotland and Ireland) just to have the honor and pleasure of doing so." —*Chicago Tribune*

"*Sports Illustrated* senior writer John Garrity retraced his roots the old-fashioned way: by poring over documents, hunting down distant relatives, and playing some of the British Isles' finest courses. Who said you can't mix family business with pleasure?" —*Golf Magazine*

"[Garrity] is a formidable talent. . . . After all, this is a man who, in an erstwhile *SI* series called 'Mats Only,' found entertaining things to write about his compulsion for beating balls at practice ranges. In *Ancestral Links,* his themes—particularly a messy family lineage and mortality—are far weightier. Garrity is more than capable of carrying that load." —*Golfweek*

"Garrity is part Irish, part Scottish, and all raconteur."

—Hole by Hole.com

ANCESTRAL LINKS

A GOLF OBSESSION
SPANNING GENERATIONS

JOHN GARRITY

NAL NEW AMERICAN LIBRARY

New American Library
Published by New American Library, a division of
Penguin Group (USA) Inc., 375 Hudson Street,
New York, New York 10014, USA
Penguin Group (Canada), 90 Eglinton Avenue East, Suite 700, Toronto,
Ontario M4P 2Y3, Canada (a division of Pearson Penguin Canada Inc.)
Penguin Books Ltd., 80 Strand, London WC2R 0RL, England
Penguin Ireland, 25 St. Stephen's Green, Dublin 2,
Ireland (a division of Penguin Books Ltd.)
Penguin Group (Australia), 250 Camberwell Road, Camberwell, Victoria 3124,
Australia (a division of Pearson Australia Group Pty. Ltd.)
Penguin Books India Pvt. Ltd., 11 Community Centre, Panchsheel Park,
New Delhi - 110 017, India
Penguin Group (NZ), 67 Apollo Drive, Rosedale, North Shore 0632,
New Zealand (a division of Pearson New Zealand Ltd.)
Penguin Books (South Africa) (Pty.) Ltd., 24 Sturdee Avenue,
Rosebank, Johannesburg 2196, South Africa

Penguin Books Ltd., Registered Offices:
80 Strand, London WC2R 0RL, England

Published by New American Library, a division of Penguin Group (USA) Inc.
Previously published in a New American Library hardcover edition.

First New American Library Trade Paperback Printing, February 2010
10 9 8 7 6 5 4 3 2 1

Copyright © John Garrity, 2009
All rights reserved

See page 293 for author copyrights and permissions.

[NAL] REGISTERED TRADEMARK—MARCA REGISTRADA

New American Library Trade Paperback ISBN: 978-0-451-22907-6

The Library of Congress has cataloged the hardcover edition of this title as follows:

Garrity, John.
    Ancestral links: a golf obsession spanning generations/John Garrity.
        p. cm.
    ISBN 978-0-451-22591-7
    1. Golf courses-History.   I. Title.
    GV975.G34   2009
    796.352068-dc22   2008046340

Set in Adobe Garamond
Designed by Spring Hoteling

Printed in the United States of America

Without limiting the rights under copyright reserved above, no part of this publication may be repro-
duced, stored in or introduced into a retrieval system, or transmitted, in any form, or by any means
(electronic, mechanical, photocopying, recording, or otherwise), without the prior written permission
of both the copyright owner and the above publisher of this book.

PUBLISHER'S NOTE
While the author has made every effort to provide accurate telephone numbers and Internet addresses
at the time of publication, neither the publisher nor the author assumes any responsibility for errors, or
for changes that occur after publication. Further, publisher does not have any control over and does not
assume any responsibility for author or third-party Web sites or their content.

The scanning, uploading, and distribution of this book via the Internet or via any other means without
the permission of the publisher is illegal and punishable by law. Please purchase only authorized electronic editions, and do not participate in or encourage electronic piracy of copyrighted materials. Your
support of the author's rights is appreciated.

To my discovered cousin, Anne Hughes,
who is too wonderful for words.

ANCESTRAL LINKS

PROLOGUE

The burial urn had caught a pretty good lie. The ground was flat, and the lawn smelled of a recent mowing. Grass clippings clung to my shoes. It was a warm, sunny afternoon. The cherry trees were in bloom, their pink branches swaying gently in a one-club wind.

The urn was a polished walnut box with a cross carved on the lid. A man in a brown truck had delivered it to my Kansas City home a week or so before, and I had wasted no time opening the package. I removed six layers of bubble wrap and a soft drawstring bag to get to the prize.

I whistled in admiration.

"It's fantastic," I said to my wife, Pat. I ran my fingertips over the box, admiring the color and grain. "It's almost *too* beautiful."

Pat had found the urn on the Web site of the New Melleray Abbey in Peosta, Iowa. Trappist monks in belted robes had labored over it for days, maybe even weeks. I pictured the monks at their work benches, doing the Lord's work with hand planes, corner clamps and squeeze bottles of yellow glue.

But now the urn was in Wisconsin—basking in the sun on a green square of artificial turf at the edge of a freshly dug hole.

"Daddy loved walnut," said my sister, Terry, who had flown up from Florida for the ceremony. "There was a restaurant at the old Muehlbach Hotel that had walnut paneling, and he'd always comment on it and run his hands over it."

I smiled and took Pat's hand. There were maybe twenty of us gathered at the grave site—friends and relatives from Kansas City, Chicago, and Minneapolis. The editor of the *New Richmond News* stood at a discreet distance, taking notes and photographs.

I had pulled into town the day before with my dad's ashes and my golf clubs in the trunk. I looked to the left as I rolled past the nine-hole New Richmond Links, a meadowland course bounded by three roads and a fenced pasture. A little farther on I caught glimpses of the eighteen-hole New Richmond Golf Club through a wall of trees planted long after my father had left his childhood home. I passed a sign: New Richmond, pop. 7,858.

The number on the sign produced a twinge of guilt. It was not much greater than the number of days that had passed since my father's death. For seventeen years his ashes had sat on a closet shelf in our Kansas City home—in the very room, in fact, where he had died of lymphoma at age eighty-five.

We certainly meant no disrespect by storing Dad's ashes with the office supplies. His funeral mass, staged by my church liturgist wife, had gotten favorable reviews. Pat had put his old wing chair at the front of the church, next to the casket. On a side table she laid out his bifocals, a bag of chocolate-covered caramels, and a few of his favorite books—Maugham's *The Razor's Edge*, O'Connor's *The Last Hurrah*, Forester's *Admiral Hornblower in the West Indies*, and Rex Lardner Jr.'s *Out of the Bunker and Into the Trees*. Against the chair she propped Dad's old sand wedge, the club he had gripped and regripped while watching episodes of *Matlock*, *Wheel of Fortune*, and

Murder, She Wrote. At the mass, Pat brought tears to everyone's eyes by singing "An Irish Blessing"—but not before Michael Farrell, editor of the *National Catholic Reporter*, had won over the audience with an Irish-accented reading from P. G. Wodehouse's *The Golf Omnibus*.

But it had always been our intention to return Dad's remains to the small town where his golf mania had taken root. So there we all were at last, on an afternoon in spring, in the cemetery behind New Richmond's Immaculate Conception Church. Looking up, I watched a westbound jet drag its contrail across the sky. "Beautiful day," I whispered to Pat.

Looking around, I scanned the headstones and monuments for the now-familiar names: Padden, Casey, Hughes, McNally, Lynch, Barrett, Reilly, Lavelle. Dad's marker, installed according to my instructions, was a small granite stone set flush with the ground:

JOHN B. "JACK" GARRITY

1905–1991

A few feet away, two older stones marked the graves of my paternal great-grandparents, Michael Garrity (1830–1883) and Elizabeth Garrity (1826–1909).

A little voice piped up: "Who's in there?"

My four-year-old granddaughter, Madeline Olsen, and her six-year-old brother, Jack, were standing at the edge of the excavation, staring at the cremation urn. Maddie had asked the question, and now she looked up at the circle of grown-ups, who chuckled indulgently.

"It's Grandpa Jack," said her mother—my daughter, Teresa.

Maddie leaned forward to peer into the depths. "Are you going to put that box in the hole?"

This time she looked to Father Jim Brinkman, standing on the other side of the grave. But I didn't hear the amused pastor's reply. Instead, I heard my father's fulsome laugh and imagined his response: "That's the object of the game, Junior."

I stared at the beautiful walnut box, sitting at the edge of the hole, and pictured God's hands reaching down with the heavenly putter for the tap-in.

The following morning, a Saturday, I slipped away from the motel and drove out Business 64 to the New Richmond Golf Club. I parked at the top of the hill in a shady spot and walked around the cedar-sided club-house to the pro shop, where an assistant pro, forewarned, handed me the key to a golf cart.

"I won't be long," I said.

I took my pick from a row of electric carts and drove back up the as-phalt path to the parking lot. Stopping only to pick up some items from my car, I steered the cart downhill through the trees, around the superinten-dent's shed, and out onto the course.

It was a golf course my dad would not have recognized. The tree-lined fairways were silky green, the bordering roughs a darker hue. The greens? I won't insult your intelligence by comparing them to the greens at Augusta National, but New Richmond's greens would hold up for speed and appear-ance against those at your better private clubs. The course was definitely prettier than most. Flowering trees and shrubs drew the eye with their fat splashes of pink, white and lavender; bright tulips rose out of memorial flower beds. The white bark of birch trees stood out against a perimeter of tall pines and spruces. My dad's affectionate appraisal of his hometown track—"possibly the lousiest damn course in Wisconsin"—was clearly out-of-date.

It took no more than two or three minutes to reach the northeast corner of the property, and even less time to find what I was looking for. I parked thirty yards or so behind the eighth green, where trees partially hid the grassy berm of the Soo Line railroad tracks, and walked straight to my tar-get: an old patch of concrete. Roughly six feet square and obscured by en-croaching turfgrass, the concrete was an anomaly in that sylvan setting. Was it part of an old foundation? A loading dock? A granary floor? Whatever it was, the concrete must have been left there for a reason. A lone worker on a Bobcat could have broken it up and hauled it off in minutes.

I knelt at the head of the slab and jabbed a hand spade into the soft turf, making repeated stabs until I had cut a rectangle a foot long and six inches wide. I carefully lifted the plug of turf with the spade and set it to one side. I then used a hand hoe to deepen the excavation. The walls of my hole were grave-digger straight. The displaced dirt formed a mound of perfect brown topsoil—a loamy substrate that probably hadn't been disturbed for decades.

When I was satisfied with the hole, I tossed aside the hoe and dusted off my hands. I picked up a clear plastic jar with a snap-down lid that I had bought at a dime store. Reaching into my pocket, I pulled out a golf ball: a shiny Top-Flite XL with a custom logo: BELMULLET GOLF CLUB, 1925–2000. I stared at the ball for a moment and then dropped it in the jar.

I reached into my pocket and pulled out another ball. This one was a Titleist NXT Tour ball with an owner's identifying mark: a single green dot. I stared at this ball until the thud of a shot landing on the eighth green interrupted my reverie. I dropped the second ball in the jar and snapped down the lid.

What do you say when you're burying golf balls? I merely observed a minute of respectful silence and then picked up the hand hoe. But as I began pushing dirt back into the hole, the refrain of a song played in my head: *Don't let me come home a stranger. . . . I couldn't stand to be a stranger.* I would have hummed it, but a big, burly guy in a University of Wisconsin sweatshirt had walked onto the eighth green and was lining up his putt. I stopped filling the hole and sat back on my haunches, watching.

A gallery of one.

CHAPTER 1

The whole course has a raw, untamed appearance, with its great wounded dunes spilling sand and still prone to move under the command of the relentless winds.

—from John de St. Jorre's *Legendary Golf Links of Ireland*

Here come the lambs to slaughter!"

Chris Birrane grinned as four men staggered onto the first tee, chins on their chests. The wind was blowing west-southwest at twenty-five to thirty knots, gusting to forty, and if you wonder why I use nautical parlance, try playing Carne on some cold gray morning when the clouds hang low and the great dunes resemble Atlantic swells in a hurricane. Chris had the collar of his quilted jacket turned up. He had a sailor's watch cap pulled over his ears. Take away his clipboard and cigar, and you might have mistaken him for a deck hand on the Shannon car ferry.

I had picked a good morning to watch Chris perform his starter duties. "We've got a couple of golfing societies, some Americans," he said, "and anybody else who wanders in from the road. I'm here to discourage them." Irish golfing societies, he explained, were golf clubs in the most fundamental sense—that is, their members came together to play golf, not to own or operate golf facilities. There were hundreds of golfing societies, many of them formed by professional organizations or large corporations. Golfing societies sponsored leagues, staged local competitions and organized coach trips to golf shrines like Old Head, Lahinch and Carne. "You can't get a handicap from a society," Chris said. "For that you have to join a club that's affiliated with the Irish Golfing Union."

Chris turned to the golfers, who were dressed in odd combinations of jeans, corduroys, flannel shirts, sweaters and rain suits. "Come on up, lads, don't be shy." He tilted his head back and squinted, pretending to size them up. "You're looking disgustingly fit for a golf society."

It soon became apparent that Chris was not a starter in the traditional sense, imbued with an officious attitude and armed with a fourteen-point list of rules and prohibitions. Chris was more of an advisor-commentator. When one golfer asked if it was safe to hit toward a husband and wife who were well up the fairway, Chris shrugged and said, "If you're going to hit somebody, hit the man. I don't like arguing with the women." When another fellow sliced his drive into a dark crevasse short of a big dune, Chris offered consolation. "It's not too bad—it's only grass there. And a rope ladder at the bottom to help you get out."

A golfer asked Chris how he had come to be a starter at Carne.

"I have a checkered history," he said. "I was born in London, the son of an immigrant. I came home to Ireland when I was thirteen and finished my education here. Went to college. Got a job. I was an industrial engineer, I did time and motion studies. I went back to England, went from there to Belgium, to Brussels and Antwerp, from there to the Haig, and then Germany, working for the same company. In between, I got married. I had one child at the time and another on the way, and I decided there was too much travel. My young fellow was about a year old, didn't know me from Adam."

He interrupted himself to greet another foursome stepping onto the tee. "You look wonderfully fit," he said. "Are you Mormons?

"Anyway," he resumed, "I wasn't exactly poor at the time, so I decided to come home. My wife was the connection to here. She's from a few miles up the road. I met her in Ballina, I came out here and discovered Erris. We live right on the beach on a big hill overlooking Broadhaven Bay. It's just a fantastic place to live, and that's where I mean to stay until I pop my clogs." He took a breath. "But this was seventeen and a half years ago, and there wasn't an awful lot here then. I took a job with the Dunnes stores and commuted to Ballina, which is our biggest town, I suppose, about forty miles away. I worked there for a while, but it just got to be too much, it wasn't worth it. I went to work for a factory here called Warner's, which has since gone to India or Pakistan or somewhere. They closed down in 2000."

Chris stopped again to watch the golfers hit their tee shots. One of them, a round man in a bright yellow windbreaker, wobbled on his backswing and hit a feeble pop-up that the wind treated like dandelion fluff. That triggered a round of hooting and abuse from his friends.

"A fellow was here a while back," Chris said, stepping forward. "Swung with all his might, hit it straight up in the air. It came down in his shadow. 'Guys,' he says, 'what did I do wrong?' His mate says, 'Crap on the end of the club.'"

Chris mimed a golfer examining a clubhead with a puzzled look. "The guy who hit the shot looks at the clubhead. He says, 'There's no crap on this club.'" Chris shook his head. "'Not that end,' says his mate. 'The other end.'"

Yellow Windbreaker and his friends broke up with laughter.

"I started golf when I couldn't play anything else," Chris said, picking up the story after the foursome had teed off. "I was always in sport, but I considered golf either elitist or something for the older generation. But ten years ago a friend of mine asked me to have a hit of the ball, so I had a hit of the ball. And I was hooked. Joined the club. Started playing, enjoyed it immensely. It became my mistress. Then that factory closed down in town."

"Warner's?" I had heard about the late, lamented clothes factory. At its peak it had employed more than a hundred workers.

Chris nodded. "I was doing nothing, really, a bit of freelance work. And then a job came up here as the starter, course ranger and gofer. I jumped at the chance." He took a puff on his cigar, expelling a cloud of smoke that peeled off in the wind.

Next on the tee was a Canadian trio—a dentist and his wife from Toronto and their friend, a car dealer. The threesome took golf holidays every summer, alternating between Scotland and Ireland. The wife, mistaking me for a local, asked me to look at her scorecard. "How do you pronounce the name of this hole?" She pointed a blunt, unpolished fingernail at a string of cryptic syllables—cryptic, that is, if you didn't speak Gaelic.

I said, "I'd pronounce it *Loch Easy.*"

"You're not Irish!" She smiled and yanked the card away.

"Try him." I nodded toward Chris, who, in answer to the car dealer's query about the location of the first green, was pointing toward Newfoundland.

Chris pronounced *Log 'a Si* for the woman, and when she said she had heard different versions of the legend behind it, he said, "My versions are absolutely the best, and they're honest ones. When I tell you there's faeries in the hollow, there's faeries in the hollow. I've seen them." He looked over one shoulder and then the other, as if he didn't want to be overheard. "There was a group of four Canadians once, lovely guys—two brain surgeons, a specialist in some other area, and a dentist. I was caddying on the occasion, and they were good golfers, but just out for a laugh. They were asking about the names of different holes we have here, and one of them was the fifteenth hole, *Tir na nóg,* which is 'Island of Youth,' if you like. They said, 'Can you explain that? What's that about?' I said, 'Well, every twenty-one years an island appears out in the bay. If you're lucky enough to see it, you gain eternal youth. You don't age.' They gave me that look—you know, skeptical. 'No, it's been told for a long time,' I said. 'It's to do with the Children of Lir and all that stuff. About every twenty-one years the island appears, but it comes at weird times, sometimes in a mist, and you may not see it.' So we have a laugh and hit the balls, and we're away down the fairway. And one guy comes up to me—a brain surgeon, literally—walks up and says, 'Excuse me. Is that story true?' "

Chris laughed. "I said, 'Absolutely!' "

The fairway had cleared, so Chris stepped back. The dentist and his wife pull-hooked their drives, canceling out the left-to-right wind and sloping terrain. In other words, they found the fairway. The car dealer, on the other hand, blasted one high and straight, but down the right side. The wind seized his ball and flung it on top of the nasty dune that guards the dogleg.

"I think you'll find that," Chris said reassuringly. "Have you got a spare ball with you?"

The Canadians grinned as they stumbled off the tee. Immediately, four middle-aged American men came up the steps, looking first to the left, where a cipher of a fairway disappeared into the windswept banks, and then to the right, where Chris waited with his cigar and clipboard.

I watched with a smile, thinking *What a start*.

CHAPTER 2

In Central County Mayo, about twenty miles east of Castlebar, is the village of Knock. The Chapel of Knock has been a place of pilgrimage since an apparition of the Virgin Mary, Saint Joseph and Saint John appeared in 1879. Even though it was raining that day, the area around the figures is said to have remained dry.

—from Richard Phinney and Scott Whitley's Links of Heaven

A sunny afternoon in September 2007. I popped the trunk of my rental car, put my right foot on the bumper and slipped the knot on my shoelace. About a dozen cars were parked on the blacktop lot, which sloped away from a two-story clubhouse nestled in the dunes. Below the lot, to my right, the land rolled off toward Blacksod Bay and Belmullet town. Grazing cattle and scattered farmhouses filled the foreground. Purple mountains defined the distant shore.

As I laced up my ratty old FootJoys, I glanced at the pole-mounted windsock, an orange-and-white-striped oracle fluttering and buckling in a westerly breeze. The windsock was a navigation aid for pilots approaching Carne's helicopter pad. It was to this circle of asphalt, at the edge of the car park, that VIPs descended from the sky, scaring the cows and donkeys with their mighty *throp-throp-throp* and grass-flattening downdraft. Film actor Hugh Grant, former FBI director Robert Mueller, British Open and Masters champion Mark O'Meara, plumbing magnate Herb Kohler and legendary golf architect Pete Dye—they all had arrived by chopper.

Or so I'd been told. Most days, the pad attracted corncrakes and ravens looking for a place to warm their feathers.

I slapped a cap on my head, hoisted my golf bag out of the trunk and stood it up on the tarmac. I put my car keys, pocket change and folded euros in the zipper pouch above the bag's handle. I tossed my cheap pay-as-you-go mobile phone into the trunk. I extracted a red-and-white business card from my wallet—JOHN GARRITY, SENIOR WRITER, SPORTS ILLUSTRATED, TIME & LIFE BLDG, NEW YORK, NY 10020—and slipped it into the right front pocket of my navy Dockers. I reached into one of the bag's waterproof pouches, felt around between the old golf gloves, scorecards and iPod earbuds, and finally came up with a logoed ballpoint pen (YOUR MARRIOTT AWAITS). I put the pen in my left front pocket.

I shut the trunk, swung the bag straps over my shoulders and marched up the hill to the clubhouse.

The golf shop at the Carne Golf Links is hidden in a breezeway underneath the clubhouse. I call it a golf shop and not a pro shop because Carne, uniquely among world-class golf courses, does not have a resident golf professional. Tee times, green fees and merchandise sales are handled by a small staff under the direction of Mary Walsh, a head-turning blonde with administrative skills. Mary was alone behind the counter, brow furrowed in concentration as she studied budget data on a computer monitor.

"How does the back nine look?" I asked.

"It should be wide-open." She tapped a couple of keys, and the day log appeared on the screen, a grid of boxes arranged along a time line. "We had a golfing society this morning, but they've finished and gone." She looked over her shoulder at a bank of CCTV monitors, which showed no activity on the first or tenth tees.

"Today could be the day," I said, backing toward the door.

Out in the breezeway, I unzipped the two bottom pouches of my stand bag. From one I withdrew a handful of tees and a divot-repair tool. They went into my right front pocket. From the other I removed five used golf balls, none bearing the mark of the same manufacturer, and a green suede golf glove of some sentimental value. The balls went into my left front pants pocket, alongside the pen. The glove I stuffed into my left hip pocket.

Shouldering the bag again, I walked up a short, steep path, which took me out of the shadows and onto a sun-washed promontory. As always, this first view of the course produced a delightful hollow sensation in my stomach. From the first and tenth tees the land plunges into shadow and then climbs again, the northwest view blocked by a line of tall, menacing dunes. The first hole, a short par 4, doglegs to the right around a big dune, its poorly defined fairway canted left to right in a nasty conspiracy with the prevailing wind. The tenth, a par 5, requires a blind uphill drive between bookend dunes, the fairway disappearing over the crest of the hill.

I paused only briefly to take in this inviting aspect. Circling around the tenth tee, I walked straight up the tenth fairway. When I reached the top of the rise, I turned to look back at the clubhouse, the sparkling bay and the distant hills, thinking *Dad would have loved this*. I then walked on down the hill toward the green, which occupies a natural bowl. The red flag, flapping gently in the breeze, stood out like a jewel against the backdrop of a forty-foot dune. Some afternoons I stopped about a hundred fifty yards out and warmed up by hitting a ball or two into the green.

This time, I kept walking. I took the steep path to the left of the tenth green and climbed up into the dunes. The trail curved to the right and then leveled off near the top. Puffing a bit from the climb, I set my bag down and took the railroad-tie stairs up to the eleventh tee. It was like stepping onto a cloud. The narrow canyon of the eleventh fairway lay in shadow, sixty feet below. Farther on, beyond a wire fence, a great swath of cow pasture sloped down to the Atlantic Ocean, which shimmered like blue steel under a hammer. Some afternoons I stopped at eleven to hit two or three drives—or simply to look out upon the sullen profiles of Inishkea, Inishglora, and the other offshore islands. But not today. I shouldered my bag and followed the trail as it plunged to the valley floor. The dunes on either side crowded in like walls, their steep sides terraced with narrow ledges sculpted by generations of sheep and cattle grazing on the Carne commonage. ("*Cows* climbed these dunes?" I asked amused locals. "How did they turn around?") Walking into sunshine, I glanced up and to the right toward the eleventh green, which sat atop a ridge some forty feet in the air. But I veered again, this time taking a low trail to the left through knee-high marron grass. That put me on a hidden track blazed by maintenance vehicles. I followed this rutted road for a hundred yards or so as it wound through sand and scrub, emerging finally at the seventeenth fairway. Peering around a dune to make sure no golfers were hitting off the tee, I walked on toward the sea. I was puffing again as I scrambled up the last steep slope. I carried my golf bag onto the seventeenth tee and stood it up behind the white tee markers.

Looking around, I drew a deep breath. Held it. Exhaled.

I strolled back past the blue tee markers and took in the sweeping coastline. A flock of birds fluttered chaotically above the adjacent cow pasture, darting and diving; they looked confused, leaderless. Beyond them, under a faint line of distant clouds, a solitary freighter rode the horizon. It looked like a bird on a wire.

Turning away, I fished the green glove out of my back pocket and tugged it onto my left hand. I then bent down for a pinch of grass, which I tossed in the air, watching the little blades drift from right to left as they spun to the ground.

Friends used to ask me for directions to Carne. "It's in the most remote corner of the Republic of Ireland," I answered, "forty miles past the EARTH ENDS HERE sign. You fly to Dublin or Shannon and drive west and north to County Mayo, maybe stopping for directions in Westport or Ballina. Then you travel west across this treeless bog that will scare you with its bleakness. . . ."

Then George Geraghty, a member of the Carne greenkeeping crew, gave me a shorter description. He said, "We're at the end of the rainbow."

I'm a passenger in a car in Colorado in the dark. Jim Engh is at the wheel. It's autumn 2002, and Engh, a golf architect of growing reputation, has just returned from a golf trip to Ireland. The highlight of his trip was a new links course on the Atlantic coast, a wild, untamed masterpiece called the Carne Golf

Links. "My favorite course in the whole world is Ballybunion," he says, naming a venerable links in County Clare, "but Carne comes a close second."

The name means nothing to me. "Where's it located?"

"It's in a little out-of-the-way village that nobody ever heard of. A place called Belmullet."

My head whips around. "Belmullet?"

I have heard of Belmullet. I have even been to Belmullet. On a two-day visit to the Mullet Peninsula in 1989, my wife and I were introduced to at least a dozen Geraghtys. One of them, a farmer's wife, took us out behind her white-washed house and pointed over the fields to a rocky beach on Blacksod Bay, saying, "That's where your great-grandfather got on the little boat to go out to the big boat to sail to America." We drove past a golf course on that visit, but it was a rudimentary layout, a little nine-holer with a port-a-cabin clubhouse and wire fences strung around the greens.

I am skeptical, therefore, of Engh's claim that my ancestral home has a world-class golf course. A few days after my Colorado trip, I go on line and type "Belmullet Golf." Within seconds, I am staring at a dreamscape—an aerial photograph of the Carne Golf Links as a heaving sea of dunegrass streaked with sun and shadow. Further clicks of the mouse produce a torrent of encomia. "Quite simply the most stunning discovery I have made in golf," writes Dermot Gilleece in the Irish Times. *Not to be outdone, Keith Ging of* The Express *writes, "If I was limited to one course for the rest of my days, this would be it." The most measured view is that of James E. Finegan, who played Carne while researching his book,* Emerald Fairways and Foam-Flecked Seas. *"I am inclined to go rather far out on a limb for Carne," he writes, "by calling it the singlemost remote great course in the British Isles."*

"Hey, Pat," I call to my wife. "Come look at this."

I looked up from the twirling blades of grass and hitched my pants in conscious emulation of Arnold Palmer. I pulled my driver out of the bag.

The seventeenth at Carne is a 436-yard par 4. You drive over a gully to a fairway that rides a ridge and bends to the right around a plateau of shaggy moguls. The green hides behind these mounds, the only hint of its existence being a solitary sand bunker set into a distant hillside. ("The bunker gives you something to aim at," a club member once told me, so now I stare at the little patch of sand the way Gatsby stared at the distant green light from his lawn in West Egg.) Sliced tee shots plunge into a blowout on the right, a monstrous cauldron of fescue and marron grass that might as well be marked with out-of-bounds stakes. Finding your ball in this wasteland is a fifty-fifty proposition, and the odds of hitting it back up to the fairway on the first try are not much better. Hooked tee shots meet a somewhat better fate, because the thirty-foot cliff on the left side of the fairway is so sheer that most balls reach the valley floor.

Refusing to dwell on either possibility, I teed up a ball, took a couple of brisk waggles and smacked a long, high fade that flirted with the precipice on the left before drifting back. The ball landed in the middle of the fairway and took a nice big hop before rolling to a halt, about 260 yards out. "He took a dangerous line there," said the announcer in my head, "but you can't argue with the result."

I fished in my pocket for another ball, teed it up, and hit a second drive, better than the first. This one, driven straight up the middle with a yard or two of draw, landed near my first drive, bounced once, bounced twice . . . and vanished. That ball, I knew, was either at the edge of the cliff, where the fairway narrowed to about eighteen yards, or over the edge.

Teeing up a third ball, I adjusted my aim a few yards to the right and tried to reprise my second drive. Instead, I got handsy and slapped a listless floater that barely cleared the sandy escarpment, disappearing into the moguls.

I'm the driver of a car in Ireland. It's a sunny afternoon in July 2005. My brother is asleep in the passenger seat. I don't want to wake him, but I've taken the coast road so he can see the cliffs at Céide Fields, County Mayo's answer to the Cliffs of Moher. I pull off the narrow road, steering around some scrambling sheep, and park on a dirt outlook.

"Hey, Tommy." I employ the caddie murmur he taught me when I was ten. "I think you'll want to see this."

He lifts his head and opens his eyes, blinking. It takes him a few seconds to process the image, but then a smile lights his face. Seagulls glide along the tower-

ing walls of primordial stone. Waves crash against the rocks and into blowholes,
launching spume high above the roiling basins.

"I thought I was taking a nap," he says, "but I must have died and gone to
heaven."

We sit for a moment, taking in the postcard view.

"There's the green." I point toward Dun Briste, a sea-stack off the tip of
Dunpatrick Head, a couple of miles away.

"That's the green?" He shoots me a glance. "If that's the green, I don't think
you have enough club."

My first ball was in the middle of the fairway, a few feet from the hundred-fifty-meter marker, a small white paver. I peeled off well short of it and climbed onto the plateau to look for ball number three. I found it right away—it was sitting in a tiny crater full of tangled fescue and withered bluebells—and took an ill-considered swipe with an 8 iron, chunking it about sixty yards.

Annoyed, I returned to the fairway and took a moment to study the seventeenth green. Cut into a huge dune, the long, narrow putting surface bends to the right around yet another nausea-inducing pit. Pulling a 6 iron for the 165-yard shot, I aimed for the center of the green and tried to hit a draw around the mound that blocks the left-front approach. Alas, I hit it slightly thin and a tad right. The ball landed on the fringe and rolled a few yards before toppling off the edge and down the steep bank.

Ball number two, the one that I had bashed over the cliff, hid for a few minutes on a grassy shelf, ten feet below the fairway. Upon finding it, I wedged it halfway to the green, staggered up the slope, and then wedged it again, the ball stopping about twenty feet short of the hole. I found ball number three in thick green rough at the foot of the moguls. I gouged it out with my gap wedge and then watched in disgust as it lost its nerve in midflight and dove into the pit alongside ball number one.

I stood for a moment with my head down. (Sometimes after a bad shot I stare at the spot where the ball was before I disturbed it, as if the ground were somehow accountable. I picked this habit up from certain touring pros.) But I kept my cool. I went down into the greenside hollow with my lob wedge, hit two slashing pitches up to the green, and scampered back up the bank. After some undistinguished putting, I planted the flagstick in the cup, fished the pen out of my pocket, and wrote the following on the back of my business card:

1) 5-5-6 (1 IN F , 1 R, 1 L, 0 GIR)

I shouldered my bag and walked straight back up the seventeenth fairway, humming a tune. When I got to the tee, I gave the sea and the offshore islands another long look. I then teed up a ball, took a couple of free and easy waggles and smacked a high fade into the fairway. "That's just perfect," said the announcer in my head. "He takes half the trouble out of play with that power fade."

Happy with the result, I teed up another ball.

Chapter 3

Many people believe [Belmullet] is called after the fish of that name because of its rather similar shape. More likely it's from the Irish word "Muileat," meaning diamond. The name was later corrupted to Béal an Mhuirthead.

—from Rita Nolan's *Within the Mullet*

The Belmullet town square was a bustling place on a summer afternoon. Cars, trucks and tractors made their slow, cautious loop around a central roundabout that served as a pediment for a twenty-foot column of mortared stone. This column was probably the single-most unattractive piece of public sculpture in Ireland, but it grew on you. The storefronts were a predictable mix: a Londis supermarket, a fast-food takeaway, a hardware store, a café, a Bank of Ireland branch, a corner pub (Denise's), another corner pub (The Corner Pub) and a computer shop. A produce truck was usually parked outside Londis, its side panels folded back to display pallets of locally grown strawberries and asparagus alongside piles of oranges, plums and grapes from Africa. In good weather, children lined up at the window of an ice-cream truck. Their moms, bank cards in hand, lined up at a sidewalk ATM.

My two-bedroom flat was just off the square on Barrack Street, two doors down from the Phoenix Chinese restaurant and directly opposite the Sheer Elegance hair salon (Ann Geraghty, proprietor). Most traffic in and out of Belmullet passed by my door, Barrack Street being the in-town name for the R312, also known as the Ballina Road. My building, like most of the structures near the square, presented as two stories with a door onto the sidewalk. Shared walls were the norm until you reached the edge of town. But for the mix of facades—whitewashed lime, red brick, gray stone, blue stucco—the streetscape was as regular as two lines of boxcars.

"I don't want to spend my sabbatical in some drafty farmhouse," I had told Pat the previous summer. "I'd like something in town, something close to the pubs." I painted her a picture of a typical Irish evening: a dinner of pan-fried salmon and boiled potatoes followed by a sunset stroll along Broadhaven Bay; a pint of Guinness and a game of darts at McDonnells. "We'll read Yeats and Joyce by a turf fire," I said. "We'll go out in the moonlight and gather cockles and mussels, alive alive-o."

"It's your sabbatical," Pat had said, smiling indulgently. "I'll only be there for three weeks."

She didn't have to add that the term "sabbatical" (which I prefer to "extended golf holiday") was pretentious. But Pat, although not a golfer herself, accepted—no, *supported*—my plan to spend several months in Ireland and Scotland investigating my bloodlines for evidence of a "golf gene."

"All I ask," she said, "is that you don't leave me out in the country with no car."

So I was in a furnished apartment at No. 8, The Docks, Barrack Street. The flat had most of the "mod cons"—washer/dryer, radiators, wi-fi, a small TV—but its best feature was a panoramic view of the town docks at the mouth of a quarter-mile-long canal connecting Broadhaven and Blacksod bays. A few brightly painted fishing boats were usually tied up at the quay below my third-floor balcony. At high tide they bobbed in six feet of water, separated by rubber fenders. At low tide, when the narrow end of Broadhaven Bay emptied, they sat, heeled over, in the mud. Two more boats—rotting hulls, actually, their masts taken by storm or pilferage—were tethered to the opposite shore, no more than two hundred yards away. Cows wandered the steep hill beyond, a single-lane road twisting up through a copse of stunted trees to a distant farmhouse.

I was captivated by this view. Every morning I drew back the living room curtains to see what the tide was up to. When it was out, birds strutted around on the mud flats, picking at piles of seaweed. Channel buoys lay on their sides like fallen tops. I was similarly fascinated by the progress of construction on the docks, which were undergoing a renaissance. A three-story apartment building was going up between the boats and the canal, affording me the opportunity to watch a warren of concrete-block walls sprout trusses, beams and gables. Yellow-vested carpenters popped in and out of view through dark holes that were not yet windows. My dining alcove, which faced east, looked out upon an even fancier block of flats nearing completion. This building, wrapped in a shirtwaist of pricey fieldstone, cried for attention with its modernist projections of glass and steel. ("Belmullet hasn't seen its like," a construction worker told me. "It's got underfloor heating, entertainment systems, granite counters. It's five star.") The daylight hours saw a steady procession of heavy machinery on the unpaved quay—bulldozers, dump trucks, backhoes, front loaders, forklifts, cement mixers, cherry pickers. Each trip to the windows promised some alteration of the marina landscape: a new mountain of gravel . . . pallets of floor tile . . . spools of orange electrical conduit . . . a truckload of concrete drainpipe.

I couldn't watch this hive of activity without remembering my first night in Belmullet. It was September 1989. The proprietors of our bed-and-breakfast had recommended dinner at the eleven-room Western Strands Hotel on Main Street, just below the square. It was twilight when we parked our rented Volvo at the curb in front of the hotel. Before going in, Pat and I decided to stroll down the street to Broadhaven Bay, a walk of about two blocks. The sidewalks were empty, and cars were few. We passed shuttered shops. Some of the buildings had rotted windowsills and padlocked doors; a few were so far gone that they resembled bombed-out structures from World War II. Broken windows, collapsed roofs. Tall weeds and rubble filled the interiors. A cow stared at us through a breach in the back wall of an abandoned store.

After our walk, we ate on white tablecloths in a narrow, dimly lit room.

The food was excellent, but the waitstaff and the other diners seemed to have come directly from a funeral. I remember the muted rattle of silverware, the polite clearing of throats behind napkins. When we left the hotel, Belmullet was dark—so dark that I invoked my dad's old expression, "dark as a yard up a stovepipe." There was a single pool of light down the street, outside the open door of a newsagent's. A few teenagers hovered at its edges, like campers around a fire.

Dad loved Ireland. That is, he loved the John Wayne, Maureen O'Hara, Bing Crosby, Barry Fitzgerald, Tin Pan Alley version of Ireland. He never missed a televised showing of *The Quiet Man*. He crooned "How Are Things in Glocca Mora" while shaving. He had once attended a concert by the Irish tenor John McCormick, and his memory of the great man's voice ranked right up there with his mind's eye movie of Bobby Jones' famous Lily Pad Shot. Dad looked Irish, with his dark eyes, narrow face and handsome features, and he invariably described his adoptive home as an Irish town. "New Richmond was Irish as hell," he'd say. "I don't think they let you in if you weren't Irish."

But of the real Ireland, he knew nothing.

"Where did we come from?" I asked him when he was pushing seventy. "Where did the Garritys live?"

"Damned if I know, Johnny." He looked puzzled, as if the answer ought to be somewhere on his person—in his wallet, perhaps, between his AARP and Social Security cards. "Aunt Jane said something about County Mayo."

Aunt Jane, he had to remind me, was Jane Hughes. Jane was a sister to my grandfather, Thomas A. Garrity, and wife to William A. Hughes, New Richmond's town clerk. When Thomas Garrity, a Minneapolis lawyer, died of typhoid fever in his thirties, Aunt Jane had taken in my orphaned dad, who was maybe four at the time. Her sister, Katherine Casey, had taken in his brother, Marshall, nicknamed "Mersh," who was two years older than Dad. The Garrity brothers grew up in adjoining clapboard houses on Greene Street, a block off New Richmond's Main Street.

But that's all my dad could give me: *Mayo*. Aunts Jane and Katy, of course, were long dead. So was my uncle Mersh, an eccentric fellow who used to limp through my imagination on a wooden leg. (My mother said that Mersh had gotten drunk in a hobo jungle during the Great Depression, and a train had run over his leg. "That sounds about right to me," Dad said by way of confirmation. "A train would explain the missing leg.") In short, if I wanted to track down my forebears, I would have to do it the old-fashioned way: by researching the family tree.

To which I said: no way.

There were people, I was sure, who found genealogy enthralling. I was not one of them. I never longed to know if my great-great-great-great-grandmother came over on the *Mayflower*. I was indifferent to the possibility that one of my ancestors tended the horses while St. George slew the dragon. When I read the Bible, I skipped past all the "begats," and I can't tell you how many presidential biographies I returned to the library because the first three chapters dwelled on paternal grandparents who had left Aberdeen in the eighteenth century to farm in Kentucky.

I didn't even read *Roots*.

In other words, I was a typical American. My brain could process two or three degrees of kinship—grandparents, grandchildren, uncles and aunts, nieces and nephews, first cousins and, with a little coaching, stepparents, stepsiblings, and immediate in-laws. Beyond that, the relationships spread like kudzu, and my first thought was to go to the garage for weed killer.

My aversion probably owed to the fact that my own family tree had split at the trunk when I was still in short pants. My parents divorced in 1952, when I was five. My father, who owned a small scaffolding company in Kansas City, Missouri, promptly married the woman who had supplied his business capital. My mother, the former Grace Helen Stuart of Minneapolis, Minnesota, responded by moving to West Palm Beach, Florida. She took with her my college-actress sister, my high-school-sports-star brother, and a precocious five-year-old with big ears and a cowlick.

Neither of my parents talked much about their immediate antecedents. There were certain secrets and private hurts that they deemed too sensitive to share. My dad, for example, who was garrulous to the extreme, had nothing to say about his mother, Mary Byrnes Garrity. ("He couldn't bear to talk about her," my sister, Terry, told me, "because she ran away to New York after his father died. No one knows why she left, but she deserted her children and ran. I think she died of influenza in the epidemic of 1918.") My mother had secrets, too. Born into a socially prominent Minneapolis family, she grew up in a big house with her utility executive father, Charles Stuart, and her elegant and voguish mother, Grace, whose name was never uttered in my presence. (Terry again: "Our grandfather had our grandmother committed to the asylum at Oconomowoc, Wisconsin. She was an alcoholic and may have suffered from bipolar disorder. She died in the asylum, and Grandfather Stuart married his beautiful secretary, who wound up with the family fortune when he died.")

The family photo album wasn't much help. There was an old photo of Charles Stuart sitting at a rolltop desk; with his square forehead, rimless spectacles and thick build, he exuded Presbyterian rectitude. There was a studio portrait of Grandmother Stuart as a stunning young brunette in a Gaslight era dress with fur scarf and matching muff. There were also some box-camera snapshots that my parents had taken of each other on a job-hunting trip to the Gulf Coast in 1937, the most dramatic being a pair of portraits taken on a scenic overlook near Natchez, Mississippi. A tall pine anchors the foreground. A river winds off through the forest below.

The rest of the photographs, dozens of them, were of golf swings. Dad swinging in a driveway beside an old Packard . . . A teenage Terry swinging in a backyard under shade trees . . . Dad swinging in a park with patches of snow on the ground . . . Dad swinging in pleated slacks, white shirt and flapping tie . . . Tommy swinging on a practice range under the watchful eye of the old tournament pro, Leland "Duke" Gibson . . . Dad swinging in a fifties-era polo shirt with alligator logo. Virtually all of the pictures of Dad caught him at the top of his backswing with his head down— "anchored," as he always put it—his hands high, wrists firm, the club parallel to the ground. "That looks like swing 19-B," Dad would say, rifling through the photos. "Here's a good one. None of that dipsy-doodle stuff with the hands. All you have to do is drop the club on the inside and bust it with the right hand." The camera, as Dad saw it, had been invented so he could check the position of his hands at the top.

Anyway, *Mayo*. That's what I had in February of 1989, when Pat and I started talking about a trip to Ireland. "There must be somebody who knows about your family," she said. "Somebody in New Richmond?"

"Who do I know in New Richmond?" I asked. "Dad took me there one time, and that was almost thirty years ago."

"What about that man who grew up with your father? The judge."

"Joe Hughes?" I tried to remember a man I had met at a California wedding in the early seventies. "Well, I guess he'd be kind of a half brother to my dad."

Half brother? It was more complicated than that. Judge Joseph Hughes was the adopted son of two New Richmond lawyers, Jamie and Billie Hughes, who had lived across the street and a few doors down from my dad's adoptive parents. I had met Jamie and Billie in the summer of 1961, when Dad and I drove up to watch my brother play in the St. Paul Open. Dad described Jamie as an older cousin, but it was clear from his respectful attitude that Jamie and Billie had played a big role in his upbringing. They were a lovely old couple who split their time between their houseful of books and a storefront law office.

So Joe Hughes, ten years younger than my dad, was a quasi-relative, and it suddenly occurred to me that Jamie and Billie, being lawyers, might have held on to documents or letters belonging to my aunts Jane or Katy, and those documents or letters might point back toward Ireland.

"It's a long shot," I told Pat, "but what the hell . . ." I climbed the stairs to my bedroom office and dialed Information. "Is there a listing," I asked, "for a Joseph Hughes in New Richmond, Wisconsin?"

There was. I wrote the number down, thanked the operator and hung up.

It was midafternoon in Kansas City. Judge Joe was probably on the bench, trying not to nod off during some protracted argument about residential easements. Or, I thought, he might be retired. He might be watching *Divorce Court* reruns in some Sun Belt condo.

Didn't matter. I dialed the number.

He picked up on the first ring. "Hello?" When I gave my name, he said, "Johnny, how are you? How's Jack?" We chatted for a few minutes, small talk, and then I got to the point: Pat and I were going to Ireland, and Dad didn't know where his family came from. Was there any way to find out?

Joe's answer was as direct as a news bulletin. "They came from Belmullet in County Mayo."

"What? Bel-*what*?" I fumbled for my pen.

"B-E-L-M-U-L-L-E-T," he spelled out. "Belmullet. And your great-grandmother was from Newcastle, just up the road. Her maiden name was Stephens."

And just like that, my world got bigger.

H ere is where I apologize to Scotland.

Forgife me, o land of gowf, keeper of the flame and sacred shore. I swear by the shepherd's crook that I will nae slight ye in the pages to come.

It's just that, growing up, I was led to believe that golf was a Garrity thing. There were no snaps of Stuart backswings in my mother's meager collection of family photos. She had nothing to say about Ernest Jones' "swing the clubhead" theory, and, aside from the purely human interest she took in Arnold Palmer after reading Herbert Warren Wind's profile of him in *The New Yorker*, she ignored tournament golf. I don't remember my mother *touching* a golf club, much less swinging one.

So I was shocked to discover, several years after my mother's death from cancer in 1971, that Grace Garrity had not only played golf, but played it well. "Oh, she was crazy about it," Dad told me on a visit to his apartment in Gainesville, Florida. "Your mother outdrove me using a 2 iron off the tee. Leonard Dodson, the old touring pro, gave Grace lessons at the Kansas City Country Club, and he said she hit the ball as far as that gal from Texas, Betty Jameson." Jameson, Dad didn't have to tell me, was a Hall of Fame golfer and one of the founders of the LPGA.

"Your mother had a very unorthodox swing," he went on. "She lifted the club very abruptly, but she had a big arc, and when she started down, *pow*! She could really bust it. But she never could hit a wood shot. I never saw your mother use a driver."

I took Dad's glowing appraisal of Mother's game with a grain of salt, but the revelation that she had been a golfer left me unsettled. It was as if I had found love letters from an old admirer in her vanity drawer.

"Why did she quit?" I asked.

Dad frowned, trying to remember. "I don't know. We used to play at Swope Park all the time."

"Was it when we moved to Florida?"

"Before that. I'm trying to recall." He shook his head. "I think Grace quit about the time Tommy started to play regularly with me, when he was eight or nine years old. I don't know if we couldn't afford green fees for all of us, or . . ." A troubled look crossed his face. "I don't think that was it. But talk about being broke," he chuckled, "I remember the time . . ."

Dad rambled on, putting as many words as possible between himself and a memory.

I knew, of course, that my mother's family had played some golf. One well-connected relative—I call her "Aunt Mary"—raised eyebrows by hitting the links six days after her husband was murdered. And if that wasn't enough to get the gossips buzzing, her golf partner and subsequent husband was the principal suspect.

My dad was the first to tell me this story, having heard it from my mother. But Mother hadn't shared all of the juicy details with him—such as the fact that Lord Darnley's corpse had been found in the garden after his house was blown up, or the bit about Aunt Mary slipping out the back door around midnight, shortly before the bomb went off. And that was a shame, because Dad, a great talker, would have made those details sing. As it was, he left me to ponder the implications of the tale with an understated "They played rough in those days."

That was certainly true of the thuggish Earl of Bothwell; although, to be fair, he was never convicted of the Darnley assassination. It was equally true of the sixteenth-century Englishmen who later imprisoned and then beheaded my golfing ancestor, Mary Stuart—otherwise known as Mary Queen of Scots. In his book, *The Complete Chronicle of Golf*, Ted Barrett provides the proper perspective: "The sad example of this beautiful and accomplished woman—she sang pleasantly, spoke or read in six languages and wrote and collected poetry—had no discernible effect on the increasing popularity of golf among all classes."

Another Stuart—Mary's father, James IV of Scotland—was, in Barrett's words, "the first golfer whose name is known to history." And yet another Stuart—Mary's son, James VI of Scotland (and I of England)—played at Perth, introduced his two sons to the game at an early age, and even authorized a royal club maker. "Jimmy Six," as he was surely known to his playing partners, was reportedly on the Leith Links when news arrived of a Catholic rebellion in Ireland. Writes the very dry Barrett, "Accounts differ as to whether he withdrew from the match or finished it."

The House of Stuart, to sum up, was a veritable golf academy. And at the risk of sounding like one of those toffee-nosed descendants of the *Mayflower* voyagers, I'll just point out that the Stuarts did their stuff long before the first written rules of the game (1744) or the founding of the Royal and Ancient Golf Club of St. Andrews (1754). My Irish ancestors, by way of comparison, didn't know a niblick from a necktie until well into the twentieth century.

"Let's say my mother carried the golf gene," I said to Pat over dinner one evening. "She meets my golf-mad dad back in the twenties. They marry and have three children. Golf mania is a dominant trait, so it follows that their children would all inherit the gene. One son becomes a PGA Tour player, the other son becomes a golf writer, and the daughter, while not a golfer, per se, writes a golf book and lands a talk-show gig at a Florida radio station."

Pat reached for a biscuit. "*The Sensuous Woman* was a golf book?"

"No, I mean her other book. *The Golfer's Guide to Florida Courses.*"

Pat knew I was being facetious, but she recognized something in my jokey musings: a desire to make sense of my own career. The wheel had spun, the steel ball had gone round and round and round, bounced, rattled and stopped with surprising finality on 18 red: "golf writer." The truth is, I was no more obsessed with golf than the next fellow, and I suspect I would have become a schoolteacher, a songwriter or an historian—*anything*—but for the facts of my ancestry.

That, in any case, is what caused me, at the start of my seventh decade, to briefly exchange the cares of journalism for the freedom of the links. And that is what landed me in a dockside flat in a little out-of-the-way Irish village that nobody ever heard of.

A place called Belmullet.

CHAPTER 4

We wind about in the dells and hollows among the great hills, alone in the midst of a multitude, and hardly ever realize that there are others playing on the links until we meet them at luncheon. Thus, on the first tee, we may catch a glimpse of somebody playing the last hole, and another couple disappearing over the brow to the second, and that is all; the rest is sandhills and solitude.

—from Bernard Darwin's *The Golf Courses of the British Isles*

My brother phoned me from Houston around Christmas, 2005. He said, "I have this picture in my mind of the seventeenth hole at Carne."

My own brain immediately provided the visual—a ridge-running par 4 of 436 yards with deep ravines on either side of a bending fairway. A long, narrow green that curled around a grassy abyss.

"I keep playing that hole in my mind," Tommy continued, his voice raspier than usual. "I hit different clubs off the tee. I lay up one day, and the next day I go for broke. Most days I want to keep the ball under the wind. If the flag is all the way back and right, it calls for a wholly different approach shot. . . ."

"I love that hole," I said, "but I don't know why. It's way too hard. It's the only hole on the course I've never parred."

"You know what I'd like to do?" Tommy's voice had that conspiratorial tone I remembered from my childhood, when he was the indulgent big brother proposing a game of bunk-bed basketball or Wiffle Ball Home Run Derby. He said, "I'd like to play the seventeenth at Carne with three balls in my pocket. I'd hit three tee shots, play all three balls into the green, and then hole them all out for a score. Then I'd go back to the tee and do it again. And again. I'd play the hole six times with three balls until I'd played eighteen holes. I think eighty would be a great score."

The idea grabbed me the moment I heard it. I pictured my brother on Carne's seventeenth hole on a sunny afternoon, a quiet man in a quiet place. I saw him hitting high cuts from the tee and low draws to a front-left pin position. I pictured him walking back toward the tee with his driver in his right hand and three balls in his left. And I saw myself walking beside him, his old staff bag slung over my shoulder.

Only later would I recast his three-ball fantasy as the Seventeenth Hole Challenge. Only later would I begin to see the rulemaker in the rules. As with most of my brother's made-up games—and he was always suggesting a friendly competition, whether it be card tossing or marble racing—this one reflected his analytical side (the sets of three, the accumulation of data, the illusion of order) while celebrating the vagaries of golf (the prickly landscape, the unpredictable weather and the prevailing vincibility). It was also typically inner-directed. Tommy hadn't boasted that he could play the seventeenth hole in fewer strokes than I could (which wouldn't have been much of a boast) or that he could beat anybody in Belmullet or County Mayo or the whole of Ireland. He had simply set the bar for a sixty-eight-year-old former tour player with one kidney, three kinds of cancer and a frozen shoulder.

"No way I could shoot eighty on that hole," I said. "Maybe ninety."

I loved the fact that Tommy was still thinking about Carne. We had played thirty-six holes there over three days in July. Carne was the high point of an eight-day car tour of Ireland that I had fashioned for him out of frequent-flier miles and Marriott points. It wasn't a golf trip, exactly, but we had enjoyed a round at the European Club in Wicklow, taken a guided tour of the luxurious Druid's Glen course near Dublin, and stopped in Clare for an hour's walk on the famous Ballybunion links. Tommy had never been to Ireland, so everything was fresh to him; he was like a child getting his first glimpse of mountains or the sea. "It was like I was holding my breath," he wrote me after the trip. "—afraid that if I relaxed, something might change. I always knew Ireland was there, I always knew it was magical. I just never thought I would experience it first hand." As for the golf, he wrote, "Carne stands out as the clearest memory of all. Particularly the back nine. I could play that stretch over and over again and be perfectly happy."

Or, as he was now saying on the phone, he could play one *hole* over and over again and be perfectly happy.

"If you're up for another trip to Belmullet," I said, "we could give it a try. I've got a million Marriott points."

Tommy's chuckle was followed by a soft cough. "Well," he said, "I'll have to get in better shape."

Twenty months later, on a cloudy August afternoon, I lugged my clubs out to the seventeenth tee at Carne. I had three golf balls in my pocket.

Ninety, I told myself, would be a good score. Eighteen bogeys seemed about right for a ten- to twelve-handicapper.

Not that I had a legitimate handicap. Years before, after a fifteen-year layoff from golf, I had briefly played to an eight on the strength of three-hundred-yard drives, two-hundred-yard 5 irons and a USGA handicapping system that averted its eyes in embarrassment when I shot ninety-five. My game then took a significant turn for the worse (don't get me started on golf schools), and I stopped keeping score. "I'm about a twelve," I told the organizers of charity scrambles. "I shoot between seventy-eight and one hundred and five."

Actually, I didn't shoot much at all. For the better part of the nineties I played most of my golf at commercial driving ranges. I pummeled range balls from Tokyo to Tampa, and I got so good at it that my New York editors asked me to write an online column for range rats, a pioneering blog called "Mats Only." It was great fun, the range life, but after four or five years of rubber tees and punks yelling "Fore!" from passing cars, I lost interest in

practice and found my way back to the golf course. But I didn't find my
way back to the scorecard. If a playing partner wanted to keep my tally, fine.
I was happy just to breeze around Turnberry or Pebble Beach in pursuit of
a two-dollar Nassau. If the United States Golf Association got wind of
it—well, they knew where to find me.

So it's fair to say that I didn't fully appreciate the challenge awaiting me.
I had played the Carne Golf Links maybe a dozen times over five years. In
that time I was probably 16 over par on the seventeenth hole, my ratio of
bogeys to double-bogeys being about two to one. I had never made triple-
bogey or worse; but I hadn't parred or birdied it, either. If there was a red
flag, it was this: I had driven into trouble only twice in my dozen attempts.
In other words, I had never parred the hole in ten attempts from the *fairway*. Typically, I blocked my approach shot into the deep pit on the
right, hacked my ball back up to the green and then either two- or three-
putted.

None of this was on my mind on that August afternoon. I began by
climbing the big dune beside the seventeenth tee and looking down into the
natural amphitheater of sixteen green. There were no golfers there and there
were none up on the pinnacle tee of Carne's postcard par 3. Satisfied that I
would not be impeding traffic, I scampered back down to the seventeenth
tee, pulled my driver and teed up ball number one. Wanting to milk the
moment, I stepped back and imagined that I was being introduced by Ivor
Robson, the Scotsman with the singsong voice who was the first-tee announcer at British Opens. ("Next up on the tee . . . John GAR-rity!")

I stepped up, took a couple of confident waggles, swung . . . and yanked
my drive so far left that it overshot the fairway and plunged into the grassy
canyon.

Huh.

Shrugging mentally, I teed up a second ball and hammered another
drive. This one followed the same line as the first and disappeared over the
cliff.

Well, crap!

My confidence shaken, I decided that on this day, under these conditions, I shouldn't be trying to draw the ball. So I aligned myself left, tightened my grip to promote a fade and smacked a spectacular push-slice that

hung out over the sandy escarpment for an eternity before exiting stage right.

I stood on the tee, staring in disbelief at the blowout and the broken clouds above. It had never occurred to me that ninety might be unattainable. My brother had said eighty would be a great score, and I had automatically added ten. (Nobody writes a book called *How to Break 94*.) Tens were such a familiar benchmark that I hadn't noticed this peculiarity about my brother's challenge: he hadn't set the bar at 79.

I, meanwhile, had told anybody patient enough to listen that I hoped to shoot ninety on the seventeenth hole. "It's a par 5 disguised as a par 4," I added, lest they mistake me for a chronic nineties-shooter. "Think of the Road Hole at St. Andrews, only tougher. Picture the Road Hole with a sand quarry in place of the Old Course Hotel, and a canyon running down the left side and a deep pit on one side of the green and tall dunes on the other with a nasty mound in front of the famous pot bunker, but with real thick rough, none of that wispy stuff." If I was that defensive about ninety, I realize now, I could never have said, "I hope to shoot a hundred." I would have felt pathetic.

But no more pathetic than I felt on that August afternoon, having hit my first three drives off the map. I found my third ball way down in the sandy waste on the right, so deep in dutch that it took me three more swings just to regain the fairway. I then shimmied down the thirty-foot slope on the other side, wielding my sand wedge like a mountaineer's ax. This canyon had a relatively level floor, but the grass was correspondingly greener and more lush. It took me five minutes or so to find a couple of balls. Not *my* golf balls, but I couldn't see how it made any difference. I wedged the first ball back up to the fairway. The second ball, buried in thicker grass, came out heavy and dropped like a beanbag, halfway up the slope.

That was when I gave up.

There is a story that Chris Birrane, Carne's starter, tells about the seventeenth hole. "We had a Japanese group here," says Chris. "Eight or ten of them. Some ladies, too, walking around with the men, taking photographs. They had more cameras than RTÉ or CBS. I was caddying on the day. One of the guys was an important course designer in Japan, and he had an entourage, and I got one of his employees or relatives. A nice guy, a lovely man. Not a great golfer, but there but for the grace of God. To the best of my knowledge, he had four words of English—'ball,' 'please,' and 'thank you.' So if he wanted to know where his ball was, he said, 'Ball?' When I told him, obviously, it was 'Thank you.' He bowed for everything. I was like a king for eighteen holes. I never had so many genuflections. But as far as I was aware, he only had those four words of English.

"So we played around. Very little conversation, a lot of sign language. Mostly pointing in the wrong directions, left and right. He was a happy guy—he laughed at everything. Finally, we got to the seventeenth. He hit his drive, and it was probably the best drive he hit all day. It went more than two hundred yards, which was fantastic. But it took a wicked bounce and kicked to the left into that big gaping hole we have on the seventeenth. But he didn't know where it went, and as we walked up the fairway he turned to me and said, 'Ball?' I pointed in the general direction of the chasm, which he wasn't aware of. So we walked on, and when we got to the edge of the cliff, he said, 'Ball?' I pointed down at the ball, which was at the very bottom. And he looked down and said, 'Ohhhh . . . *screwed*!'"

Chris smiles. "So apparently he had five words of English. But he was a lovely guy."

I kept thinking of the Japanese golfer in the days after my three-ball fiasco. If he had been in my shoes, I imagined, he would have kept playing, regardless of the score. He had spirit. He had spunk. I, on the other hand, had responded to a mild screwing by throwing in the towel.

Actually, I didn't so much quit that day as regroup. *You aren't ready,* I told myself. *You don't have the game to play this hole.* I collected the balls from the fairway and tossed them over the cliff. I climbed down and wedged them back up to the fairway. Climbed up, collected the balls, threw them back down. And so on. "What a player does best, he should practice least," Duke Snider is supposed to have said. "Practice is for problems."

A few days later, on a Saturday morning, I got out to Carne early and found Chris in his little office at the end of the breezeway. A stocky man in his fifties, Chris sported a military buzz cut and performed his official duties in sneakers, jeans, and, when the weather called for it, a quilted nylon jacket and watch cap.

"I'm having a little trouble with the seventeenth hole," I told him. "I think it's cultural."

He looked up from a club that was clamped in a vise for regripping. "That's probably it," he said. "A group of guys came here recently on some kind of package tour. They were Americans like yourself, lovely guys, and they said they were playing some of the best links courses in the northwest of Ireland—Westport, Ballina, and some course I can't even remember. And those courses, you know, they aren't links courses at all—they're parkland. So they came out here, and it was a beautiful day, and they decided they wanted to play thirty-six holes. I said, 'Okay, fine, boys, we'll see you later on.' So after eighteen holes I met them in the bar, and they weren't going *anywhere*. They'd been out there five and a half hours. We were going to issue them flares so we could find some of them again."

"They were overwhelmed," I ventured.

He nodded. "There's many come here, especially Americans and Canadians, your side of the water, who are not acquainted with real links courses. They've played some man-made links, which are completely different, and they've played some fantastic courses with superfast greens and manicured fairways. But they're totally unprepared for this. They play for the pin, which doesn't work here. They're off the back of the green. They hit it up in the wind and it blows back to their feet. Or they hit it in the junk and can't dig it out. They just can't get the hang of it at all." He opened a box of Prince Albert cigars and took one out. "But they love it, and they come back."

I zipped up my rain jacket. "So what advice do you have for an American playing the seventeenth at Carne?"

"Don't! It'll only bring you grief."

He stuck the cigar in his mouth and smiled.

CHAPTER 5

Muirfield's great quality is its frankness—its honesty. There are no hidden bunkers, no recondite burns, no misleading or capricious terrain. Every hazard is clearly visible. Chiefly for this reason, the course has always been extremely popular with foreign golfers, and especially Americans; it has a sort of "inland" flavor that makes visitors feel much more at home.

—from Herbert Warren Wind's Following Through

The week before the official start of my Irish sabbatical, I flew from Ireland to Scotland to cover the Senior British Open for *Sports Illustrated*. The venue was Muirfield, a great old links in East Lothian at the edge of Edinburgh's suburban sprawl. I was familiar with the course, having worked the 1992 and 2002 British Open Championships, won by Nick Faldo and Ernie Els, respectively. On neither of those occasions, however, had the combination of course setup and weather been as demanding as it was for the Senior British. The wind was relentless, blowing the creases off trouser legs and making flags pop like small arms fire. The rough was thigh-high in places and so thick that three-time British Open champ Gary Player all but demanded that it be tested for drugs. "It surprises me," he said, "that they have made the Senior Open so much tougher than the regular Open."

Muirfield played so hard in Friday's belt-loosening wind that first-round coleader Nick Job, who started at three under, shot eighty-five and missed the thirty-six-hole cut. On Saturday, when the gale blew straight off the Firth of Forth, only sixteen of seventy-seven players managed to par the 449-yard first hole, and the last two threesomes were collectively 9 over par before they reached the second tee. "The situation of only one semicut is stupid and over-the-top," said Job, referring to Muirfield's mowing scheme of short rough turning abruptly to knee-deep hay. "It's too demanding, really. The fairways are narrow in the best of times."

Tom Watson, after a second-round seventy-one, had a different take: "I loved it out there. It was just a great day on the golf course."

But that was a *five*-time British Open champion speaking. And even Watson admitted that he had not always cherished the linksland. "When I first came over here," he said, "I tried to fight the wind and the general conditions. But that didn't work." So the young Watson had decided to give in. "Not surrender, mind you, but to go with it, to use the wind. Once I did that, my links game improved."

I jotted down Watson's remarks in my reporter's notebook.

Watson looked all of his fifty-eight years. His eyes had that squinty look that old golfers get, and his forehead was lined like a field of winter wheat. Watson's default expression was a tight-lipped smile, but at Muirfield he flashed a boyish grin from time to time—when his ball flew as he wanted, say, or when one of his shots took an unexpected bounce. On Saturday evening, Watson hit a 3 iron from the seventeenth fairway, trying to reach the green of the par 5 in two. The sun was at his back, firing golden rays from its position above the firth, but the sky ahead roiled with dark clouds from a furious squall that had passed over the course. Watson held his follow-through and watched the flight of his shot with absorption, as he always does. He then lowered the club and turned to his caddie, Neil Oxman, saying, "Didn't my ball look beautiful against that dark sky?"

Standing a few yards away, behind the ropes, I swallowed hard. I remembered another Tom, another course, another sky.

———

I barely know Tom Watson, which is surprising. You would expect that two Kansas Citians of roughly the same age, who attended Stanford University at the same time, might be acquainted—particularly when one of them becomes a Hall of Fame golfer and the other dodges respectability by becoming a golf writer. But I never laid eyes on Watson at Stanford, and I was not yet a golf writer in the late seventies and early eighties, when he was winning his money titles and major championships. My dad and I followed his career closely, but we did so while eating off TV trays in the living room of a turn-of-the-century shirtwaist house in Kansas City's Hyde Park neighborhood. (Dad watched his golf from a wing chair while clutching an old Wilson sand wedge. The club's leather grip was worn to a shine and was as hard as oak.) For perspective we turned to the sportswriters at *The Kansas City Star* and *The Kansas City Times*, who followed Watson as assiduously as they did the baseball Royals, the football Chiefs and the basketball Kings.

My friend Mike McKenzie, the *Star*'s cheeky sports columnist, knew Watson better than I did. "I'm careful not to abuse my position and pester Tom," Mike told me over press box hot dogs at Royals Stadium, "but he understands that he's Kansas City's fourth franchise. He's always got a few minutes for me at a tournament, and I've got his home number." When Watson invited him to play at the exclusive Kansas City Country Club, Mike, a nongolfer, disarmed him by stepping onto the first tee with a Dial-a-Club, one of those variable-loft gadgets you adjusted with a coin.

Jo-Ann Barnas, the *Star*'s golf writer, also knew Watson. If he was dining with friends on the road, Watson might ask Jo-Ann to join them. "Kansas City was a very provincial place, and Tom was comfortable with that," says Barnas, who now covers sports for the *Detroit Free Press* as Jo-Ann Barnas Taylor. "He knew he was the only reason we covered the majors, so he'd always take a few minutes after a round to make sure I had what I needed."

I did *see* Watson around town. At the downtown Lyric Theater with his first wife, Linda, and their children, Michael and Meg. At Arthur Bryant's Barbeque with his brother-in-law and agent, Chuck Rubin. In the auxiliary press box at the ballpark, where Watson could watch his beloved Royals without being pestered by fans. (The Royals' George Brett, who always asked for a corner-facing chair in the back of a restaurant, said that he once looked over his shoulder in a Kansas City eatery and spotted Watson on the other side of the room—in a chair facing the corner.) At the ballpark, Watson liked to hone his competitive edge by making small wagers. Fly ball or grounder? Foul or fair? Swing or take? During a weather delay, Watson and a pal might watch two raindrops as they trickled down the press box window, a buck or two riding on which one reached the bottom first.

But for my dad, as for me, Watson was both the raindrop and the window. "I remember Tom Watson as a teenager," I'd tell people. "Short pants. White tennis socks and golf shoes." But after all those years, did I really remember Watson, at the age of fourteen, playing a bunker shot at the 1964 Missouri Amateur? Or was it the yellowed clipping that I remembered? The one with the photograph captioned "Costly Mistake—Tommy Watson hit sand on his backswing on No. 4, costing him the hole in his third-round loss to defending champion Jim Colbert from Santa Fe Hills."

Dad kept the old clippings in a fat manila envelope, which he never put away. They were not snippets, but whole broadsheet pages that measured fifteen inches by twenty-four inches when unfolded. One such broadsheet, the front page of the Sunday sports section of *The Kansas City Star*, dated June 28, 1964, bore the banner headline GARRITY SHOCKS JIM COLBERT, followed by a subhead DEFENDING CHAMPION LOSES, 5 AND 4, TO BLAST OF BIRDIES. A second story, GARRITY FINDS HIS GOLF SWING, had three subheads, including CHANGE IN GRIP EARNS SPOT IN FINALE OF STATE AMATEUR. At the bottom of the page was a three-column photograph of my brother holing a birdie putt on the fifth green at Indian Hills Country Club, and then both stories jumped to page 5B, where there were more photographs, more play-by-play, more quotes, and a sizable notes section. And then, just to put things in perspective, the inside page offered this one-column AP dispatch: NICKLAUS TIES ARNIE IN OPEN.

It was the *Cleveland* Open, but you get the idea. Amateur golf was still a big deal in Kansas City.

Anyway, when I say that Watson was both the raindrop and the window, I mean that Dad and I viewed him as a surrogate. When the cameras followed Watson into Amen Corner, we imagined a different Tom winning three Masters titles. When the cameras caught Watson running onto the seventeenth green at Pebble Beach, his hands raised in triumph, we dreamed of someone else hoisting the U.S. Open trophy. Dad and I didn't know Tom Watson, but we knew, in the jargon of the day, "where he was coming from."

Watson, I have since learned, shared our nostalgia for the Kansas City captured in those yellowed clippings. I met him for the first time in the mid-eighties, when *SI* sent me to Orlando to do a "slumping Watson" story—the slump feature being a dubious honor bestowed on great golfers when they go a few months without winning. I talked with Watson in the locker room at the Bay Hill Club after the first round of Arnold Palmer's Bay Hill Classic. When the interview was over, Watson asked how my brother was doing.

"Great," I said. "Tommy is head of sales and marketing at MacGregor. Two kids, two cars, a life."

"When you see him," Watson said, "tell him that I was in the gallery the day he beat Jim Colbert at Indian Hills. It was the best golf I'd seen up to that point, and it inspired me. It made me want to become a tournament player."

I felt a surge of family pride, but journalistic detachment carried the day. I waited until I was outside the locker room door to scribble down Watson's words in my notebook. And I waited a good thirty seconds more before running back to the press tent to phone an old man in Kansas City.

"Time is free," a motivational speaker once observed, "but it's priceless." Standing on a dune at Muirfield, I took in the golden linksland, the golfers and the crowd, and I asked myself how forty years could evaporate faster than a puddle in a car park.

On Saturday night, in my room at the Edinburgh Marriott, I unzipped my computer bag and pulled out a file folder labeled FAMILY. Among the birth certificates and death notices were a few old clippings from Dad's stash, including GARRITY OUTLASTS CARR: MISSOURI GOLF TITLE GOES TO BLUE HILLS BELTER ON 5 AND 3 DECISION. I put that one aside and unfolded the broadsheets with the semifinals coverage. "Garrity's performance against Colbert was nothing short of amazing," wrote the *Star*'s golf writer, Dick Mackey. "[One down after two holes], the lanky, powerful belter from Blue

Hills took over, ramming a birdie of 3½ feet on No. 3, winning No. 4 with a par, taking No. 5 with a three-foot birdie and following suit with an eight-footer on No. 6. . . . Colbert maintained his poise, playing sharp golf himself, and battled on even terms from 7 through 10. Then Garrity cut loose with a twenty-five-foot birdie on 11 and sank an eighteen-footer on 12 to go 5 up. . . ."

On the inside page, in the Notes column, I found an item I didn't even remember:

> **Tom Garrity and Jim Colbert were waiting to tee off when they were asked if they had ever played a prior match.**
>
> **Garrity said, "Yes, in the second round of the state in 1958."**
>
> **"I didn't think you'd remember it," said Colbert.**
>
> **"But I sure do. You beat me, 6 and 5."**

Snorting with amusement, I sank into the armchair by the window and picked up the front page again. This time I studied the photograph of my brother rolling in his birdie putt on No. 5. My first observation was that he was sartorially sound: dark slacks, a pale polo, brown-and-white wingtip shoes and no hat. (The fashion gaffes of the polyester seventies were still a long way off.) His dark hair was combed laterally from a left-side part. It was a style that I tried to emulate, but on Tommy it looked good. The photo reminded me that he had been a very handsome man.

My second observation was that Tommy's putting style was from another era: the Slow Greens Epoch. He bent over the ball, his knees flexed and hands close to his thighs in the question-mark posture favored by Nicklaus and Palmer. I couldn't tell anything about his swing path from the photograph, but his head was down as the ball neared the cup, his eyes burning a hole in the grass between his feet. His putter was an old-fashioned hosel-at-the-heel blade with a flat lie angle—not, I was surprised to see, the bronze Bull's-Eye putter he had employed when I caddied for him.

Behind Tommy in the photograph, spectators were lined two deep under a canopy of elms. Most of them were men, and most were hatless. I let my eyes wander over the faces, expecting to see my dad or Tommy's wife, Joanne. Instead, I found . . . me? I had to hold the paper under the bedside lamp to be sure, but—oh, yeah. Pale, beanpole youngster with pencil neck, nerd haircut and glasses. Two-tone sport shirt of a style favored by retired jewelers in Miami Beach. There I was, three weeks out of high school and two weeks into a summer job fabricating insulating panels in a grimy warehouse.

Smiling to myself, I remembered how Tommy, who was four inches shorter than my six foot seven, would often introduce me to friends and business associates with the line, "I'd like you to meet my *little* brother."

And I remembered how much I enjoyed hearing him say it.

The final round of the Senior British Open was a test for Watson. Weighing on his mind—lurking, perhaps, behind the cloud formations that fascinated him so—was the still-fresh wound of his final-round collapse at the U.S. Senior Open in Kohler, Wisconsin. (Watson had shot forty-three on the final nine to hand the tournament to Brad Bryant.) Asked at Muirfield if he wanted to erase that memory, Watson had nodded. "I hate failure," he said. "I need to get even."

But first he had to catch Stewart Ginn, the third-round leader. Ginn, whose wire-rimmed spectacles and long, frizzy hair made him look like a hippie candle maker, was an Australian-born pro who lived in Malaysia. He had done nothing much in 2007—he was 121st on the Champions Tour money list—but he was a former winner of the Ford Senior Players Championship, which the seniors treated as a major. "I haven't done stoutly well on links," he conceded, "but I guess as you get older you understand it a bit more."

Ginn soon learned that some things surpasseth all understanding. Watson caught him on Sunday with a birdie on the third hole. As sun followed rain and the wind blew up again, Watson pulled out to a four-shot lead over Ginn, Eduardo Romero and Mark O'Meara, another former British Open champ. Watson was 2 under and still three strokes to the good when he drove into a steep-faced fairway bunker on the par-4 eighteenth. Suddenly it was interesting. It took Watson two shots to escape the sand, and his fourth, from the fairway, bounced a few paces to the right of the final green.

No matter. Using his bigheaded putter, Watson rolled his ball over the fringe and down to tap-in range. When neither O'Meara nor Ginn managed to scare the hole with their long birdie putts, Watson bumped his ball into the cup for his third Senior British title and his fifty-ninth career win. Parenthetically, it was the first Watson victory of my golf-writing life.

Through it all, the wind and sky performed their wonderful tricks. Waiting on the sixteenth tee, Watson's threesome had watched a spectacular rainbow fan out from horizon to horizon, the brightest segment pouring color onto the Muirfield clubhouse. "You notice those things when you're older," Watson told me after the trophy ceremony. "You're not so focused on birdies and bogeys and all that stuff."

Yes, I thought. That had to be it.

CHAPTER 6

Thus we leave what was mortal of the brave and lovable soldier, far out in the rolling veldt, simply resting—resting after his short life's work was done.

—from J. L. Low's *F. G. Tait, A Record*

One morning, when the shadows were long and cool, I lugged my bag out to the seaside dunes and played the seventeenth three times with three balls. I didn't write down my scores, but I couldn't help peeking every time the imaginary standard bearer walked by with a sign reading GARRITY E or GARRITY +2. Of course, that was plus-or-minus *bogey*, not par. Sign Boy smirked as he slid the +4 card into the clip. GARRITY was out in 49.

I played the par-5 eighteenth for fun—and birdieing it was fun—and then stopped in the golf shop to chat with Mary Walsh.

"Did you already play?" She stopped rearranging shirts on a circular rack to gape at me. "You must have gone off in the dark."

"I only played a couple of holes," I said truthfully. "I actually came out to see about Sunday."

Which was also true. As an honorary lifetime member of the Belmullet Golf Club, I was eligible to play in the Sunday competitions. But there was a catch: I needed a handicap. Not a pulled-out-of-my-butt handicap, either, but a valid, you-can-look-it-up, signed-by-an-authority handicap issued by the USGA, R&A or GUI.

"It won't be a problem," Mary said. "I talked to John Hanley, the handicap chairman, and he said you can play three rounds here with a member, turn in the signed scorecards, and you'll be good. And I talked to Terry Swinson and Gary Stanley, and they said you could play with them this Sunday at nine-oh-seven, if that would suit you."

Swinson, a retired facial surgeon, was the club's honorary secretary, and Stanley was a past captain of the club and current greenkeeper of the Carne Golf Links. I had played with each of them on previous visits and found them to be serious golfers and good company.

"Wonderful," I said.

Mary smiled as she tapped my name into the Sunday log.

Next on the day's to-do list was . . . well, nothing. I had an idea of how I wanted to spend my sabbatical—looking into old records, chasing down distant cousins, playing golf—but I didn't want to feel as if I was on assignment. "I've been scribbling in reporter's notebooks for forty years," I had told Pat while packing for Ireland. "I'd like this to be looser, less structured." When she asked how many notebooks I was taking, I shrugged. "I don't know. Six."

My first month off the company leash, August, had been a total sloth-a-thon. Pat had taken three weeks off from her job as a church liturgist and choir director to help me get settled in Belmullet, and the two of us had played host, for ten days, to Teresa, Jack and Maddie, who were—how do I put it?—*tourists*. We'd visited the Guinness Brewery in Dublin, climbed the winding stone staircases of Bunratty Castle, shopped for take-home gifts in touristy Westport and explored the mountain bog at Céide Fields, a Neolithic site thirty miles up the coast from Belmullet. Then, suddenly, my family members were gone, and my apartment on the docks was a quiet bachelor flat.

The apartment was where I was headed when I left the golf shop, but I changed my mind before I had driven five hundred yards. The little winding road that joins Carne to the Blacksod Road makes a sharp turn about halfway down. The jog is dictated by the Carne cemetery, a walled plot about a hundred yards square with an iron gate and a patch of tarmac out front. I had visited the cemetery several times, most recently with Teresa, but some impulse made me pull over again and park outside the wall.

The Carne cemetery is orderly and well maintained. The burial plots are demarked by garden pavers and filled with ornamental stones, potted plants and small statuary. The headstones are of polished granite or marble, varied in size and shape. None is taller than five feet or thicker than a dictionary, but what the markers lack in heft they make up for in loquaciousness. "In our hearts you will live forever," reads one tombstone, "because we thought the world of you." Another, above a lengthy list of survivors, practically sings, "The happy hours we once enjoyed / How sweet their memory still / But death has left a vacant place / This world can never fill." At the back of the cemetery, rising out of a fieldstone plinth, is a naturalistic sculpture of Jesus on the cross. Behind Jesus is the wall, and farther up the hill the golf clubhouse and the jagged green line of the Carne banks.

I walked back and forth between the headstones, reading the now-familiar names: Padden, Casey, Hughes, McNally, Lynch, Barrett, Reilly, Lavelle. I lingered at the graves of presumed kinfolk. A white marble headstone remembered Martin Geraghty of Elly as "a dear father" and gave his age, at his death in 1978, as "80 YRS." A slab of red granite recalled that Tim Hughes of Binghamstown had died in March 2000, "Aged 80 Years," as if he had been a fine wine. Not far away, under a black stone topped with a white Celtic cross, lay the earthly remains of Catherine Diamond "and her daughter, Mary Geraghty, Died 15 Feb. 1986, Aged 70 Yrs."

Finally, I stopped at a plot flanked by small statues of kneeling angels. Pink cosmos bloomed in pots on the white gravel.

IN LOVING MEMORY OF
JOHN GERAGHTY (JACK)
TIRRANE
DIED 23 APRIL 1993
AGED 77 YRS.

His Wife NORA
Died 16 May 1998
Aged 82 years
In Heaven You Rest, No Worry No Pain.
In God's Own Time We Will Meet Again.
R.I.P.

Who, I wondered, *was buried here with my dad's name by a golf course he never knew but would have loved?*

As was so often the case when I stood over an Irish tombstone, I thought back to 1989, when a friendly farmer had led Pat and me to the bleak, lonely Mullet Peninsula. I had three clear memories of that day. The first was of farm wife Annie Geraghty pointing across the fields to the bay, saying, "That's where your great-grandfather got on the little boat to go out to the big boat to sail to America."

The second was of Martin Geraghty, a tall old man in a tweed jacket and flat cap who stood on the dirt road outside his house and pointed his cane at an empty pasture on the other side of a stagnant lake. "There used to be twenty-seven Geraghtys living there," he said. I looked across and saw nothing but a spot of rubble—some old stones stacked a foot or so high.

The third memory was of an even older man, a stooped character who stood in the road with his dog. Old Paddy Geraghty had on a tattered sweater and scarf, but what grabbed my attention was his narrow, weathered face, his ruddy complexion, his white stubble of beard . . . and his ears. "You have my father's ears," I blurted, trying to control my excitement. "I know those ears!"

Old Paddy had rewarded me with a toothless grin.

Where, I wondered as I gave Jack Geraghty's headstone one last, long look, *is Paddy buried? And who else has those ears?*

CHAPTER 7

Health and life to you.
The mate of your choice to you.
Land without rent to you.
And death in Eirinn.
—Irish Drinking Toast

It didn't take five minutes to drive along the bayshore and back into town. I parked on the docks beneath my balcony and took the stairs up to street level. Halfway up, on a big deck that fronted the neighboring flats, I bumped into Eamon Mangan as he came out of an apartment door with a mop in his hand. Eamon, sometimes known as "Mr. Carne," was a founding director of *Turasóireacht Iorrais* (Erris Tourism), the nonprofit entity that owned and operated the Carne Golf Links. I had met him in 2002, when I was on assignment for *SI*. "Eamon has a furniture store," someone told me at the time, "but his passion is Carne." So I expected some brawny Irish promoter along the lines of Fred Corcoran, the Boston-born charmer who guided the careers of Sam Snead and Ted Williams while running the old PGA tour.

Instead I got this Mangan fellow—a slight, bespectacled man with a manner so unassuming that you could have easily mistaken him for a ribbon clerk. He reminded me of Art Wall Jr., the Pennsylvania pro who birdied five of the last six holes to win the 1958 Masters.

The mop, Eamon explained, did not signal a career change. He owned a couple of flats on the docks, and he was sprucing up an apartment that had just been vacated by Polish immigrants. "I saw your car at the course," he said. "Did you play?"

"I played seventeen nine times," I replied. "Then I played eighteen."

He showed no surprise. He was up to speed on my seventeenth-hole obsession.

"I have a question for you." I pointed down at the quay, where a dozen fishing boats were tied up—double the usual number. "Why the sudden traffic?"

"The weather must be turning. They usually anchor at Ballyglass"—a tiny harbor a few miles away, near the mouth of Broadhaven Bay—"but it's quite exposed. When a winter gale threatens, they anchor here for shelter." The local fishing fleet, he added, was minuscule. "There's no infrastructure. The big processing plants are in Galway."

My interest in the boats was not entirely academic. On my original trip to Belmullet I had asked the Geraghtys at Cross Lake to speculate on my ancestors' life on the peninsula. "I asked if they would have been farmers or fishermen," I told Eamon, "and they said, 'Farmers. The Geraghtys were farmers.'" I looked across the quay to the mouth of the little canal that bisected the isthmus. "But there's so much water around here, the ocean and the bays. There must have been some Geraghtys who went to sea."

Eamon thought it possible, but he reminded me that an Irish fisherman of the nineteenth century, emigrating to the United States, would have found little opportunity to practice his trade on Wisconsin farmland.

I conceded the point. "Do you fish?" I asked.

"I did," he said. "When I came back from London I had a little boat, a cabin cruiser. I joined the angling club. We caught mackerel, pollock, haddock, all sorts of stuff. But I found a new hobby, and that was the end of that."

"A new hobby?"

"Golf." He gripped the mop as if it were a putter and made a practice stroke.

I left Eamon to his domestic duties and climbed the steps to the street. Normally I would have turned right and ducked into my flat, but I crossed the street instead and popped into McDonnells pub. It was the lunch hour, so there were only a few old men at the bar and several more, in faded jumpers and wool jackets, enjoying a political argument by the door. "Padraig's not here," said the lass behind the bar, "but you can probably catch him in an hour."

"No problem," I said. "I just want to ask him some questions about funerals."

She nodded—again, showing no surprise. Padraig Conroy, Belmullet's most prominent publican, was also co-owner and director of McDonnells Funeral Home, just up the street.

My next stop was Carey's on Main Street. This little shop, on the Blacksod side of the square, is a newsagent, but there was a small book department in back, where I liked to browse. On a Saturday or a market day the shop does enough business to keep two young female clerks hopping at the cash registers. I usually bought the *Irish Examiner*, partly out of loyalty—the Cork-based national daily occasionally reprinted my golf stories—and because the *Examiner* had a lively sports section. For happenings in Erris I depended on *The Mayo News*, a nonsensational tabloid, and *Western People*, a weekly broadsheet packed with compelling dispatches such as MAN DROVE WITH DEFLATED TYRE and CLONBUR MAN STUCK FINGER UP AT THE GARDAI.

From Carey's I crossed the street to *An Builin Blasta* (The Tasty Loaf), a busy bakery and tea room. I stopped there two or three times a week to pick up salad rolls at fifty cents each. "Any brownies today?" I asked.

"No, sorry," said one of the aproned ladies behind the display case. "Try tomorrow."

Clutching my newspapers and my bag of rolls, I strolled past the Centra and Londis supermarkets and crossed the square to Atlantek Computers Ltd., a tiny storefront tucked between Snoopy's fast-food takeaway and Hegarty's convenience store. Atlantek's door opened on a narrow aisle cluttered with pegboard displays of computer accessories, but the back widened to accommodate a wall-mounted desk where customers tapped away on rent-by-the-hour PCs.

"Is Alan in?" Alan was Alan McGrath, the store's owner and head technician.

"I'm afraid not," said Sarah Ferguson, the pretty young woman behind the service counter. "He's at the Ballina store today."

"That's fine," I said. "I just wanted to thank him for lowering the firewall on my modem."

Alan had popped around the corner to my flat and plugged a couple of these into one of those and tapped on his keyboard, and five minutes later I was video-conferencing with my astonished wife in Kansas City. "It's incredible," I said. "It's going to save us a fortune in phone bills."

"Alan will be happy to hear that," Sarah said with a smile.

I turned to leave, but some notices on a corkboard caught my eye: WIRELESS BROADBAND FROM I EURO PER DAY . . . SUMMER BINGO, BROADHAVEN BAY HOTEL . . . ERRIS WALLCHASING, NO DUST, NO MESS. I was reading these notices when Eamonn Kelly backed through the shop door with a loaded dolly. This Eamonn, I was about to learn, was a deliveryman for Fastway West Couriers in Tuom, County Galway. Five days a week he drove his truck the length of Erris, delivering parcels from Ballycastle to Blacksod Point.

As Sarah signed for the packages, I caught fragments of their conversation—something about the soon-to-be-demolished power station at Bellacorick and the stone bridge that crossed a stream there. "That's the musical bridge," Eamonn was telling Sarah. "You rub a stone along the bridge, and it's supposed to play a tune. And you're not supposed to drop the stone. That would be bad luck."

"Why bad luck?" Sarah asked.

"Well, you see, the bridge itself was never completed. If you look at it, you'll see that a stone was left off the top of the railing at one end. Because of the curse."

Eamonn, I noticed, was about the same age and build as Chris Birrane, and he had the same ironic way with a yarn.

"I'll bite," I said, stepping toward the counter. "What's the curse?"

Hearing my American accent, Eamonn turned and smiled. "Well," he continued, "they say an old woman went out and knelt on the bridge, and she cursed it. And that's because her two sons worked on the bridge—they helped build it. But they drank their money away in the little pub that's there. So she cursed the bridge, and part of her curse was that no man would ever hold a license in that pub again. So all the licensees were women after that."

Sarah cocked her head. "Why didn't they finish the bridge?"

"Well"—he took a breath—"I was told that three different men tried to finish the bridge, and two died within the year. And the third, he got extremely ill—he was on his deathbed. So someone in his family went out and knocked a stone off the end of the bridge. And he immediately recovered. So that's why there's no stone there, and the bridge remains unfinished."

I was tempted to play the part of the brain surgeon and ask, "Is that true?"

"You should go up there and have a go at it," Eamonn told Sarah. "Listen for the tune. But *don't* drop the stone, whatever you do." He looked at me and shrugged. "I'm just passing on what I was told."

Sarah was giggling now, which only encouraged Eamonn. "Don't use a sharp stone," he told her. "Use a round, smooth stone so you won't drop it. And don't take one that's too big to hold in your little hand. But make sure it's not too small, either, or you'll break a nail or bloody your knuckles. You've got to get the correct size." He wheeled his empty dolly to the door. "Just don't drop the stone."

Eamonn parked the dolly on the sidewalk and stuck his head back in the shop. "If you don't turn up on Monday," he said, "we'll know what happened!"

He gave me a wink as the door swung shut.

Back at the apartment, I sliced some tomatoes and mozzarella for lunch and drizzled balsamic vinegar onto the plate. I ate in the dining alcove on a table piled with books, newspapers and file folders. The east windows provided an end-on view of Broadhaven Bay, from the boat ramp on out to the distant hills. Only now I couldn't see those hills; a curtain of rain had dropped, rinsing the color out. Sky and water were the same shade of gray, with only the flashing green lights of the channel buoys to break the monotony. When I was finished eating, I cleaned up, put the dishes on the countertop to dry, and stretched out on the leather couch for a nap.

I awoke fifteen or twenty minutes later. The rain had intensified. The wind was howling across the harbor, creating wide, flat waves that darted one way and another before feathering out on the banks. Shaking off my torpor, I sat again at the dining table, this time with the window at my back. I woke up my PowerBook by poking the shift key. When I opened iChat, the names on my buddy list were in shadow; no one was available for a video chat. I launched Google and then sat for a moment or two, staring at the familiar white screen with the letterboxed search line and blinking cursor.

I typed "McDonnells Belmullet" and hit return. In 0.23 seconds I got a list of 102 results. The first was an eleven-second MySpace video from someone named Lucky Col, who had apparently thought that his friends would find meaning in a cacophonous clip of boozy strangers shouting at one another in front of a wobbly camera. Number two was a blog titled "Post-Mayo Depression," which employed a photo of a full glass of Guinness in an otherwise empty McDonnells to illustrate the author's sadness upon leaving Mayo at the end of a summer holiday.

Neither extreme characterized my visits to Belmullet's destination pub. I dropped in sometimes in the afternoon to see if anyone was playing darts. (Jim Engh, the aforementioned golf architect, was both a McDonnells fan and a darts hustler. He carried his own darts in a velvet-lined case.) My usual drink was a 7-Up—a liquid so pallid that Padraig Conroy invariably waved off my attempts to pay.

I was about to start another search when my eye caught a string of Chinese characters. I clicked on the link and got a different photograph of McDonnells, this one showing Padraig, a strapping fellow in his thirties, wiping a beer glass with a bar towel. I recognized the picture as one that had appeared in *Golf* Magazine. This, apparently, was the Chinese version of a tasty article about Carne written by *Golf* associate editor Lisa Taddeo.

Out of curiosity, I clicked on a link titled TRANSLATE THIS ARTICLE. I was immediately rewarded with a new headline: CARNE WILL LET YOU TEMPORARILY STOP BREATHING.

It took me a second to figure out that this curious sentence was a literal translation from the Chinese of CARNE WILL TAKE YOUR BREATH AWAY. Taddeo's article, previously translated from English to Chinese, had now been restored to English by a computer program. The effect was stunning:

Stadium by the color of green and brown components . . . occasionally covered by the sand dunes. When your eyes with the ups and downs and changes in the slope, they will find a big turning point suddenly dropped, and then there is a great risk of cave-valley, the same as Ma crater, is like guns scars left by the bombing.

Another descriptive passage seemed to refer to my visit to the cemetery, hours before:

This piece of land was once a piece of Christian burial on the mortality of the children's cemetery, now it is a unique Stadium, standing on the court, you will feel like to return to space-time tunnel, from another world. . . . Yes, when this has stood the ancient cemetery, the Atlantic chill morning rushing toward us, as if we could touch our past lives.

The autotranslator's take on McDonnells was also spot on:

McDonnells of the room dark, damp. But here contains dynamic atmosphere. . . . Here are the scene of Irish music performances, accordion, Wuxianqin Khan Lee and those of music and After the performance, they will pick up the beer, take a musical instrument, joyful drinking.

Enthralled, I saved the translation to my hard drive for later study.

I then reached across the table for a file. The top document was my birth certificate, issued by the Kansas City, Missouri, Department of Health. It said I was born at St. Joseph's Hospital at four twenty-two a.m. on January 11, 1947. My father was John Byrnes Garrity, a forty-one-year-old white man born in Minneapolis, Minnesota. "Usual Occupation: Real Estate

Broker." My mother was Grace Helen Stuart, age thirty-seven, same birth-place. "Usual Occupation: Housewife."

The next document was a copy of my father's birth certificate, issued by the Minnesota Department of Health. "Garrity," it said—no given names—was born in Minneapolis on September 7, 1905. The "attending physician or midwife" was H. B. Swertsen. The father was T. A. Garrity, age thirty-six, occupation lawyer. The mother was Mary Garrity, age twenty-nine, no occupation. No address, either.

I put aside the birth certificates and picked up an old letter from my dad. Dated March 19, 1954, it was three pages long and typed, single-spaced, on J. B. GARRITY SCAFFOLDING CO. letterhead.

> Dear Kids: Sure sorry to hear Terry and Johnny are sick. Glad, however, that the chicken pox weren't too bad. . . . Things are quiet here. News obscured by dust storms. Yesterday a se-ries of tornadoes hit all around us, but no damage. And only a sprinkle of rain. The Kan-sas City lawns have the texture of sand traps. Dry and powdery. We are using shovels instead of carpet sweepers to clean the apartment. Furniture and clothes are all a mess. Even worse, dust gets on the grips of my golf clubs and makes them slippery. And scours the paint off golf balls in a matter of minutes.

In another paragraph, Dad made a confession.

> It just occurred to me to mention that I ate your Valentine present. I had gotten a carton of the Cadbury milk chocolate almond bars, the first in Kansas City, and was planning on mail-ing them down; but a shortage of chocolate-covered peanuts in the house one Saturday night

```
proved too much, and the present disappeared.
Will try to get a replacement and send it off
before temptation strikes again.
```

Smiling, I got up and walked into the kitchen. Opened a cupboard. Found a Cadbury whole-nut bar on the shelf. Peeled back the foil wrapper and took a bite. Tossed the paper sleeve in the plastic trash bin.

Dad's birth certificate was still out, so I sat back down and studied it. *T. A. Garrity, lawyer.* A Minneapolis lawyer, I said to myself, should have left behind some sort of public record. Had I ever Googled my grandfather?

I typed "Thomas A. Garrity" in the search window and hit the return.

The first two or three pages of results were a hodgepodge of tangential links. There was a Pennsylvania gastroenterologist named Thomas McGarrity, and a mathematician named Thomas A. Garrity, who had written a book for the Cambridge University Press, and yet another Thomas Garrity in Kentucky, who had published a study titled *Pet Ownership as a Protective Factor Supporting the Health of the Elderly.* I was going to pack it in when my eye caught a link titled PAW NOVEMBER 22, 2006: MEMORIALS. The URL was princeton.edu, and the Garrity listed in the extract was not a Thomas A., but a Thomas C.

I clicked on the link, and this appeared:

```
Thomas C. Garrity '59
     Tom died May 25, 2006, at the M.D. Anderson
Cancer Center in Houston.
     Few of us knew Tom. He left Princeton early
in our sophomore year, when he roomed briefly
with Stu Hutchinson and Dave West. Born in
Kansas City, Missouri, he came to Princeton
from Palm Beach High School following his fam-
ily's move to Florida. According to Dave West,
Tom was a prominent member of the freshman
golf team, a point borne out by his later ca-
reer accomplishments.
     After leaving Princeton, Tom attended the
```

University of Missouri, where he also excelled
at golf. His obituary in the Kansas City Star
notes that he "dominated the Kansas City golf
scene in the late 1950s . . . played on the
PGA Tour in 1960 and 1961, but . . . gave up
tournament golf to establish a stable environ-
ment for his family." He then earned a degree
in landscape engineering from the University
of Florida, became a golf course architect and
later moved into executive positions in the
golf equipment industry.

    Tom is survived by his wife, Joanne; his
daughter, Anne; his son, Jeff Goss; a sister;
a brother; and two grandchildren, to all of
whom the class extends its sympathy.

—The Class of 1959

    I don't know how long I stared at the screen, but I eventually became
aware that the room was brighter. The rain had moved across the bay and
up the coast. Gulls were strutting around on the gleaming mud of the tidal
flats.

    I walked out on the balcony and inhaled deeply. The air was cool and
fresh, the wind down by half. The sun was peeking through the clouds. I
fished my mobile phone out of my pocket to check the time: four thirty-five
p.m. Sunset was at least three hours away.

    Plenty of time to drive out to Carne and play the seventeenth hole.

CHAPTER 8

The defendant, represented by Mr. Brendan Flanagan, told the court that on the night in question he had drank between eight and ten pints at the Neale. He did not bring his jeep to the pub as he intended to get a taxi home. He told the court that his jeep, which he had been using earlier on in the day for herding cattle, was parked roughly a mile from the pub. He also said that his house was about a mile to a mile and a half from the pub. He decided to walk home and went to his jeep. He stopped there as he wanted to hop into the jeep and take a rest and keep warm.

—from "Man Who Was 'Revoltingly and Disgustingly' Drunk Had No Intention to Drive Car Home," *The Mayo News*, July 24, 2007

Speaking of Michael Geraghty," Pat said during one of our video chats, "when are you going to visit that records place?"

"The what?"

"The genealogy place. I looked it up for you on the Web."

"Oh, right." I fumbled through a pile of papers, looking for the brochure I'd gotten from my friends at Erris Tourism. "Soon," I said. "Very soon."

I wasn't stalling. It had been my intention to do a records search on

Michael and Elizabeth Geraghty at the very start of my sabbatical. But I wasn't going to waste a day in some musty library while my daughter, Teresa, and my grandkids were in Ireland. Who would hold Jack's hand walking up the circular stone steps of Bunratty Castle? Who would chase a giggling Maddie across the lawn at St. Stephen's Green? Anyway, since their departure, as I tried to explain to Pat, I had been playing catch-up. "Every round of golf at Carne adds another piece to the Geraghty puzzle. Every par on seventeen draws me closer to my clan."

But Pat was right to remind me of my mission in Ireland. The very next morning I grabbed a notebook, tossed the brochure for the North Mayo Heritage Center on the passenger seat of the Toyota and motored up to Crossmolina, a distance of fifty kilometers. I made a right in town, just past the little bridge that crosses the River Deel, and drove back out into the countryside on the R315. Four miles later, I spotted the sign for Enniscoe House and turned into a narrow lane that wound through thick woods— the first trees of any consequence I had seen in weeks. I parked in a graveled lot outside the estate wall, beyond which I could see the upper stories of a six-chimney manor house. The mansion was pink and had vines running up its walls. A marker at the edge of the car park informed me that ten thousand sessile oaks had been planted on the estate "to conserve Ireland's heritage of broad-leaved trees."

There was an open door in the stone wall, and just inside the door was an oak lectern serving as a reception desk. A few people wandered around the lobby, perusing the book racks or staring out the conservatory window at a garden with a trimmed lawn and gravel paths. They were older couples, mostly. Some carried little notebooks. One white-haired lady clutched a document envelope that looked as if it had spent a century in an old trunk.

I told the elderly woman at the desk that I was looking for anything she might have on a Michael Geraghty of Cross or Belmullet, born in 1830, or his wife, Elizabeth Stephens of Glencastle, born in 1826. "That's all I have," I said. "They ended up in Wisconsin, and there's a line in a book that says that Michael Geraghty was wounded in our Civil War."

The woman behind the desk picked up a thick book, *Surnames of North Mayo, A–H,* but she immediately put it down. "We won't have a record of any births before 1830," she said. "Those records were destroyed in church fires. Do you know when they were married?"

"I'm afraid not."

Thumbing through another book of names, she came up with a possible link to my great-grandmother. "There were two families of Stephens in the 1800s." She turned the book around for me to look at. "There was a John Stephens of Kilmore Parish and a Patrick Stephens of Ardowen."

She picked up the phone, read off the names and towns to someone and hung up. "It will take a few minutes," she said. "The tea room is open, and you're welcome to look through the museum while you wait."

I chose the museum, a single room devoted to Mayo's rural heritage. Anything that might have been in a nineteenth-century barn was in the museum—old horse tack, sidecars, pit saws, turf cutters. There was a closed door at the far end of the room, and every few minutes the old woman crossed the museum and disappeared through the door, emerging a few seconds later with computer printouts.

On her fourth trip, the receptionist came out of the back room with bad news: "There's no record of the marriage." All she had for me was a single page with the heading, *Index to Griffith's Valuation of Ireland, 1848–1864,* and the names of the two Stephens.

I drove away disappointed.

That afternoon, I opened the windows to let in a cool September breeze and sprawled on the couch with the latest copies of *Western People* and *The Mayo News.*

I loved the county weeklies. I was especially fond of the minor crime stories, like WOMAN HAD NO DOG LICENSES, which ran to surprising lengths and quoted liberally from the sentencing remarks of the judges. The reporting was rich with details. The witnesses to an assault were outside the pub because the brother of one of them was dating a girl from Castlebar, who was late getting to the cinema due to road works on the N5. The father of the man who punched the Garda was the owner of a takeaway frequented by one of Mayo's better hurlers, who could have testified to the character of the victim if he had not been cracking heads at Dublin's Croagh Park. The mother who had left her daughter in the pub was scolded by the judge for allowing the underage girl to buy a vodka and coke, but the publican was believed when he testified that his wife had asked the girl and her brother's girlfriend's children to leave the pub at nine p.m. and that, furthermore, no underage patrons were served, although the Gardai had testified that the girl in question was uncooperative and they could smell alcohol on her breath.

It took me a while to notice that the characters in these accounts—the witnesses, the police (or *gardai* in Gaelic), the judges and even the authors of these rambling articles, expressed themselves in locutions and rhythms that were, to a certain degree, my own. And to an even greater degree, my dad's.

I thought back to my Kansas City summers with Dad. He'd walk up the street to the Westport Bank, where he was revered as a check kiter of unsurpassed skill and charm, and return ten minutes later with a narrative to rival the *Iliad*. ("And I said, Jesus Christ! It shouldn't cost three dollars to stamp 'Insufficient Funds' on a little piece of paper!") He'd pop into the A&P for a steak and wind up delivering a shopping-cart elegy for the sirloins he used to get from a friendly butcher at the Brookside Milgrams. ("He'd cut them on the bias, Johnny, and when we had Tommy's gang over to the house in Crestwood, they couldn't believe their eyes. Those sirloins were *literally* five inches thick and lightly marbled with fat. . . .")

He was not a bore, my dad. He made his golf partners laugh. He coaxed smiles out of the grumpy mailman, the tired cashier and the soon-to-be-bankrupt masonry contractor. When Dad entered a park with his 5 iron and three perforated plastic balls, children ran over to see what he was up to, and usually they stayed—not so much to watch as to listen. Dad talked as he addressed the ball ("I've been taking it too far inside, which can happen if you don't drink enough whiskey") and he talked during his backswing ("I think I'm going to bust this one"). But he never talked on the forward swing—or at least not until the follow-through, when he would pass judgment on the ball in flight, issuing a jaunty "Oh ho!" for a good shot, or a disappointed "Oh, balls!" for a stinker.

Living with Dad, I never lacked for entertainment. His soliloquies anticipated the radio musings of Garrison Keillor, whose *News from Lake Wobegon* airs from St. Paul's Fitzgerald Theater, not far from where my dad bought his first golf club. Dad, like Keillor, mined the banalities of small-town life for epic themes. But Dad's delivery was heartier than that of the lugubrious Keillor, and his tone more legalistic—a reminder that Jack Garrity, a lawyer's orphaned son, had spent a year or two at the University of Minnesota Law School. Sometimes Dad sounded like he was testifying—all those details, the emphatic hand gestures, the precise, clear language of cross-examination. "I don't know that this is pertinent," he would say, "but . . ."

Before Ireland, I had assumed that his distinctive phrasing and florid vocabulary were drawn from his favorite books and movies. When he referred to a woman across the room as "a good-looking tomato," he was borrowing from Ring Lardner. When he talked of "a youth misspent in the pursuits of commerce," he was channeling P. G. Wodehouse. Sometimes I had to guess at the influence. Robert Benchley? *The Philadelphia Story?* Bob Hope? Spike Jones? Or was it pure Jack Garrity? One time, a Hillcrest Country Club member lumbered onto the first tee in Bermuda shorts and a pith helmet, prompting my dad to crack, "The last time I saw somebody dressed like that, he had one foot on a dead elephant!"

But now, as the weeks of my sabbatical flew by, I began to hear my father in the locutions of Mayo folk. Seamus Cafferky, for example. Answering a question about the notorious Black and Tans constabulary of the 1920s, the Belmullet clothier told me how his uncles had been robbed and threatened by the British bullies, and how similar indignities had been visited upon his own father. He added, "But I believe they were not very pleasant times in this area, you know?" Seamus had my dad's knack for understatement.

Chris Birrane had his glibness. Chris was standing with his clipboard outside the starter's office one morning, when an Irish gent of about sixty complained that he couldn't find "the girl" in the golf shop.

"Gone to put on some makeup," Chris said without blinking. "She saw you comin'."

The simplest exchanges sounded scripted. My brother, on his first afternoon at Carne, had struck up a conversation with a barmaid who was loading a tray of sandwiches for a boisterous bunch of children in the Spike Bar. "Excuse me," she said, lifting the tray. "I have to attend to the wee horrors."

They call it *blarney*, and my dad had it in full measure. But in modern Ireland the gift of gab is subsumed in something called *craic* (pronounced *crack*)—broadly defined as good times. "What's the craic?" means "What's up?" "There'll be good craic" signals that fun will be had—the kind of fun you'd expect to find at Paddy's Eagle Inn or at a wedding party in the Broadhaven Bay Hotel. The Irish spelling is annoying to some, who denounce *craic* as a Bord Fáilte attempt to promote Ireland as a land of tin whistles, cozy pubs and souvenir linens. But most everyone in Belmullet used the term. The locals liked to joke about the Sligo man who flew to America and got stopped by Homeland Security when he asked, "Where can I find some good craic?"

Actually, that was becoming my question. As I explained to Pat in our next video chat, "Genealogy is a dead end. Even if I trace the right Michael Geraghty, what have I got? A couple more names? Some birthdates?" A few minutes in a shop or pub, on the other hand, opened the spigot of Irish charm and made me feel connected. "Everybody's got a story," I said. "It might not be Michael Geraghty's story, but it's a story." I shrugged for the camera. "And who's to say?"

"Isn't that what you always do?" Pat looked up from her paperwork. "Interview people?"

"When I'm working, yes. But this is different. This is . . . *craic*!"

Afterward, watching some children throw a red ball around on the quay, I remembered my first visit to the Mullet and my astonishment upon meeting Paddy Geraghty, the old man who had my father's ears. I was too excited at the time to recognize that he also had my father's tongue.

So I crossed the square one rainy afternoon and walked down to Cafferky's, a clothing store on Main Street. Big "SALE!" stickers were plastered on the display windows. Inside, a female clerk ushered me to a little room behind the shop, where Seamus Cafferky himself was pouring a cup of tea. "It's not the lap of luxury," he said, not getting any argument from me. The room was barely large enough for a fridge, a kettle, a tiny table and a couple of wooden benches.

I sat, and Seamus squeezed in opposite me. A man of about my age with a square face and gray-to-white hair not unlike my own, he looked at ease in a pair of flannel slacks and a burgundy sweater bearing the four-swans logo of the Belmullet Golf Club.

"I've been making a feeble effort to track my ancestors," I said. "Do you get many roots-seekers in Belmullet?"

"Yep, it still goes on." He blew on his tea. "Hand-knit sweaters used to be a big item for American visitors, and you needed a receipt to get them through customs. Some months afterward, somebody would write to us. 'My in-laws visited your store, and my great-great-grandfather came from your area, and his name was so-and-so, and if you have any information . . .'" Seamus made little etcetera circles with his free hand. "Because they were working on a family tree. My mother was knowledgeable about various areas and different names, and we were successful in helping quite a few people." He chuckled. "The funny side was that you'd tell a family here in Mayo that somebody from America was making inquiries, and they would automatically think, 'There's a legacy here for me!' "

I smiled, remembering how nearly every Geraghty we had met in eighty-nine could vaguely recollect a great-grandfather Michael or Martin who had wound up in the American heartland, "possibly in Wisconsin." They made these assertions, one of them merrily pointed out to me, only after taking full measure of our rental car, a spanking-new four-door Volvo sedan.

"Does the Cafferky family have an American branch?"

Seamus nodded. "My dad had two sisters who emigrated to Chicago. One of them never came back. The other came back in the early seventies, toward the end of her life. I remember driving to Ballina with my mother and father to collect her at the train. It was very teary that day." He looked sad. "Forty years, you know."

"But you never left?" I was thinking of George Geraghty, who had picked potatoes in England, and of Chris Birrane, who had done time and motion studies in Belgium, and of Eamon Mangan, who had followed four brothers to London.

"I've lived here in Belmullet all my life," Seamus said. "My father was a carpenter at a local joinery shop. My mother was a dressmaker. So there's probably a piece of the rag trade in me." He took a sip of his tea. "We were a family of seven, and my parents always said, 'You'll stay with us. You won't leave us alone.' I was always conscious of that. But if I had to stay in Belmullet, I made up my mind that I would try to work for myself. I started working when I was sixteen years of age, and in 1968 I took the plunge, I opened my own drapery business. And now I'm here forty years"—he paused to let the number register on me—"and I don't regret one minute of it. At one stretch I had two shops in the town here, and I used to stock golf wear for Carne, before they opened their own shop. And for years I ran a cinema."

My head came up at the mention of the cinema. In 1989 I had taken a photograph of the old movie house on Main. It had no marquee or ticket window—just a hand-painted sign, CINEMA, over a small door. (When I showed the snapshot to my father, he told me that he had worked briefly as a movie projectionist in the 1940s, losing the job because he had allowed a reel of film to ignite. "I practically burned down the Dickinson Theatre," he said with a laugh, "which in those days was frowned upon.")

"This room was part of the cinema." Seamus looked around. "I had a shop at the front and the cinema was at the rear, and I must say it was very good to me. Sometimes we ran for three nights a week, sometimes we ran for seven nights, depending on the film. We sold popcorn and minerals and sweets, and people came from all over Erris. I had it open for twenty years from 1970. I took it over from my two good friends, who were the butchers next door."

I asked Seamus what sort of films he had shown.

"I suppose the one that stands out in my mind mostly was *Jaws*. And the other one was Jack Nicholson in *One Flew over the Cuckoo's Nest*. They would have been seven-night runs. The first film ever I showed was *The Greatest Show on Earth*. A local man came to see it, but he thought it was all about horses, and when he found out what it was, he didn't come in." Seamus gave me a wan smile. "But life was different at that time. When I opened the cinema here, my good friend Eamon Mangan had built the Palm Court. All the big bands played there, they came from different parts of Mayo and from outside. People would come to the cinema, particularly on Sunday night, and after the movie was over they would go to the Palm Court to dance." He nodded. "They were actually very pleasant years, because people knew how to enjoy themselves. They didn't have to go to the pub and get drunk."

Seamus got up to rinse his cup at the sink. "I was twenty-six when I started my own business in the drapery trade. Or a clothing store, as you call it in the States. We had a very mixed bag—curtains to menswear to sportswear to boys' wear. You couldn't afford to specialize, because the area's too small."

"The store was right here?"

"Yes. This had been a grocery store, but that was long gone when I took over. There was a tiny area out front. No back entrance, just the front door. And no storeroom. I had to use my parents' house to store stuff. I'd bring it down by car."

Seamus conceded that his experience was not typical; most young men of his generation had been forced to leave Ireland to find work. "Thankfully, all that has changed. I attribute an awful lot of that to the free education that was introduced in our country. Now it doesn't matter where you come from or what you are, you get the same chance as the millionaire's child." He put his cup down to dry. "Not that there's anything wrong with the millionaire's child, but in the earlier years, if you didn't have the money, you didn't get the opportunity. Now the young people are going to college, they're qualifying in whatever field they've chosen. And now the emigration is practically nil."

Seamus excused himself for a minute to help close the shop. When he came back, I turned the subject. "When did you get interested in golf?"

"In the middle seventies or so." Seamus squeezed under the table. "Up to that time, Gaelic football was my sport. It was the thing to do in my time, and I loved every minute of the Gaelic. But when I was finished with football, people said, 'You have to join the golf club.' " Seamus feigned astonishment. "I hate to admit it now, but my thought was, 'All these fellows are so *old*. There's nothing there for a fellow my age.' So I paid my fee for maybe three or four years without ever playing. But eventually I started playing a bit. Eamon Mangan and Pat Cafferky and myself were probably the three people that started off, and we all got hooked on it. We had a lot of great times down there."

"That would be the little course at Cross?" I had glimpsed some golfers from a car window in eighty-nine, along with a farm fence, dark clouds and a lonely flag flapping in the wind.

"That's right. It was a nine-holer owned by a couple of farmers down there. The tees were built on a scheme by the Mayo County Council. The fairways were never cut. There would be rabbits on the greens, cattle running around the place. All the greens would be wired-in. Sometimes you could lose your ball in the droppings of a cow."

Apart from the fenced-in greens, I thought, Seamus could have been describing the nine-hole New Richmond course that my dad had helped build.

"As time went on," he continued, "a lot of people even younger than me joined. I became captain in 1986, and that year we had a record number playing in the Captain's Prize—forty-eight, which we thought was a lot."

"You were in the tavern then?" I recalled a structure in Binghamstown that had an old-time golf scene painted on its north-facing gable.

"That's right. We didn't have a clubhouse, but eventually—and again, I don't want to sound boastful—but the year I was captain we got our first shelter on site. It was a caravan we bought for a hundred pounds, and we took it down there and decorated it, and we used that for quite a while. But we used the local pub in Binghamstown for the nineteenth hole and for presentations. It was called the Golfer's Tavern." He smiled wistfully. "I have a lot of memories of the old course. They were good times and a stepping-stone to get to Carne."

He paused, as if searching his mind. "I remember a particularly lovely, sunny day. This gentleman comes into the shop, he says, 'I was told to approach you, that you would direct me. I want to play golf here in Belmullet.' He happened to be a German, and I said to him, 'Are you long in this country?' He says, 'I've been here for the last ten days.' I said, 'What courses have you played?' He says, 'I came into Shannon, and I played Killarney. I played Waterville. I played Lahinch. I played Ballybunion. Now I'm in Westport, and I decided to come to Belmullet.'"

Seamus shook his head. "All those great courses! So how can I tell this man that this is not a course for him? So I said, in a polite way, that he shouldn't be thinking about playing here. But he says, 'I just want to play golf in this area, and I believe there's a nine-hole course.' " Seamus heaved a sigh. "So I directed him to the golf course and told him that he'd find a post box on the side of the caravan, and he'd find envelopes in a box beside it, and he should put three pounds in the envelope and put his name on it and put it into the post box. And he could play away until it got dark."

Another pause. "Nearly five or six hours later, I saw him coming through the door, and I think I'm going to have to take it on the chin now. So I says, 'How'd you get on?' And he said, 'What a *marvelous* day I've had.'" Seamus' eyes sparkled. "He says, 'Where in this world would you get to be all by yourself on a golf course, the birds singing, the cattle running around, the smell of the sea and the rabbits nearly coming to be petted on the head. Where could you get that in this world? I *thoroughly* enjoyed it.'" Seamus smiled, showing his dimples.

The story of the German visitor captured my own feelings about Carne on a sunny afternoon. "I was out yesterday," I said, "and the breeze was so sweet I could almost taste it." When I told him about the seventeenth-hole challenge, he listened attentively, chuckling when I described my forays onto the slipfaces of the giant dunes. It was obvious that he missed the golf trade. He said, "I miss meeting the people that come by to buy something and to talk about where they come from and how they found the course. Unfortunately, I don't get to do that much anymore."

We chatted, Seamus and I. His words flowed easily, like notes from a horn. As we walked through the darkened shop, it struck me again, this idea that my dad was in Belmullet—or, rather, that Belmullet had somehow been in my dad.

"Take care," Seamus said outside the store. He waved and walked off toward his bayfront house, which was just around the corner on Shore Road.

The rain had moved on, but a blanket of clouds remained. I strolled back to my flat on wet sidewalks, stopping several times to look in shop windows. I had the key out when I got to my apartment door, but I didn't put it in the lock. I turned instead and watched as cars and trucks rolled by, their tires singing on the pavement. Lifting my eyes, I stared across the street at the hair salon. Lights were on in the shop, and through lace curtains I could make out several women in adjustable chairs with other women moving around them. Above the shop was a wide sign that faced my bedroom window.

SHEER ELEGANCE. PROPRIETOR: ANN GERAGHTY

My eyes darted from the sign to the window and back to the sign. Then back to the window. I stood there for another moment or so, staring. Finally, I pocketed the key.

And crossed the street.

CHAPTER 9

Be kind to thy father, for when thou wert young,
who loved thee so fondly as he? He caught the first accents
that fell from thy tongue, and joined in thy innocent glee.
—from a poem by nineteenth-century poet Margaret Courtney

John Harrity brought two of his sons to Carne. Brian, twenty-six years old and bearded, wore a scruffy green cap that had belonged to his maternal grandfather. Patrick, twenty-three and clean shaven, wore a tan baseball cap. The boys were there to caddy—Patrick for his dad, Brian for his dad's realtor friend, Rick Boulé. They were all from Worcester, Massachusetts, where John owned an appliance service company. John and Rick were members of Tatnuck Country Club, founded in 1898. "It used to be an old WASP course where they wouldn't even let Irish clean their toilets," John told me before our round. "My father-in-law, John Tagney, led the first successful caddie strike. He got the caddies a boost from ten cents to twenty cents a bag."

It was a sunny late-summer morning, and if you stood on one of the mounds behind the ninth green, you could look across Blacksod Bay to the far shore, where black-roofed tract houses met farmland and cattle grazed in green pastures. To the south, the glossy bay broke into fingerling channels that disappeared around dark stacks of land.

I had been corresponding with John Harrity for several years. He was one of the readers with Irish surnames who had written *Sports Illustrated* to comment on my Carne story of 2003. "I played here for the first time a year before I read your story," John told me in the breezeway outside the golf shop. "My cousin, Jimmy Egan, has a farm down in Louisburgh, below Crogh Patrick. He doesn't play golf, but he said that Carne was getting good reviews. So I brought eleven friends from Worcester up to Belmullet—"

"Back in Worcester," Rick Boulé interrupted, "John is known as His Royal Highness, the Tour Director."

John acknowledged Rick with a smile. "I've made thirty-seven trips to Europe, and thirty-six of them have been to Ireland. I made my first trip twenty-two years ago with my grandfather, Patrick Harrity, and now I come about twice a year, usually in the spring, before the tour buses arrive. When I take friends to Lahinch, it's easy. We come off the course and there's six glasses of Guinness lined up on the bar." John jabbed with a finger as he silently counted the six beers. A solidly built man with a square face and a gray mustache, he reminded me of the old movie actor, Howard Duff.

"As I was saying, my cousin told me about Carne, so we drove up. It was our last round of the trip, and I went out with two of my best friends. The wind was howling on the first tee. The other guys are sitting in the shelter of that little mound, sitting on the ground, watching us get blown away trying to get off the tee. Laughing their asses off."

"A typical day at Carne," I said.

"We played the front nine in rain and sleet," John continued, "and then it cleared up. We got out to twelve and thirteen, where you play to the sea, and I sort of looked around as if my eyes had just opened, and I said, 'Oh, my God. This is paradise.'"

Brian, who had been listening attentively, said, "Dad was really surprised when he read your story in *SI*."

"I loved the story," John said, "but I thought, 'Oh no, Garrity has let the cat out of the bag. The parking lot will be full of tour buses.'"

"Then *SI* published his letter to the editor." Brian gave his dad a fond glance. "That really boosted his ego."

I turned to John. "You said you've made thirty-seven trips to Europe, thirty-six of them to Ireland. Where did you go the other time?"

"Scotland," he said. "To play St. Andrews."

Ask me what I remember about my round at Carne with John Harrity and Rick Boulé, and I'm duty-bound to say, "The Shot."

We had arrived at the seventeenth hole near the end of a satisfying if not always elegant round. On the path up to the tee I explained my special fascination with number seventeen, retelling the story of my brother's phone call and providing a synopsis of my first attempts to shoot ninety for eighteen balls. "I par the hole about one time in six," I said, "but I still haven't made a four in an actual round." The Harritys absorbed this information calmly, leading me to believe that tribal rites and arcane compulsions were not unheard of at Tatnuck Country Club.

I don't recall the order in which we teed off, but Rick drove short and straight, John hit a snap-hook that bounced and vanished at the edge of the big pit, and I pounded a high fade that came down in the rugged moguls above the fairway. John quickly found his ball in light rough at the edge of the chasm, so I was up among the mounds, searching for mine, when I turned to watch him hit. Patrick had handed him a hybrid club—a questionable choice, since John had about two hundred yards to the front of the green with patches of Celtic terror down either side.

John swung, and the ball came out of the rough as if propelled by an explosive charge. It whistled by me, still climbing, and then started its pure descent, gliding down to the bumpy neck of fairway and landing just so, getting a forward bump from the dark side of a knob, bounding past the citadel mound on the left, rolling onto the narrow front of the green, and stopping, finally, about twenty feet short of the flagstick.

I make my living in the backwash of Tiger Woods and Phil Mickelson, so I can't say that John Harrity's approach on seventeen was the greatest shot I've ever seen. But it was certainly the best shot I'd ever seen on that hole. I raised my arms and clapped in appreciation. Minutes later, after

John narrowly missed his birdie putt and tapped in for par, I told him I hated him.

But aside from The Shot, I remember John's sons. The boys were not golfers, although they obviously had been exposed to the game by their keen father. Brian worked for his dad at Harrity Appliance Service and toiled evenings and weekends at a liquor store. "He's a huge fan of the Dave Matthews Band," John said. "He travels to their concerts. He's seen them dozens of times." Patrick, who was in his fourth year at the Massachusetts College of Art, was an artist, part-time bartender, songwriter and musician who played club gigs with local bands. John said, "I tell him that when he makes it big, all I want is a steak dinner, a bottle of cab and a fine cigar."

Tipped off to their bohemian tendencies, I looked for signs of boredom in the boys. And saw none. Patrick, a self-described naturalist, took in the dunescape and sea views with hungry eyes. "I'd love to come back and paint this," he said. "I could easily lose myself in this light." Brian was similarly enchanted, stopping from time to time to do a 360 with Rick's bag on his shoulder. We were halfway through the round, however, before I picked up on the father-son vibe. Brian and Patrick weren't bored as caddies, it struck me, because they weren't bored by their father. They fed him lines. They smiled at his jokes. On the thirteenth tee, with nobody behind us, John handed his driver to Brian and told him to tee one up and take a rip. With no self-consciousness, Brian took a couple of practice swings and then smacked a creditable drive up the left side of the fairway.

"Wow," said John. "Rick should be carrying the bag."

Brian handed the club to Patrick, who grinned sheepishly and hit a banana ball that screamed over the fence into the adjacent cow pasture. "Take a mulligan," said John, tossing his son a ball. Patrick teed it up, performed a couple of Ed Norton–style gyrations over the ball, and duffed another drive. He laughed and handed the club back to his father.

John smiled indulgently. "Patrick is our artistic son."

After the round, the artistic son swapped his sneakers for flip-flops and joined us for drinks in the Hackett Lounge. "My feet were killing me," Patrick said. "I get blisters wearing shoes." John walked over from the bar with a pint of Guinness in one hand and a half-pint glass of 7-Up in the other, and we sat around a table, our chairs turned toward the big windows and the terrace. The red flag on the eighteenth green waved gently in the sunlight. In the distance, way up between the bookend dunes, a foursome prepared for their descent into the dark hollow.

"I was disappointed the weather was so nice," Rick said, his legs splayed. "I had this forty-nine-dollar rain suit, but my girl friend talked me into buying a new Dry Joy for the trip. Three hundred dollars later, it's dead weight in my bag." He smiled to show he was being facetious.

John took a sip of his foamy brew and sat back, a contented man. "You can see why I just keep coming back to northwest Ireland." He glanced at me over his shoulder. "There's no finer place in the world when the sun is out."

Brian and Patrick nodded in unison.

I suppose I was the artistic son.

Oh, I loved sports as much or more than most boys. I collected baseball cards. I played sandlot baseball, touch football, and practiced my hook shot by moonlight on an outdoor court. I could tell you how many points Bob Pettit averaged for the St. Louis Hawks and how many yards Jim Brown gained for the Cleveland Browns. When the Kansas City Athletics slugger Bob Cerv broke his jaw in a home-plate collision in fifty-eight, I counted the days that he played with his mouth wired shut.

But I was also the kid who rode his bike to school with an open book on the handlebars, the kid who played the guitar, read *The New Yorker* and owned original-cast recordings of Broadway musicals. My mother, who dragged me through a succession of rented houses and apartments in the Palm Beaches, played Chopin waltzes on a baby grand purchased on the installment plan. At least one night a week she entertained actors, musicians, artists and writers, leading them in conversation from a wicker chair, her glass of sherry and a pack of Parliaments close at hand. As a little boy in pajamas, I would creep from my upstairs bedroom to the top of the stairs to watch and listen, edging down step by step until someone took notice and swept me up for a tickle session and a late-night cookie.

My father wasn't so big on the arts with a capital A. He'd take a barbershop quartet over a string quartet, and he could never understand why my mother, who could sight read classical music, couldn't improvise an accompaniment to "Stardust." One summer, when my Princeton-bound brother announced that he had a date with the granddaughter of a painter named Benton, Dad said, "Jesus, I thought I knew every painting contractor in town." It turned out that Tommy was dating the granddaughter of Thomas Hart Benton, the renowned painter and muralist.

But Dad was a reader. He subscribed to *Collier's*, *LIFE*, and *The Saturday Evening Post*. He bought paperback mysteries by Rex Stout, Erle Stanley Gardner and Mickey Spillane and read them with his feet up on his office desk. At our Crestwood home, the built-in bookshelves were crammed with biographies, histories and hardcover fiction. (My stepmother, an accomplished decorator, insisted that the books be shelved according to height, a policy that my dad accepted with a minimum of grousing.) As a second-generation bibliomaniac, I read what Dad read: W. Somerset Maugham, J. P. Marquand, Damon Runyon, C. S. Forester's Hornblower books, Rafael Sabatini's swashbucklers, P. G. Wodehouse, and the sainted Charles Van Loan. And it wasn't just books and magazines. When Dad and I lunched at Winstead's or Sydney's, we'd each take a folded section of the *Star*'s early edition and read while eating our hamburgers, looking up occasionally to share a bit of news or a funny line from Bill Vaughan's "Starbeams" column. ("Suburbia," Vaughan wrote, "is where the developer bulldozes out the trees, then names the streets after them.")

My brother read, too—the sports pages, comic books, golf instructionals—but Tommy's bigger passion was fishing. When I was a toddler and the family was intact, we lived on a tree-lined cove at Lake Lotawana, a man-made lake near Lee's Summit, Missouri. Tommy spent hours on the lake in a rowboat fitted with a smoke-spewing outboard motor. Terry, who fancied herself an artist, painted big green polka dots on the boat, and I contributed to my brother's mortification by occasionally tagging along in a black Hop-along Cassidy outfit with a white cowboy hat, cap gun, holster and orange life vest. ("If they'd had satellites back then," he told me when we were grown up, "they could have seen us from space.") The boat and I must have scared the fish, because Tommy never seemed to catch anything when I was along. Terry says that he came off the dock one evening with a little bass dangling from a line, prompting me to run up to the house yelling, "Mother, he *found* one!"

It wasn't until we moved to Florida and I started grade school that I saw Tommy as anything more than a good-humored babysitter. I started noticing the trophies on his dresser, the scrapbooks full of newspaper clippings and scorecards. The blue curtains in his bedroom—courtesy, again, of Terry, who had a certain facility with fabric paint—were decorated with numbered flags, golf expressions ("Fore!") and an angry cartoon rabbit popping out of a burrow with a lump on his head and a golf ball in his hand.

Where and when Tommy played all this golf, I couldn't figure out. He did enough homework to make the honor roll, and he gave his autumn and winter afternoons to the Palm Beach High School basketball team. (He played forward, center and guard for a Wildcat team that had future New York Yankees manager Dick Howser at one of the guard positions. Tommy's coach told the *Palm Beach Post-Times*, "If Garrity continues to improve, he'll be one of the best high school players in the state.") The spring months, then? Tommy's scrapbook had page after page of three-paragraph clips with headlines like WPB GOLFERS RIP EDISON, 17 TO 3½ and CAT GOLFERS NOW A STATE THREAT. But he must have been afraid that I would scare off the birdies and eagles, the way I did the fish. As far as I can recall, he never took me out to West Palm Beach Country Club, where the high school team practiced. I never saw him play in a high school tournament.

Golf, I would eventually figure out, was something that Tommy did with Dad. And Dad was in Kansas City.

This discovery was in no way traumatic for me. I was comfortable in the kid brother role. My sister, on the other hand, had witnessed the sword-in-the-stone moment, the incident that had sent lightning crackling across the Missouri sky and changed the family dynamic forever.

"I was sitting on the concrete porch of the house in Lee's Summit," Terry told me years later, "and Daddy was in the front yard, hitting those woolen practice balls. Tommy, who was five, was chasing the balls and running them back to Daddy. All of a sudden, Tommy picked up one of Daddy's clubs, gripped it way down on the shaft and took this perfect swing. And the ball flew up in the air." Terry thrust an arm out, suggesting a bulletlike trajectory. "It was incredible. I looked at Daddy's face, and it was as if his whole world had changed."

She laughed. "I said, 'Uh-oh. I'm no longer Daddy's little girl.'"

Things *had* changed. Dad bought a couple of old hickory-shafted irons and had a pro cut them down to kid size. "Daddy was just set on fire," Terry recalled. "He started teaching Tommy, and Tommy loved it. He loved the attention."

That was in 1942. A decade later, despite geographic removal and the dislocations of divorce, the father-son golf connection endured. The proof was in the "Dear Kids" letters that Dad banged out on his Royal typewriter. Every missive had paragraphs directed to each of us individually, but Tommy's section tended to read like an article in *American Golfer* magazine. "Tommy is right not to change his golf swing at this time," Dad wrote in March 1954—

> . . . . His ultimate goal should be the Nelson three-quarter swing with not quite so much lateral shift. But the changes should be made gradually over a period of months, or even years. Tommy can tell by looking in the movie viewer that there is no sway whatsoever in his own swing. At the top his head is still directly over the ball and his right knee is flexed and angled forward in the direction line. In years to come he will probably reduce the shift somewhat, but even that isn't too important. Narrowing the stance, as he did this winter, eliminates much of the shift. . . . If he can't get the Byron Nelson book from the local library, I'll send mine down. Also, I believe that he will do better with the ¾ punch on ALL irons. Much better flight to the ball and, of course, far better accuracy. Ask him to recall his 4 iron into the 12th green at West Palm Beach this winter. Right on the pin all the way, and not ten yards off the ground. Better to use one club stronger and keep the ball down and on target. A full swing on iron shots, particularly the medium and short irons,

```
produces a high lob shot that looks like hell
and is out of control.
```

Reading those words in my Belmullet flat, I thought of the prototypical "sports dads" I had written about over the years. Fathers who gave their sons or daughters public tongue lashings (Jack Brett, father of George). Fathers who took financial advantage of them in their teens (Marc O'Hair, father of Sean). Fathers who pushed them into multimillion dollar endorsement deals when they were too young for the prom (B. J. Wie, father of Michelle). Fortunately, Jack Garrity was not that kind of sports dad. He was more like Earl Woods, father of Tiger—a blend of loving parent, amateur coach, and devoted fan.

With John Harrity and his sons still on my mind, I thumbed through Dad's letters, looking for pertinent passages. Writing in July 1952, Dad had tried to console Tommy over his failure to qualify for some tournament in Miami by pointing out the personal shortcomings of another Kansas City player, a young amateur of growing reputation. "As you know, he has done nothing but play golf, winter and summer, since he was twelve," Dad wrote of the player. "He's good. Awfully good."

```
His family has spent a tremendous amount of
money on the development of his game. He has
either quit or been kicked out of three colleges
in the last two years, and he hasn't amounted
to a tinker's dam in any other respect. True,
he has gotten a lot of publicity, some silver
mugs, and a warped viewpoint; but I think he
has completely lost sight of the fact that golf
is just a game, not an end in itself.

   My ambition for you is quite different,
even though most of the local pros agree that
you could get to the top. I would like to see
you develop your game to the point where you
can qualify for, and hold your own, in occa-
sional tournaments. I would like to see you
```

```
play on your college team, and by that time
have brought your game to the point where it
will be a real source of pleasure to you the
rest of your life. Beyond that, the price is
too high. To be a real top-notcher you would
have to spend most of your time on the practice
fairway or the course proper—working hour after
hour, year after year. It would mean curtail-
ment of all your other activities, like fish-
ing, basketball and baseball, that you enjoy
so much and that make for a well balanced in-
dividual. These specialists in sport are kind
of a cracked crew, anyway. I think it far bet-
ter to be proficient in a number of activities
than [to be] a star in any one.
```

A "Dear Tommy" letter, dated a week later, mentioned the site of my brother's disappointing round—"That Biltmore Golf Course sounds like quite a layout"—and made light of his failure. "I think your mother was a good scout to arrange the trip for you," Dad wrote. "She said it cost about fifty bucks. So it's just as well that you shot a 92 instead of a 75, as it reduces the cost per shot considerably."

But it was the next paragraph that really put things in perspective:

```
Don't ever feel, Tommy, that you are letting me
down. You played the best you could under the
circumstances, and that's O.K. You would have
had lots more fun, of course, if you had been
on your game and scored well. But the darn thing
comes and goes, and you never know what you are
going to come up with in any given round.
```

"Lots of love," the letter ended. "Write again soon. Your letters mean a lot." And then the typed signature:
"Daddy."

CHAPTER 10

The great Gaels of Ireland
Are the men that God made mad
For all their wars are merry
And all their songs are sad
—from a poem by G. K. Chesterton

Every journey has its playlist. I kept my car radio tuned to Midwest Radio, a station in Ballyhaunis. Between farm reports and funeral notices, Midwest Radio broadcast music from Nashville's salad days: Ferlin Husky, Hank Williams, Patsy Kline, Buck Owens, Tammy Wynette, George Jones. In the hour-plus it took me to drive to Ballina or Westport, I'd hear Johnny Cash singing "Ring of Fire" or some Irish cover band paying homage to Conway Twitty with a syrupy rendition of "As Soon As I Hang Up the Phone."

"Midwest Radio is a time machine," I told Pat during a video chat. "It's a wormhole. You can live in modern Ireland and 1950s America at the same time."

So I had the radio. But when I wanted music that spoke to the circumstances of my Irish sabbatical, I'd burn a CD for the car. I listened to the Chieftains, Van Morrison, the Clancy Brothers, Christy Moore, U2, and Maura O'Connell. Two songs, in particular, had me hitting the repeat button. The first was Mary Black's cover of "Don't Let Me Come Home a Stranger."

> *In this place so far from home*
> *They know my name, but they don't know me*
> *They hear my voice; they see my face*
> *But they can't lay no claim on me*

I loaded this haunting tune onto my iPod Shuffle, which I clipped to my golf cap when playing alone in the afternoon. Sometimes I'd climb the dune above the seventeenth tee—to stare at the sea or to wait for other golfers to play through—playing the song over and over, as if it held the answers to questions I would never think to ask. *Don't let me come home a stranger. . . . I couldn't stand to be a stranger.*

The second song was "American Wake," pulled off a CD of the same name by the Elders, a Kansas City–based rock band fronted by the Wicklow-born singer/songwriter Ian Byrne. Up-tempo and almost belligerent in tone, "American Wake" pulled at the scab of the famine years, when thousands upon thousands of Irish had boarded the so-called "coffin ships" bound for America. "An American wake was all they had," mourned Brent Hoad's lyric. . . .

> *Then a jig was danced, a one last chance*
> *For the father to face the son*
> *As the keener wailed they could make out the sails*
> *In the rising of the sun*
> *There were blessings and toasts, they buried old ghosts*
> *As they drank to the now and then*
> *As the minutes passed by they tried to deny*
> *They would never see Ireland again*

I was listening to "American Wake" one evening as I drove the Blacksod Road, the main artery on the Mullet Peninsula. My destination was Cross Lake, a brackish lagoon tucked behind a stretch of dunes about three clicks south of Carne. My tourist map of Erris touted Cross for its "scenic view, birdwatching and angling," and I suppose the birdwatching part was true.

The sun was an orange disk as I drove past the Carne banks. The windsock was limp. There were more houses on the Mullet than I remembered, and more houses being built—vacation homes with fieldstone walls, paved driveways and tidy gardens. A couple of kilometers along I rolled through tiny Binghamstown, named for the heartless English landlord who had controlled much of the peninsula in the early 1800s. (The village's Irish name is *An Geata Móre,* for the "big gate" that Major Bingham installed at the entrance to the town's fairgreen—a gate that opened only upon payment of a toll.) Just past Binghamstown, the road took a hard right at a bare-bones marina. I pulled off the road and parked at the water's edge by a sign on a pole: CE SAILIN.

Saleen Harbour was nothing to look at. An ugly concrete basin offered protection to a few small boats. A stone quay poked its stubby nose into Blacksod Bay. There was a gray beach, its drabness ameliorated by a verge of varicolored stones tumbled smooth by waves and storm surges.

I got out of the car and walked out on the quay.

This is the spot he would have gone from, George Geraghty had told me in 2003. *They used to go out here in small boats. The children, they had just a label with their name on it, a label hung from their necks. A label for the relatives in America.*

There were no boats on the bay and no signs of life on the quay. A few vessels were tied to the inside walls of the basin. One of them, a white, 30-foot cutter with an orange float attached to its forecastle, caught my eye. GERAGHTY CHARTERS read the legend below the aft starboard rail. SEA ANGLING AND PLEASURE TRIPS.

My dad's generation were all sailors, George had said. *They went out in currachs, little fishing boats.*

I tried to picture Saleen Harbour in the nineteenth century: a crowded wharf, a three-masted schooner anchored in the bay, wagons and donkey carts, and everywhere you looked a ragged mass of the dying and destitute.

"Human wretchedness seems concentrated in Erris," a visiting Quaker had written in March of 1847, when the Great Famine was in its third year. "The culminating point of man's physical degradation seems to have been reached in the Mullet. . . . They had no homes, no shelter, no land, no food; they slept at night in the streets and begged for support during the day. . . . Six people had died in the streets in the previous few nights. Several I saw there were beyond the reach of earthly calamity. The ghastly smile which momentarily played on the countenances of these living skeletons, at the prospect of a little temporary relief, I cannot easily forget."

My great-grandmother, George had said, *saw two of her sons thrown on the back of a donkey, dead.*

The way to Cross was marked by a little white sign: MAINISTIR NA CROISE. I drove up a gravel road, past isolated farm houses and fenced pastures. The sun was balanced on the dunes across the lake when I parked at water's edge in front of George Geraghty's house.

Or should I say houses? There were three. The first, which he had built upon his return to Ireland after thirty years as a builder in England, was the cozy cottage I had visited in 2003. The second, right next door, was the old stone house I remembered from 1989, the house of Martin and Mary Geraghty. The third was a roofless maze of concrete block surrounded by weeds and piles of building materials.

Why, I asked George outside his front door, was he building a new house?

He shrugged. "I want a change."

I snorted. The view was immutable: the lake, a line of dunes, the sky. There were two houses on the north shore, a few hundred yards up the road. You had migrating birds, clouds and, on a clear night, the moon and stars.

"The old house here, that's coming down." He nodded toward the middle structure, dark since the death of his mother in 2006. "It's where I grew up. Five brothers and sisters. My granddad built it, Mickey Geraghty. Mickey's the Irish for Michael."

George hadn't changed much in the four years I'd known him. A lean, sharp-edged man with close-cropped brown hair, he looked younger than his fifty-six years. He coached a Gaelic football team, and he worked full shifts as an assistant greenkeeper. And when he said he was building a new house, he meant block by block, stick by stick, from foundation to chimney cap.

"These were great old houses," he said, leading me around the middle one. "Just stones and dried cement. The walls are about eighteen inches thick." He showed me a section of wall where the finish had fallen away to expose the rough stones. "That's the original wall. The stones came from here. They used to bring them over from the shore."

The wall resembled a jigsaw puzzle. The rocks were of various shapes and sizes, the gaps filled with thick gobs of wet-lime mortar. "What do you use for plaster?" I asked.

"The same exact stuff. Lime, feathered out in a finish coat and painted." He turned and gestured toward the stacked blocks of his new house, which resembled a three-dimensional game of Tetris. "The construction now is concrete block with a cavity. You fill the space with two-inch polystyrene to keep out the damp."

We walked around the middle house to an old stone barn. "The milk cows used to be in all winter," George said. "We'd feed them dry hay. The horses and the donkey were in, too, because they worked hard. They're all out now."

"You have horses?"

"Six," he said, "fed on silage and crunch." Crunch, he explained to the clueless golf writer, was a special meal for horses.

His new house, George continued, would have three bedrooms, a utility room, a kitchen and a lounge. "It's self-designed, like the one I'm in." But unlike his previous house, the new one would conform to modern building codes and environmental regulations promulgated by the European Union. "I have to put in a rank of small windows instead of one big one," he said, looking annoyed. "What's the sense of that? It goes back to the old tax, where they taxed you for light." I must have looked baffled, because he added, "The bigger the window, the more tax you paid." He shook his head. "It's stupid."

The sun was gone by the time we walked back out to the road, but pink clouds hovered over the distant dunes. We stood where Pat and I had stood almost two decades before, the spot where George's dad had pointed his cane across the corner of the lake. When I reminded George of that, he nodded. "My dad was great for stories, and he had a good memory. It was a pity he didn't write things down."

"Funny you should mention that." I flipped open my reporter's notebook. "I remember your dad talking about the Black and Tans"—the thuggish militia hired by the Royal Irish Constabulary to suppress revolution in the ugly times of 1920–21.

"The Black and Tans were here," George said with a curt nod. "They shot a man in Binghamstown. He was putting his cows in the field, and they shot him in the back. Another time, they took a young lad, just before Mass, I think, and tied him up and dragged him from a jeep." He scratched his chin. "There was also a story about old Mark Geraghty, who was sick and wouldn't get out of bed. The Black and Tans claimed he had a gun in his bed, under the mattress. So they set fire to the mattress."

I stared across the water at the acreage where so many Geraghtys had lived precarious lives. "Did they find a gun?"

"No, but those boys had no pity." He pointed toward the hollow up the road. "Anyway, that's where my granddad was born. They had two old stone houses, and there was a loft in one where they kept hay."

"Was it just Geraghtys? Were there other houses?"

"Oh yes. There was a family, the Lyons, when the British were here. They were very rich. They lived in a big two-story house just next door to us. They used to have parties, and there'd be horses and traps and side cars all the way around and up the hill. Massive parties, people from all over Mayo. Local people played the music and served the guests." He glanced my way. "This would have been a long time ago, when my grandfather was young."

I asked what had become of the Lyons.

He shrugged. "They weren't landlords like the Binghams and Carters. They were probably just rich English people who came and built a house, like rich people now have holiday homes." He must still have been thinking about the parties, because he added, "My dad was a fiddle and accordion player."

The problem, George went on, was that what little he knew about his forebears was anecdotal, and it didn't cover how they came to be in Cross. He didn't put much faith in those who traced the Geraghtys to the neighboring county of Roscommon, where a twelfth-century clan chief with aspirations allegedly changed his name from O Roduibh to Mag Oierachtaigh (for "son of a court or assembly member").

"I suppose we came from the sea at some stage," George said. "Some of us are very dark skinned. We may be from Italy."

"Or Spain?" The Spanish Armada had been blown onto Erris's rocky shore in 1588, and hundreds of shipwrecked sailors had never made it back to the Continent.

We stood for a moment, looking across the water. "What year was the famine?" George asked. "I can't think of it."

"1846 and '47," I said, "the worst of it."

"Oh, it was *wicked*." He practically spat the word. "An English landlord said one time, 'To Hell or to Connaught.' It was just as well to go to one or the other."

George fell silent. I picked up a stone and gave it a listless toss. It went *plunk*, and we watched the ripples spread in concentric circles. "Is it true," I asked, "that the Geraghtys of that time were farmers?"

"They were," he said. "They each had their own land, and they had a share of commonage in the sandy banks on the other side of the lake." He pointed toward the fading colors of sunset, which crowned the dunes. "There's a lovely strand there."

I had never walked the dunes at Cross, but in 2003 I had caught a glimpse of the banks from the old Cross cemetery, an untended boneyard that was falling into the sea. From a distance, the Cross banks had looked like a junior version of Carne. "Is there enough land for a golf course?"

He nodded. "Might put one in myself, when I retire." He smiled to show he wasn't serious.

It was getting chilly, so we walked back to the first house, the one with a light in the window and blue smoke curling out of the chimney. But as I followed George through the front door, I took one last look over my shoulder at the Carne banks, thinking . . . well, just thinking.

CHAPTER 11

Visiting golfer: "What's the course record?"
Irishman: "Two days without rain."
—Joke told at every links course in Ireland

It was blistering hot in Tulsa.

That's what it said on Golf.com, anyway: BLISTERING HOT IN TULSA FOR 89TH PGA CHAMPIONSHIP. Triple digits every day. Spectators staggering into first-aid stations. Course marshals pressing wet towels to their foreheads. "We've started more IVs on people than I would have expected," said the tournament's head of triage—a doctor specializing in Mad Dogs and Englishmen Syndrome.

The heat didn't seem to be bothering Tiger Woods. He was torching the field at Southern Hills Country Club with a second-round sixty-three, and he was well on the way to winning his thirteenth major title. I read the details on my laptop while munching cinnamon toast in my Belmullet flat. Comfortable in a black V-neck sweater, I couldn't remember the last time I had perspired.

Golfers, I don't have to tell you, are like sailors and farmers. We're always studying the sky, sniffing the air and listening for the distant rumble of thunder. We are weathermen in a figurative sense—men and women of the weather—but literally, too, in that we can be counted on to know the daily, three-day and five-day forecasts for various points on the globe, points where we plan to play golf, as well as distant venues where professionals are scheduled to play for our amusement. My father was a finger-in-the-wind meteorologist, and sometimes I catch myself reciting his tropes. "The wind's swinging around from the north," I say, or "Look at those frontal clouds." I fix my eyes on the treetops, pretending to see what he saw in their orchestrated swaying.

It is with an air of confident authority, therefore, that I make the following claim: Western Ireland has the best weather in the world.

Not everyone will agree. Some will point to afternoon temperatures that rarely top 65 degrees Fahrenheit and damp cloudy days that succeed one another like wet clothes on a line. Others will grouse about the winter storms with their hurricane-force winds and rampaging tides. CBS golf commentator and author David Feherty—a Northern Irishman living in Texas—e-mailed me that I was "daft" for vacationing in Mayo "at this time of the year"—i.e., summer.

But when I say that Western Ireland has the best weather, I mean golf weather. There are destinations that are sunnier (Hawaii), drier (Dubai), warmer (Arizona), cooler (Sweden) or less windy (Zimbabwe?), but those same destinations are often too soggy, too hot, too cold, or too perilous for golf. Tulsa, for example, suffers from both thunderstorms and ice storms, either of which make Southern Hills unplayable. The Mullet, by way of contrast, rarely thrills to the peal of thunder. Carne's fairways and greens remain firm and puddle-free in the heaviest of rains.

Granted, the conditions can be trying. On my third round at Carne, in the summer of 2003, I was out by myself on the back nine when an Atlantic squall came ashore, blowing my ball cap off, toppling my golf bag and pelting me with rain. By the time I buttoned up my rain jacket and struggled into my rain pants, the rain had moved on. A half hour later, I was on the oceanside thirteenth hole when another squall blew in. This one blew my umbrella apart and coated my eyeglasses with clingy droplets, effectively blinding me. But I played on, finishing an hour later in a jubilant mood and a steady downpour. I was in the changing room, laying out my soggy clothes, when *SI* photographer Bob Martin and his assistant, Mick Gandolfo, walked in. Martin, a large Englishman who bears a superficial resemblance to the golfer Colin Montgomerie, chortled at the sight of me. "You look like a drowned rat," he crowed. But then a look of concern crossed his face. "You aren't going to write about playing in the rain, are you?"

I patted my still-dripping head with a paper towel. "I don't know. Probably."

He turned morose. "They won't like it in New York if we don't have pictures of that." The corners of his mouth turned up again. "Any chance we could persuade you to go back out and play the eighteenth again?"

"You aren't serious." I looked at him. I saw that he was serious.

So Bob and Mick went to get their gear while I struggled back into my saturated clothes. Ten minutes later, in a driving rain, I climbed the steep hill to the eighteenth green for a second time while the photogs, in foul-weather gear, snapped me from above. Water streamed off my golf bag and dripped from the bill of my cap. "Lose the hat!" Bob yelled. I took off the hat. At five o'clock in the afternoon it was as dark as dusk, save for the occasional pop of the flash. "Do it again!" Bob yelled when I reached the top. "And lift your chin!"

I scaled the hill three more times in the rain, my goofball grin frozen for posterity by Bob's white lightning.

L inks golf, the locals never tired of telling me, was all about the elements. There were days when Carne played to its listed 6,800 yards, but most days it did not. The par-4 ninth hole often called for a drive from an exposed and elevated tee into a twenty-five- or thirty-mile-per-hour headwind. The par-5 thirteenth, on a shelf of land near the sea, commonly taunted golfers with a two- or three-club crosswind. "The prevailing wind is from the southwest," Gary Stanley told me during one of our rounds, "but it's not that simple. Some days you can stand on the eleventh and twelfth tees, which point in completely different directions, and the wind seems to be into you on both tees. It's just the way it comes around the hills."

In Carne's first decade, it wasn't just the golfers who had to cope with the wind. The golf shop was in a tiny Portakabin on a dune next to the clubhouse, where the wind swirled with demonic fury. "The cabin was secured to a concrete pad with two belts," Mary Walsh told me, "and when the wind got high, they'd start rattling so loud you couldn't hear people on the phone. When the computer monitor started rocking, it was time to start running."

The challenge was even greater for the greenkeepers, who were being paid—or underpaid, some would say—to stabilize a dunescape that had been shape-shifting for eons under the steady attack of wind, waves and rain. One winter storm, I read in a book, had dumped several tons of sand and salt on the fourteenth tee. "It was literally destroyed," Gary confirmed. "We had to completely rebuild the tee, and it took us six or seven months to get the thirteenth green back in reasonable condition." Reinforced with steel mesh, the seaside holes had survived subsequent storms, but Gary said the club might install some mounds behind the green. "Eddie Hackett didn't want a bank there because he thought it would spoil the ocean view. But maybe a *small* bank at the back, to deflect the wind and salt. It wouldn't have to be that high." He shrugged. "Or you can put in sprinklers and simply wash the salt and sand off the grass."

The sprinkler solution, I gathered from his expression, would be a last resort.

My own weather strategies, informed by my skin-soaking round of 2003, were easier to implement. First off, I bought an exorbitantly expensive rain suit—one that actually repelled water—and stowed it in my golf bag. Second, I bought a Carne-logoed knit cap that wouldn't blow off in high winds (and which I could pull down over my ears on frosty mornings). Third, I bought a pair of Rain-Grip golf gloves, which, as the advertising copy promised, provided "optimum grip for those rainy, wet conditions." Fourth, I made sure that I always had my snap-on rain cover ready for deployment on the golf bag. Fifth, I bought a new golf umbrella—one with ribs as thick as rebar.

The properly equipped golfer, I soon discovered, could handle most weather contingencies. In July of '06 I played a round at Carne with Gary, Jim Engh, and the 1974 U.S. Open runner-up, Forrest Fezzler—a round that devolved into pure high jinks as the weather deteriorated. Jim and Forrest were playing with seven clubs each, while I had just four—a driver, 5 iron, 8 iron and 52-degree wedge. (I borrowed their putters without shame.) We played from the championship tees, of course. It was cold and windy when we started, and the wind only picked up as we staggered around the front nine. At the turn, Gary made an educated guess about the wind speed—"probably a steady thirty miles an hour with gusts of forty or more"—and then got my attention by adding, "The storm's gonna get here soon."

And it did. The first drops hit us as we played the tenth hole, and then the first major squall arrived as we fought our way up the canyon fairway on number eleven. (I'll never forget Forrest trying to play his second from the peak of the giant dune on the right—a tiny figure braced against the wind and laughing like a lunatic.) The full fury of the storm hit us on number twelve as we left the protection of the dunes. Gary had the only umbrella, and it was useless against the stinging rain. We played the par-5 thirteenth, the most exposed hole on the course, like so many CNN hurricane reporters, lurching left and right and shouting quips that were carried away on the wind.

It was the most memorable stretch of golf I've ever played, and not just because the weather was, as the British say, "bracing." With only my four clubs to battle the storm, I played holes ten through fourteen in birdie, bogey, par, par, par. Ever since, when anybody asks me what was the best score of my life, I say, "An eighty-seven at Carne."

Sometimes, when I was out on the course by myself, I watched the squalls line up over the Atlantic and speculated on what it must have been like to live on the Mullet in, say, the nineteenth century—to live under a thatched roof in a little stone house, surrounded by ragged children, farm animals and piles of peat. I wondered if my great-grandfather, as a boy, had ever wandered out on the banks at Cross or Carne during a storm. I wondered if he had ever felt giddy in the lashing rain or thrilled at the sight of the big waves crashing at Annagh Head.

The closeness of the Atlantic made the strongest impression on me. The Mullet was as exposed as the prow of a ship, and there were stretches of shoreline that spelled danger whether you approached them from sea or land. I drove out past Corclough from time to time to park on the cliffs and stare out at Eagle Island, a hunk of rock about a quarter-mile off shore. The island's principal feature was a lighthouse, whose stubby white tower poked out of a cluster of buildings on the island's windward side, a couple of hundred feet above the waves. Legend had it that a rogue wave had pummeled the island in the 1890s, a wave so immense that it shattered the tower glass, destroyed the lamps, and funneled so much water down the stairs that the lightkeepers couldn't open the tower door and had to drill holes to let the water out.

The story was preposterous, but whenever I asked a local about the rogue wave, I'd get an "Oh yes, indeed" or "Which occurrence would you be referring too?"—as if two-hundred-foot waves were as common as counts in castles. So I began to assign my weather discoveries to two categories: credible and not credible. One morning at Carne, for example, an American who had driven down the coast from the Stella Maris Hotel told Chris Birrane that it had been a stressful drive because of all the sheep in the road. "I'm afraid I'll hit one," the American fretted. "Why don't they stay on the grass?" To which Chris replied, "The tarmac absorbs the heat of the sun. The sheep like to lie on it at night."

I found that to be credible.

Similarly, I detected genuine emotion when Erris folk spoke of an October evening in 1927 when a fleet of two-man currachs had set out from Inishkea on an overnight fishing trip. "An unexpected storm swept down, and ten young men were drowned," they would say, "and it so shattered the islanders that they petitioned for a move to the mainland and left Inishkea to the birds and the seals." But just to be sure, I thumbed through Rita Nolan's *Within the Mullet* and found two whole pages on the tragedy. "The hurricane came screaming out of the night," Nolan wrote, "and tossed their currachs around like paper boats."

Totally credible.

But submersible lighthouses I took with a grain of sea salt. Or I did, anyway, until I met Ted Hawkins.

"There's a great old guy you should talk to," a Belmullet Golf Club member had told me. "He was club captain, he was honorary treasurer and he ran a ladies' and children's clothing store for more than thirty years. He'll have plenty to say about the old nine-hole course." The club member gave me Hawkins' phone number, and a couple of days later I sat down with Ted in the parlor of the little house he shared with his wife in Belmullet town.

"I'm eighty-six," Ted said without prompting, "but my memory's pretty good still." A slender, accommodating man with white hair and a slight stoop, he walked without shuffling in answering the door and showing me in. He had quit golf two years before, having reached the conclusion that Carne, great as it was, was no track for an octogenarian. "Pulling my caddie cart up to those high tees didn't suit me," he said with a laugh. "I found myself out of breath all the time."

Ted's golf biography was not unlike my dad's. Ted had fallen for golf in County Sligo, where from the ages of seven to twelve he attended the national school at Rosses Point, near the celebrated eighteen-hole links course of the same name. "My father was the lightkeeper on Oyster Island," he said, "and every day I'd take the boat to the mainland at half eight, walk on into school, walk back at three and take the boat back to the isle. It was a very happy time."

"And the golf?" I leaned forward.

"They played the West of Ireland every year at Rosses Point, and to me it was the world's biggest event. I got to watch Cecil Ewing, who was Sligo's famous Walker Cupper, and John Burke from Lahinch. All the great amateurs." Ted's eyes got big. "And Joe Carr! He came to Rosses Point every year."

Joe Carr was the name I recognized. A Dubliner, Carr played for Great Britain & Ireland in a record 11 Walker Cups (1947–67); won the British Amateur three times; reached the semifinals of the 1961 U.S. Amateur; became the first Irishman to play in the Masters (1967); became the first Irishman to gain admittance to the World Golf Hall of Fame, and—I had to look this up later—turned heads in County Sligo by winning twelve West of Ireland titles.

The examples of those great players had inspired Ted, but he hadn't played the game regularly until he was grown up. "But I was very keen when I started off," he said with a nod. "I had aspirations to be a professional." He shrugged. "I started too late."

Perhaps the fact that I was looking for stories about the Belmullet Golf

Club explains why I didn't follow up when Ted mentioned that his father was a lightkeeper. But then Ted said that he, too, had been a lightkeeper in his youth, stationed at Blackrock in County Sligo, St. John's Point in County Down, Maidens Rock in County Antrim, and finally at Eagle Island, a few miles from where we were talking.

"All right," I said, "you can clear this up for me. Did you ever hear of a big wave that crashed over Eagle Island and filled the lighthouse with water?"

"Twenty-ninth of December, 1894," he said without hesitation. "And it wasn't one wave—it was several. One after the other. There were two towers in those days, the east and the west, and the east tower was damaged beyond repair. The sea broke the lantern glass and poured down the stairs. Afterwards, the men couldn't open the door for the water, so they had to drill holes to drain it."

I felt my jaw drop. "Ted, that's not a flat island, it's a pretty tall rock. How high was the tower?"

He got out of his chair. "I think it was two hundred fifty feet high. I can check that for you." He disappeared into the next room and returned a few moments later, turning the pages of *Bright Light, White Water*, a book about Irish lighthouses. "Here it is," he said, pointing to a paragraph as he handed me the book.

Eagle Island, I quickly read, was a high, exposed rock close to the Continental Shelf and a lighthouse that had suffered "more damage than most" in its nearly two centuries of service. Storms in 1836 and 1850 had damaged both towers and terrified the lightkeepers and their families, and then a great wave had risen up on March 11, 1861, shattering twenty-three panes of glass in the east tower and washing the debris down the stairs. "This was truly an incredible wave," wrote the book's author, Bill Long, "to have risen 220 feet and retained enough force to inflict such damage."

But the wave of 29 December 1894 was even bigger, according to the book. Ted said, "In those days, four families lived on the island—husbands, wives and children." He handed me an old *Western People* clipping headlined GRAPHIC ACCOUNTS OF STORM TERROR ON EAGLE ISLAND. Letters written by the island's inhabitants after the storm recalled how at two thirty a.m. the sea had bashed in the roof and hall door of one of the houses, tumbling the residents out of their warm beds and into knee-deep sea water. "The whole roof was gone by this time," one of the wives had written. "To see the sea boiling down stairs and into all the rooms . . . was something frightful."

I looked up. "And you lived on that island?"

He nodded as he settled back into his armchair. "I loved it. Summertime was lovely, you couldn't find a nicer place. In mushroom season, all you had to do was take a pan out, pick a bunch of mushrooms and fry 'em up."

"But the storms! Did you ever get hit by waves like these?"

"Nothing that bad. But we took precautions. We tied a rope between the living quarters and the tower so that you could hold on if you were caught in between by a wave. Anything you left outside would be broken to bits and washed out by the sea. I saw three-by-three Yorkshire flagstones lifted up and thrown ten yards."

I shook my head and resumed reading. Bill Long described the Eagle Island station as he had found it after one spring storm. "Windows had been shattered, ironwork twisted beyond recognition, doors and gates ripped from their hinges and flung across rocks and into the sea."

I laughed out loud. "It says here that Eagle Island used to have a miniature golf course, but it was destroyed in a storm."

Ted nodded, but said nothing. I put the mini-golf yarn in the "pending" category.

When I returned to the flat that night, I had the book under my arm. I read it cover to cover in a couple of days, absorbing enough lighthouse lore to impress tourists and Irish preschoolers. If you asked me about the Black Rock lighthouse, just up the Mayo coast, I'd tell you that it sat on a rock so forbidding that neither boats nor helicopters could land for months at a time. If you expressed an interest in the Blacksod light, down at the tip of the Mullet, I'd babble like a tour guide about the 1944 weather forecast issued by the Blacksod Point Meteorological Station that had enabled the Allies to pick the right day for the D-Day landings in France, and how in 1969 it was the Blacksod lightkeeper Ted Sweeney and his son Vincent greeting Tom McCleane, who had rowed single-handed across the Atlantic, and how they had later appeared as guests on the American TV show *This Is Your Life*. And if you asked about Eagle Island, I pointed out that it, like most of the Irish lighthouses, had been "demanned" in the 1980s. It's now operated in automatic mode.

That's if you asked.

"I'm going to drive out there some night and see how it looks in operation," I told Pat, adding, "Some *starry* night, when the waves are lapping at the shore."

I wanted nothing to do with it in a storm.

CHAPTER 12

Just as the sand dunes, heaped upon one another, hide each the first, so in life the former deeds are quickly hidden by those that follow after.

—from Marcus Aurelius Antoninus' *Meditations*

The golf gene," I confessed to Pat, "is an unproven concept."

"How so?" The picture on my laptop wobbled as she adjusted her webcam.

"Well, I've been doing a little research on the subject of golf in Ireland, and there wasn't a hell of a lot of it until recently. There may have been a nine-hole course at Portmarnock in 1858, and there's evidence that golf was played on the Curragh a few years before that. But Ireland's oldest golf club, Royal Belfast, only dates to 1881. So there's not much chance that Geraghtys were playing golf in Ireland before the twentieth century.

"It's quite possible," I added with a note of awe, "that my father was the first Garrity to touch a golf club!"

I was joking, but it struck me afterward that I might have hit the mark. Jack Garrity smacked his first golf shot in a Wisconsin pasture around 1918. At that time, America's first golf course, the St. Andrew's Golf Club in Yonkers, New York, was just thirty years old.. Sitting at my table in Belmullet, I Googled "Garrity and St. Andrew's" and got 29,600 results, the top three being links to my own books and articles and the fourth leading to one Mike McGarrity, a Chevy dealer in Andrews, Texas. ("READY TO BUY A NEW AUTO OR TRUCK?")

I jumped to Golf.com and read that Tiger had shot a third-round sixty-nine at the PGA Championship. He led Stephen Ames by three.

It felt odd, not being in Tulsa. I had missed only one major championship since 1989, and that was the 2004 PGA. (I covered the Russian Open that week, fulfilling my dream of walking across Red Square in golf shoes.) Furthermore, Southern Hills was only 240 miles from Kansas City; I had driven that far for cheese fries.

But I already had plenty of memories of steamy Southern Hills. I was there for the 2001 U.S. Open, won by Retief Goosen. (I remember it being hot.) I was there for the 1994 PGA Championship, won by Nick Price. (Hot again.) And I was there for the 1958 U.S. Open. (Very, very hot.)

Yeah, 1958.

I'm not a sports writer in the summer of fifty-eight. I'm a sweaty eleven-year-old in scuffed loafers, khaki pants, a plaid cotton shirt (untucked) and tortoiseshell glasses. But the golf gods love a chuckle, so they've put me fifteen feet behind Ben Hogan as he addresses a tee shot in the final round of the U.S. Open. The only thing that separates the two of us is a gallery rope and Hogan's legendary self-absorption.

You'd think I'd be happy, but I'm not. On the last hole someone clicked a Brownie camera, causing Hogan to turn and stare into the gallery with a look that could have melted glass. Now I've got this tickle in my throat and the great man is waggling his driver. I can see the front page of tomorrow's Tulsa Daily World: HOGAN MURDERS YOUNGSTER WHO COUGHED, *and the subhead,* CHOICE OF DRIVER SECOND-GUESSED BY POLICE.

Hogan! White cap, pleated slacks, polo shirt with tight sleeves, weathered face, tight lips. Hit it, I silently pray, trying to ignore the allergens dancing on my larynx. Hit it! Hogan finally swings, and my asthmatic wheeze overlays the crack of impact as his driver sends the ball flying. With everyone's eyes focused on the shot, I slip between the grown-ups and sprint into the trees, where I cough until my eyes water.

When I come out again, Hogan is gone.

D id I mention that my long-term memory is not so hot? Not as good as my dad's, anyway. A few years ago I volunteered to write an eyewitness account of the 1958 U.S. Open for *Sports Illustrated*, only to discover, when faced with a blank Word file, that I had about two paragraphs' worth of memories. Needing help, I phoned my brother in Houston. "Crank up the Wayback Machine," I said. "I need everything you can remember about the fifty-eight Open."

"Southern Hills?" Tommy's tone was quizzical. "I don't remember that much."

"You were a couple of weeks shy of twenty-one," I prompted, "a hotshot golfer at the University of Missouri."

He laughed. "That I remember."

"And we didn't call it the U.S. Open back then. We called it the *National* Open."

"That's right!" He took the bait, disturbing some waters that hadn't been fished for a while. "I've still got the hang tag somewhere. A little piece of cardboard on a string." That first nibble led to further strikes, and soon Tommy was remembering on his own. He remembered, for instance, that we weren't at Southern Hills for the first two rounds of the Open, just the final thirty-six holes on Saturday. "Dad never missed an opportunity to see the pros play," Tommy said, "but this wasn't a carefully planned trip. We just drove down from Kansas City in the Buick and bought tickets at the gate."

Mention of the Buick sent me back. The car in question was a red-and-white fifty-six Buick Special with three chrome portholes behind the front wheels. Dad always liked to get an early start, so we would have been out of bed and into the car an hour before dawn. We probably stopped for waffles and ham steaks at the Toddle House diner on Sixty-third Street, filled the tank at the Brookside Sinclair station, and then sped out of town on two-lane Highway 71. I was sure we were past Harrisonville by the time the sun cleared the wooded hills of western Missouri.

"The car radio was tuned to WHB," I said, remembering Kansas City's rock 'n' roll station and the hyper deejays who insisted that the call letters stood for World's Happiest Broadcasters. "Remember the station ID?" I sang it over the phone, " 'Yours tru-ly, double-yew . . . aitch bee!'

"Sounded better with the Hi-Lo's harmonies," I conceded.

And as we talked it came back, in dribs and drabs, memories of a very hot day in the heartland.

We get to Tulsa around ten in the morning and fight the traffic to Southern Hills. We park in a dusty field choked with cars. At the gate we pay for three cardboard rectangles bearing the words "58th USGA Open Championship." We hang them from our belts. We then climb a sun-baked slope to the clubhouse, which sits up on a ridge like a Tuscan palazzo. It is very, very hot— close to a hundred degrees and muggy. The spectators on the sidewalk behind the first tee smell of sweat, suntan lotion, cigarettes, popcorn and beer.

Dad, studying the pairing sheet, sets a time and place for us to rendezvous. Tommy and I head for the tenth tee. Dad walks back down the ninth fairway to look for the Masters champion, a young pro from Pennsylvania by the name of Arnold Palmer. When we catch up with Dad around noon he wears the earnest frown he reserves for moments of profound discovery. "This kid's going to be good," he tells us. "He takes a healthy cut at it, busts it a mile."

I'm equally excited about my own discovery: "Daddy, the swimming pool's got a water slide!"

Dad stands in line at a concession stand and buys us hot dogs and potato chips. A fourteen-ounce Coke costs twenty-five cents and is mostly ice, but Dad doesn't complain. He's having a great time.

The man of the hour is Tommy Bolt, a club-throwing cracker from just up the road in Haworth, Oklahoma. Bolt has opened with rounds of 71–71 on a par-70 Southern Hills course that has been tricked up with thick Bermuda rough and talcum powder bunkers. The scoreboard outside the clubhouse, meticulously updated by a man with calligraphy pens, reads as follows: 211, Tommy Bolt; 214, Gene Littler; 216, Gary Player; 218, Julius Boros.

I loved watching Littler," Tommy said over the phone. "His swing was compact, but beautifully measured, and he had incredible hand action."

My brother's interest in Littler had been more than academic. Tommy Garrity, then twenty, was just three months away from playing as an amateur in his first PGA event, the 1958 Kansas City Open. Littler was his swing model, the template on which he was building his own graceful action. Littler's ball went out low, rose, hung . . . and then fell softly, as if dropped by an angel.

So did Tommy's.

But it was the lumbering Boros, my brother recalled, who taught him something that day. On the seventh hole, a short par 4, Boros' approach had caught the left fringe, no more than thirty feet from the hole. Only it wasn't "fringe"—it was thick, tangly Bermuda rough, a nightmarish chipping medium. "Boros took what amounted to a full swing in slow motion," Tommy remembered. "The ball popped out, trickled down the slope, and stopped a couple of feet from the hole. I was bug-eyed."

I, on the other hand, am droopy-eyed. Having dodged the wrath of Hogan, I'm keeping to the shade, sitting against a tree whenever I get bored, wiping my sweat-streaked glasses on my shirttail. I catch a glimpse of an eighteen-year-old amateur named Jack Nicklaus, but who is he? I'm more interested in Dr. Cary Middlecoff, the former dentist and two-time National Open champ. I'm morbidly fascinated with Middlecoff. He's a snappier dresser than my hometown dentist, a pain merchant who saves his Novocain for the adult patients.

Eventually I join the crowd following Bolt and the Australian sourpuss, Bruce Crampton. The famously volatile Bolt disappoints me by not wrapping a club around a tree, but watching him is hardly a waste of time. His gallery has swollen to thousands, so it takes me a while to spot Dad and Tommy walking up the sixteenth fairway behind the golfers and rope marshals.

"I do remember the finish," Tommy said from Houston. "We were right behind the tee on the seventy-second hole, right behind Bolt."

Dad and Tommy have made a space for me to kneel between them, so I have a terrific view of Bolt as he steps onto the eighteenth tee. He's a powerful man with thick black hair and a ruddy face, and his caddy totes a leather golf bag as big as a trash can. Bolt has a four-stroke lead over Player, who has finished his round, but Littler and Boros, playing behind us, still have several holes to make up ground. The eighteenth, meanwhile, is a monster finishing hole, a lengthy par 4 over two streams and three cross bunkers to an elevated green.

"He double-bogeyed this hole yesterday," Dad whispers. Impressed with the gravity of the situation, I hold my breath.

"The minute Bolt hit his drive," Tommy said on the phone, "we took off running around the tee and into the fairway to get into position for the shot to the green."

"We *ran?*" I couldn't imagine such a breach of decorum.

"Oh, yeah. This was a shot that Dad had to see. He had this sense that it would be historic."

Dad had witnessed an historic shot or two—most notably at the 1930 National Open at Interlachen, where he saw Bobby Jones skip his famous Lily Pad Shot across a lake to the ninth green.

"I don't know if Bolt's shot was historic," Tommy continued, "but it was certainly exceptional. We were behind him again in the fairway, right behind the rope. Bolt whipped a 4 wood up there, and there was a big roar at the green when the ball landed."

My brother's description was like a long-forgotten play acted out in my mind. Years later, I had stood not far from where we were on that steamy afternoon and watched Nick Price spank an 8 iron to the final green to secure his victory at the 1994 PGA Championship. My memory of Price's shot was so clear—the spectators on the slopes above the green, the meandering creek, the deep bunkers, the big trees on either side of the fairway— that I could put Bolt in Price's shoes and see 1958 with the same clarity.

"That shot was the end of the tournament, as far as we were concerned," Tommy said. "That's what Dad had wanted to see. That's why he drove all those miles."

We're in a hotel restaurant in Joplin, Missouri. It's air-conditioned. I'm gnawing on fried shrimp and french fries while Dad and Tommy ignore their steaks and continue the obsessive dialog begun on the hot, dusty walk back to the parking lot at Southern Hills. (Dad stays excited for hours after a tournament, smoking through a couple of packs of Camels and knocking back a few bourbons.) I listen eagerly as they analyze the performances of the players they

have followed—Frank Stranahan, Lloyd Mangrum, Charlie Coe, Marty Fur-
gol, and, of course, Tommy Bolt.

"Bolt has a temper," Dad says, "but he's got a sense of humor. A couple of
years ago he was playing in the Crosby when some lamebrain told him that all
the putts at Pebble Beach broke toward the ocean. Bolt just looked at the guy
and said, 'Why don't they fill it in?' "

Tommy and I laugh. And then Dad starts to say something about Hogan.

"Hogan?" The shrillness of my voice makes them turn, forks poised between
plate and mouth.

CHAPTER 13

[The locals] are, without exception, warm, witty, and welcoming, exemplars of the human qualities of the modern Irish who somehow manage to combine effortless efficiency with beguiling charm. On a cold, blustery winter's day, there is no better place to have a pint of Guinness and a sandwich than with a few club members and a couple of quick-witted barmaids enjoying the craic in Carne's Spike Bar.

—from John de St. Jorre's *Legendary Golf Links of Ireland*

There are 382 members of the Belmullet Golf Club," Terry Swinson told me one afternoon at Carne. "There are nine honorary lifetime members, of which you are one." He gave me a nod and a smile. "There are seventy-eight overseas life members, two thirds of them from the U.S. and a third from England and Germany. Of those, forty-two are active, frequent users. There are seventy-two country members, which means they are full voting members of another club in Ireland. There are also fifty-five or fifty-six junior and juvenile members under eighteen, a number that has increased the last five years. Which is good."

He flipped to another page. "The total membership hasn't changed much in my six years as honorary secretary, but there is a trend. We have a very big turnover of local members, mostly juniors and young people. They go off to university or off to Dublin to work."

"But not to Australia," I said. "Not to England."

"No, very few have to emigrate now."

Terry, a slight, handsome man of sixty-eight with a full head of brown hair and a perpetual look of amusement, said that about fifty members played every Sunday in the club competitions. "And I mean *every* Sunday, hail, rain or snow." The local members, he continued, were "great people, very self-sufficient, noncritical. We have no marked spaces in the car park, which I think is a great thing."

The lack of airs, he acknowledged, might owe to the fact that the club did not own the Carne Golf Links. "The Belmullet Golf Club is almost unique in that respect. We're the resident club, but if things got difficult Erris Tourism could dump us out of here."

"Are there any Polish or Lithuanian members?" I was thinking of the immigrants from central Europe who were coming in droves to feed the Celtic Tiger—the housekeepers, waitresses, roofers, and technology line workers.

"Not yet," he said. "But they'll be welcome."

Terry Swinson, I was surprised to learn, was neither a lifetime golfer nor a Belmullet native. He was from a little village outside Belfast in County Down, Northern Ireland. In the late nineties, when he had a thriving facial surgery practice in the North, he was looking for a holiday home—preferably in scenic Donegal, the most northern county in the Irish Republic. "I was down in Galway in December of 1997," he told me, "shoving a fellow's jaw back for him. Nicóla, my third wife-to-be, was with me, and she wanted to see Achill Island." Achill, I knew, was a mountainous isle off the south Mayo coast that could be reached by bridge from Westport.

"We were driving home," he continued, "and by the time we got to Belmullet it was dark. So we spent the night at the Western Strands Hotel." He smiled. "The only time I'd ever heard of Belmullet was in the shipping program."

The next morning was gray and dreary, but Terry and Nicóla decided to check out the peninsula, the so-called Mullet. They drove down the

R313, hardly turning their heads as they passed Carne, and motored through the population patches of Binghamstown, Cross, Leam, Clogher and Aughleam. Just shy of Blacksod Point, Terry turned right on a farm road and drove around and up the treeless, fog-shrouded hills, and suddenly they came upon the standing stones—giant boulders arranged in a circle on a barren, rock-strewn promontory. "I thought it was Neolithic," Terry said, "until I noticed the poured concrete."

They had stumbled upon Deirble's Twist, one of fourteen outdoor installations comprising the North Mayo Sculpture Trail.

"I'm very interested in astronomy and archeology," he went on, "so we parked and got out. The visibility was terrible, but from the heights I could just make out this little seaside cottage, out on a point." And not much of a cottage, at that, but a little tissue box of a place on a patch of sea meadow.

Intrigued, Terry and Nicóla drove back down to the main road. Employing guesswork, they turned into another country lane and wandered up more hills, past isolated farms, and back down to the little white cottage. They parked and got out for a look around. "There was no door on it," Terry recalled, "and there was a puddle of water in the kitchen. It was . . ." He paused. "It was exactly what I was looking for."

What was the appeal?

"Its remoteness," he said. "The utter primitive kind of place it was. And it faced down south, which is what an astronomer wants. There was absolutely no light pollution."

Back in Belmullet, Terry made inquiries and was told that the man who owned the cottage was, at that very moment, in the Corner House Pub. A call was made, and Terry and Nicóla walked straight across the square to the pub.

"Three hot whiskeys were waiting for us," Terry remembered. "I said, 'Would you like to sell the cottage?' He said, 'I would need to ask my wife.'" The farmer went to the phone in the back of the pub, talked for a few minutes, and came back with the necessary permission.

"How much do you want for it?"

"I'll need about twenty thousand pounds, but you'll get the land, as well."

"Okay. I'll buy it."

"I thought about it for about a millisecond," Terry told me, "and it was by far the best decision I've made in my whole life. But I wasn't so sure at the time. I thought, my God, this is going to be a five-hour drive from home. But two weeks later, on a clear day, I came over the brow of the hill, and there was Achill Island in front of me, the hills, the sea. The view was stunning."

"And so," I interjected, "you've been happily stargazing ever since?"

He smiled wistfully. "To use a five-hundred-power telescope, the atmosphere has to be dead calm. You need warm, calm weather for four or five days, and that doesn't happen often here. The first time I put the telescope up, the sky was just shimmering. So I was like a golfer without a putter. I couldn't use my telescope.

"And that," he joked, "is how I came to be honorary secretary of the Belmullet Golf Club."

"Back up," I said. "How do you go from frustrated astronomer to fairway factotum?"

"Oh," he waved in dismissal, "it's not a full-time job." Terry still worked a couple of days a week at Letterkenny General Hospital in Donegal, tweaking deviated septums and ironing out wrinkled foreheads. "I don't have a staff anymore, and I never do major cases. It's very limited."

"But in ninety-seven, when you bought the cottage . . ."

He nodded. "At that time I played virtually no golf, but Carne had just opened, and I thought I'd take a look. I played a few times and decided to join. It cost very little."

"And you got hooked?"

"I did. But I'm quite a shy person, and I felt a bit of an outsider, at first—what they call a 'blow-in.' " Most of the locals, he discovered, spoke Gaelic as fluently as they spoke English, and they took it on the golf course with them. "Irish is a bewildering language," he said. "It's incredibly difficult." Anxious to fit in, Terry had tried out a common welcoming phrase of Gaelic on a neighbor, who replied, "That's *Donegal* Irish. We don't speak that."

"Mayo Irish is more related to Kerry and the southern Irish," Terry said. "A lot of the population were shoved up here by the early English."

As a consequence of his shyness, Terry played most of his golf on weekdays, either filling out a foursome or playing solo. He might have gone on that way indefinitely but for the regular calls he made to the local *Met Éire-ann* weather station to check on the relative humidity in his role as a field reporter for the Irish Astronomical Society. Three members of the Belmullet Golf Club worked at the Met station—Donal Shine and past captains Kevin Donnelly and John Hanley—and they invited Terry to play with them in the Sunday competitions. "They're all meteorologists," he explained.

One thing led to another, and Terry wound up on the golf committee. Some time later, he was offered the position of honorary secretary. "That's still a mystery to me," he said. "I happened to mention that I had a computer, and in the Belmullet of 2001 that was apparently enough to get a tick beside your name."

A more likely reason, I thought, was that nobody was as golf daft as Terry, or played Carne as often as he did. When I went out to the seventeenth hole in the afternoon, I sometimes found Terry playing the closing holes by himself, a visibly contented man in close pursuit of a single-digit handicap.

"I love my work as secretary," Terry said, "because the club is a very happy, contented club. They're great people, and it's an honor to serve them."

He stood up and crossed the room to switch off the radiator.

"Did you hear from Gary?" He looked back at me. "Sunday morning, nine something?"

"Nine-oh-seven," I said, having committed my first club-competition tee time to memory. "I'll be there."

Meanwhile, I was beginning to reach an understanding with the seventeenth hole. "You're not a par 4," I would mutter to myself on the tee. "You're a par 5, and if I treat you like a par 5 you won't be half as scary." This was a necessary self-deception, because I missed the fairway two out of three times.

"For the big hitter, the fairway just gets too narrow," the greenkeeper Gary Stanley told me during one of our rounds. "When the ground is hard, a good, long draw just keeps going until it runs over the edge."

"You're saying the hole is not fair?"

"There isn't much fair about golf," he said with a chuckle. "It's a horrible game."

I knew I wasn't blazing any trails by treating seventeen as a three-shot hole. "I'm not gonna get there in two, and I *know* I'm not gonna get there in two," club member Terry McSweeney had told me. "So why try?" McSweeney always hit a fairway wood off the tee and laid up with his second—although, as I saw it, hitting the throat of fairway in front of the green was almost as difficult as hitting the green itself. "It's the hardest hole on the course," Seamus Cafferky told me, "but one of the greatest holes anywhere."

Great . . . and yet flawed? That was the opinion of Jim Engh, who, although he loved Carne without reservation, thought it would take only thirty minutes with a bulldozer to make seventeen a better hole. "I'd shave the mounds to create ten more yards of fairway on the right," Jim said. "As it is, a really good drive is punished as often as it is rewarded."

Jim, if you haven't guessed, is a big hitter who favors a draw.

Other visitors—and more than a few members—had suggested that No. 17 would be more winsome if the huge cavity short and right of the fairway was filled. "Eddie Hackett came to visit us after the course was open," Seamus said, "and we said there were a lot of complaints about that area, and was there any possibility of maybe filling it in? 'No, no, no,' he says. 'When I'm dead and gone you can do what you like, but while I'm alive, that will not be filled.' Now he's dead and gone, but it's not filled in, and probably never will be."

Nobody, I noticed, wanted the seventeenth to be changed from a par 4 to a par 5. That would have solved the problem, but it would have also slapped the pens out of the hands of the visiting writers, who used words like "brutal" and "demonic" to describe Carne's penultimate hole. If it were a par 5, seventeen would be demoted to "tough but fair," "challenging" or—God forbid— "birdieable."

"It shouldn't matter whether it's a par 4 or a par 5," I told Terry Swinson. "It's the same wind, the same fairway, the same hazards."

"No, it shouldn't matter," he said. "But it does."

Thinking of seventeen as a par 5 was entirely different. I was keeping score now on the back of my business cards, and I noticed that 5 was invariably my mode score, the most frequent outcome. On the afternoon of

September 8 for example, I opened with 5-5-7 and finished my seventeenth-hole round, two hours later, with ten 5s and an eighteen-ball total of 95. That worked out to three pars, ten bogeys, a double-bogey, and three triple-bogeys. But if I tricked my cerebellum by putting a 5 in the par box, the round reset as three birdies, ten pars, a bogey and three double-bogeys. (Much better!) What's more, the results were about what I would expect if I played a generic par 5 eighteen times.

Unfortunately, the par-is-five ploy was effective only as a micro-strategy. "It helps me sleep at night," I told Pat during one of our video chats, "but do the math. Five times eighteen is ninety, and that's my target score: *ninety*. I'll have to shoot par golf to reach my goal." Seeing that she didn't get my reasoning, I said, "I've never shot par in my life. There's no way I'm going to par the toughest hole at Carne eighteen straight times."

"I'm not following you at all." She was opening mail at my desk in Kansas City—paying bills, throwing out junk mail, keeping the gears of our domestic life turning.

"I'm just saying that I can't shoot ninety on seventeen if it's a par 5. I have to think of it as a par 4 and try to shoot eighteen over par. I can shoot eighteen over par."

I waited for her reaction.

She looked up. "Do you want me to renew your subscription to *Golf World*?"

"No, really," I said. "I can shoot eighteen over par."

But I wasn't as confident as I sounded.

Chapter 14

Hi John. I am writing you about the article in the New Richmond News. It was interesting to read that your family came from Belmullet, as did my family. My grandfather originally spelled the name Geraghty, but my father changed it to Gherty, as our mail was always mixed up. We have visited Belmullet cemetery and found a cousin there, and we stayed at a B and B one night. An interesting note: In 1890 the Erin, Wisconsin, post office listed 72 families with the name Geraghty. It is no wonder the mail got mixed up! Reading some of the history we have been able to track down, it can get very confusing. I wish I had been more interested in our heritage growing up, but living on a farm, my life was busy. My dad had lots of stories, and I'm so sorry I never got to record them.

—from Colleen Larson's e-mail of October 22, 2007

Nobody I met in Belmullet knew about New Richmond. When I told the dart throwers in McDonnells that I had seen their names on headstones in a Wisconsin church cemetery, they showed interest; but no one said, "I've heard of the place" or "There's Reillys there who are five of kin to me." When I asked about the American wakes of the nineteenth century, I was told that the emigrants' destination had been of little interest to those who stayed behind. "It was like dying," an old Irishman told me. "You never saw them again."

To be fair, New Richmond folks were no better informed about Belmullet. The New Richmond Heritage Center, led by an indefatigable archivist named Mary Sather, had published several volumes of history and oral history, but the Irish town was mentioned in none of them. The histories made it clear that New Richmond had been settled by immigrants from Western Ireland and Scandinavia, but there was little documentation for the early settlers. Church fires had destroyed many of the parish records from the mid-1800s, and then the tornado of 1899 had flattened the town and destroyed whatever letters, photographs and keepsakes the Irish had brought with them from the old country.

I did find a teasing reference to my great-grandparents in *Sesquicentennial Tales: 150 New Richmondites, 1857–2007.* The capsule biography of a fondly remembered town librarian began, "According to her Grandmother Garrity ..." and continued, "On Tody's maternal side, Michael and Elizabeth Garrity came to Erin in the 1850s by way of Hammond [a farm town a few miles southeast of New Richmond]. Michael was a disabled Civil War soldier."

Catherine "Tody" Casey, I deduced, was the daughter of my father's aunt Katy.

Another tease came in the form of photocopied pages from a memoir by William J. McNally, a former columnist for the *Minneapolis Tribune,* that were forwarded to me by attorney Tom Doar, a New Richmond Golf Club member. In a chapter titled "The McNallys," the author reported that in 1847 one Myles McNally, "accompanied by his son William, a young man of twenty," had sailed for the United States from Galway City—the "desperate famine conditions" prevailing in Ireland at the time accounting for their "plunge into the unknown." The McNallys, the account continued, had been living near Belmullet for decades, "possibly since Cromwell's time. They had been small farmers there, no doubt never doing much better than eking out a bare existence." And then there was this paragraph:

> *I am indebted to the late M. P. Early of New Richmond (who lived to be a hundred and two years old) for an eyewitness account of the leave-taking at the McNally place. M. P. Early was seven years old at the*

time and was taken along by his parents when they made a call at the McNally place for the purpose of saying farewell and wishing Godspeed to Myles. According to Mr. Early, Myles executed some sort of a jump, sinking deep into the mud in front of the McNally cottage, saying, "There, where my foot prints are—there, no matter where I am, my heart will always be."

Myles McNally, I knew from the town histories, was the progenitor of a prominent family of New Richmond lawyers, one of whom was a charter member of the New Richmond Golf Club. What's more, my dad had often mentioned that he had gone to school with the flamboyant John McNally, who would later play his way into the NFL Hall of Fame as "Johnny Blood, the Vagabond Halfback." (John McNally inspired the character played by George Clooney in *Leatherheads*.) That meant, in terms of the Kevin Bacon game, that there were only three degrees of separation between the sentimental Mullet man, Myles McNally, and myself.

Unfortunately, the McNally anecdote in this obscure book was the only strong evidence I had of the New Richmond–Belmullet connection. Most passenger manifests and church records from the nineteenth century identified Irish immigrants only by their county of origin, making no distinction between bog-dwelling Bangorites and seafaring Westporters. To make things worse, most of the descendants of New Richmond's Irish had followed my father's example and scattered across the U.S., taking with them their family records and whatever remained of the Irish oral tradition. Nevertheless, I remained convinced that the Mayo town and the Wisconsin town were two sides of the same coin. Maybe heads couldn't see tails, but New Richmond could just as easily have been called New Belmullet.

"Even the golf courses seem to have evolved in tandem," I told Pat during one of our video chats. "The New Richmond Golf Club got started in 1924, and the Belmullet Golf Club was founded in 1925. Nine-hole golf courses, both of them. On pasture land." I had a sudden thought. "Hey, if Michael Geraghty had stayed in Ireland, my dad might have been the Belmullet club champion."

She agreed that he might have been, but she asked, "Was he ever a club champion here, in America?"

"I don't think so," I said. "I don't know." I had no idea how he ranked among the New Richmond golfers of the 1920s.

"Maybe," I said decisively.

That night, after washing the dishes, I read a few pages of the latest *Western People*, taking particular pleasure in a story headlined GARDA TOLD TO DO A REAL F***ING JOB. I then sat at my laptop and pondered the situation. I had two names to work with—Michael Geraghty and Elizabeth Stephens—plus the unvetted testimony of a small-town judge who had passed away and was now buried a few steps from them in New Richmond's Immaculate Conception cemetery.

"It's not much," I said to myself. I dragged my forefinger across the touch pad and clicked on the iTunes icon. When the window opened, I scrolled down through the Artists list to JOHN B. "JACK" GARRITY. Positioning the cursor, I double-clicked with my thumb.

I sat back and listened.

The only darn thing I know about the Garrity family is my two aunts and my father," he begins, sounding apologetic. *"I don't know a damn thing about my grandfather. I think he was first generation, Johnny, which would mean they were all born in Ireland."*

The pitch of my father's voice rises and falls, and he stresses certain syllables to express a practiced incredulity. Every thought has just arrived at Dad's door, and he is delighted.

"Now Mr. Hughes—my aunt Jane's husband, if I have this straight—was a very, very famous scholar, a professor of English at Dublin University. And when he came over here. . . ."

Dad pauses. "Johnny, I don't know why the hell people came out to this little town in west-central Wisconsin. But there he was, and he was a scholar. He spoke six languages fluently, and he taught Greek to some of the students at both the parochial school and the public school. Do you remember Jack McNally? He was Johnny Blood of the Pittsburgh Steelers. Well, Jack McNally and I were in school together, and he's since moved to Green Bay, but he was graduated from high school before he went to St. John's College in Minnesota, and he used to come over to our house and take Greek lessons."

Another pause. "Why the hell would they want to learn Greek in those years? Greek was the scholar's language, of course, wasn't it? Well, my uncle talked it fluently. I was—oh, hell—eight or ten years old when he died. An old man with a goatee. He looked like one of the Supreme Court justices."

"What happened to him?" The second voice is mine.

"He just turned up his toes."

Yet another pause. "You say your aunt lived to be ninety-two. What did she do?"

"She was a housewife. They all were in those years, as far as I know. Unless they went on the stage. That's the only thing women did, wasn't it?"

I give it a moment's thought, knowing that my dad, twice divorced, believes that women are a separate and not fully understood species. "Some of them wrote novels," I say.

"Damned if they didn't." He laughs. "Look at the Brontë sisters!"

Dad does not speak with a brogue, but his voice has a throaty timbre and air waves clarity. There is not another voice like it. My bestseller-writing sister, who has her own drive-time talk show on a Florida radio station, says that Dad could have been a radio star.

"Auntie and Aunt Casey," Dad continues, "were sisters to my dad. Their names were Janie Garrity and Katy Garrity. My dad was Thomas A. Garrity. They called him 'Tag.'"

"How old were you when he died?"

"Two months." Dad's tone is matter-of-fact. "My mother two years later, they tell me. But an odd thing." A half-note rest. "He was right in the middle of a very important trial. I used to have the newspapers, the St. Paul Pioneer Press and Dispatch *and the* Minneapolis Journal, *and I've forgotten the nature of the trial, but it was a criminal proceeding. He hated criminal law, but he was damn good at it, apparently. And they had a typhoid fever epidemic over a weekend, from bad water. Court adjourned at Saturday noon, and the papers reported that my dad was dead at midnight."*

He clears his throat. "Not sick a day in his life. Thirty-two years old."

I ask what has become of the newspaper clippings. Dad says he doesn't know. "I used to have quite a few pictures of him. There was a publication called the Northwestern Reporter *in Minneapolis, and it covered all the cases—not from municipal court, but from the federal and state courts. Year after year, a perma-*

nent record. And when you went to the Supreme Court of the United States, instead of being . . . not accuser and defender . . ." He searches for the words. "Appellant and respondent, I believe it was. And, of course, they reported verbatim. He was representing this side or the other, and it was always T. A. Garrity. I was only in seventh or eighth grade at the time, but on the occasional trip to St. Paul and Minneapolis I had access to the Northwestern Reporter, *and it was fascinating reading for me. So I was going to be a lawyer, you can imagine."*

He waits a beat. "I was so proud of a dad I never even saw."

I clicked on the iTunes controller to pause the recording. Reaching across the table, I opened a file folder and sorted through some old letters and documents until I found my dad's 1905 birth certificate. It gave his father's age as thirty-six. Four years older than Dad remembered.

Pushing back my chair, I got up and went to the balcony. A couple of street lamps cast pools of light on the docks, but Broadhaven Bay was inky black. There was the occasional green flash of a channel buoy.

I slipped a finger under my eyeglasses to scratch my nose.

The recording had to be what—thirty years old? I misplaced the original cassettes around the time of Dad's death in 1990, and years of searching in shoe boxes and file drawers had yielded nothing but dust and self-recrimination. Then, while packing for my Irish sabbatical, I had found the tapes in a cupboard under a pile of speaker cords and microphone cables. I didn't have time to listen to them, other than to ascertain that the audio had not been corrupted, but I excitedly connected my laptop to our cassette player and made a Garage Band recording of the contents. "This is incredible," I told Pat. "I'd given up hope."

Now, through the miracle of digital technology, the memories flooded back—my memories of making the recording, and my father's memories of New Richmond.

I returned to the table and clicked PLAY.

Well, I don't remember much," Dad says, "but I must have been two or three. I remember standing by the stove in New Richmond while they were discussing whether or not they were going to adopt me."

"The Hugheses?"

"That's right. Jamie and Jane, my aunt Bessie. And they finally decided to."
A poignant pause. "A funny thing. You and I were up there in 1961 to see
Tommy play in the St. Paul Open, and I never thought to look at the house I
was raised in." Pause. "Funny."

"Do I remember right? Did you and your brother grow up across the street
from each other?"

"No, side by side. In two houses. Aunt Jane and Aunt Bessie and I lived in
one, and the Caseys and Mersh were right next door."

"It was an Irish town?"

There is a pause while he pretends to count on his fingers. "I think there
were two Swedes. St. Croix County was mostly Irish. The county seat was Hud-
son, sixteen miles from New Richmond, and there were the little towns of Rob-
erts, Hammond, Star Prairie . . . farming communities with populations of
seven or eight hundred. There was a French-Canadian town, Somerset, seven
miles straight west. They had the best corn whiskey in the bootlegging days. Corn
whiskey and frog legs."

Pausing the recording again, I thumbed through one of the New Richmond books to check Dad's facts. He was wrong about the two Swedes.
The town of his boyhood had a significant Scandinavian population, many
of whom toiled in New Richmond's two major enterprises, a flour mill and
a lumber company. The ethnic boundary was the Willow River, which cut
through town a few hundred yards north of the clapboard houses where my
dad and uncle lived. (The Main Street businesses were on the south side,
the Irish side.) Logs often clogged the river by the sawmill, Dad had told
me, turning that stretch into a glassy lake called the Widespread. He remembered swimming there with a schoolmate who got trapped under a log
raft and drowned.

I made a few notes and then pushed the book aside. Clicked PLAY.

And you ask about the Irish. Johnny, I don't recall a single non-Irish that was
in the parochial school, and damn few in the public school. Howard Smith
was one of my classmates, he had an English name. I don't know, maybe he was.
He played football for St. Mary's. . . ."

I listened contentedly while the old man rambled on. Sooner or later, I knew, my younger self would ask him about the New Richmond Golf Club, and Dad would start, as he always did, with, "Well, I've told the story many times. . . ."

Sitting alone in my Belmullet flat, I pictured a sand-greens golf course bounded by three cornfields and the Soo Line railroad tracks.

CHAPTER 15

Sunday was golf day. In those times, everybody worked six full days—even the children, who usually had summer jobs almost as demanding as those of their elders—so there were few opportunities to play during the week. But on Sunday we could play from sun-up to sun-down, as long as there was no snow on the ground. There was no formality about starting times. At dawn, those who were ready just stepped up and belted the ball down the first fairway. We usually played nine holes in less than an hour and a half, and there were no tie-ups so typical of today's play: no practice swings, no temper tantrums, no showboating. We simply hit the ball in the general direction of the flagstick, pitched up to the green, and putted out.

—from John B. "Jack" Garrity's Remarks and Reminiscence on
the Founding of the New Richmond Golf Club

Sunday was golf day. I'd find the Carne car park filled with trucks and vans, their side panels splashed with colorful ads: FRANK HEALY CONNACHT GOLD MILK . . . PAUL JOHN CONSTRUCTION . . . TEACH JOHN JOE TAVERN. The breezeway under the clubhouse was similarly crowded with stand-up bags and pull carts ("trolleys" in local parlance), many of them

motorized. Another difference: no starter. Chris Birrane, minus his clipboard, was always in the Sunday field.

Every club competition had a sponsor ("The Bank of Ireland Captain's
Prize") and a format (stroke play, match play, scramble or Stableford). To
enter, you went to the men's changing room, tapped out your membership
number on a touch-screen monitor, and dropped a little brown envelope
with your six-euro entry fee into a slot. You arranged your own tee times.

The first-tee protocol was similarly brisk. Each player declared what ball
he was playing—"Bridgestone 3!"—and handed the ball to a selected member of the foursome, who would then toss the balls over his shoulder to
make up better-ball teams. (The two closest balls were partners.) The typical side bet was ten euros with no presses, skins or greenies, and—at least
in my foursomes—no handicaps. As soon as the first fairway cleared, someone teed up, belted the ball, and stepped aside. Mulligan, whoever he was,
did not come from Mayo. If you topped your first shot, you played your
second from the ankle-high rough in front of and below the tee.

Most Sundays I played with the honorary secretary, Terry Swinson, the
head greenkeeper, Gary Stanley, and some wild card recruited by Terry—
usually a young slugger with a 90-degree shoulder turn and a good short
game. Gary, who I knew from previous visits, was a thin, gnarly man with
a homemade swing and a taste for Guinness that made him a fixture
in Belmullet's pubs. Gary was easy to play with—good-tempered, self-
deprecating—and easy to underestimate. Every Sunday he would yank two
or three drives into the deepest grunge and somehow escape with a par or
bogey, scrambling being his forte. He was also a master at finding other
players' balls when they drove into trouble—a skill that saved me a stroke
or two per round.

Counting strokes, as I have mentioned, was a habit I had gotten out of.
I fancied myself a ten handicapper, and my Stateside rounds bore this out.
On a good day I made a couple of birdies and broke eighty. On a bad day
I made three double-bogeys and topped ninety—a score, by the way, that
would have been discarded under the USGA's Byzantine handicap system.
My eighteen-hole totals, when written down at all, went home with my
playing partners. When I signed a card it was next to the word "Attest,"
never by the word "Player."

I was a little out of my depth, therefore, when I waded back into the waters of golf accountability. I played my first two Sunday competitions for handicap purposes only, but I still felt like a rookie pro at the first stage of Q-School. The fairways seemed narrower, the wind gustier, the rough deeper. To make things worse, the Irish played by the rules—to the admirable extreme of holing all their putts. Three-footers that were routinely conceded in America (by players facing their own three-footers) had to be canned at Carne. I made most of these putts, but the heightened pressure and the need to study the little knee-knockers from all angles wore me down. By the fifteenth hole I was usually glassy-eyed and knackered.

The no-warm-up paradigm probably cost me a stroke or two, as well, but I loved that aspect of Irish golf. "You see very few golfers going to the practice ground before we play," Gary said during one of our rounds. "It's just the way we're brought into golf. It's sign in and right up to the first tee." When I observed that the locals rarely blamed a bad shot on "coming over the top" or went through a mental checklist before swinging, he chuckled. "I suppose that's the difference between the American golfers and the Irish. We don't go to the teaching pros the way you do, and we don't analyze the swing a lot. We just stand up and hit it and hope it goes the right way."

Keeping the game simple, unfortunately, did not make it any easier. My first scored round, on a fairly windy Sunday morning, foundered on a double-bogey, double-bogey finish. I signed for an eighty-nine, tapped my hole-by-hole into the handicap computer, and dropped my attested card into the slot.

The following Sunday I made an even bigger hash of the finish. The greater disaster, surprisingly, came on the eighteenth, a roller-coaster par 5 that climbs between two mighty dunes before plummeting into a shadowy pit deep enough to hide the tallest building in Belmullet. After losing a ball off the tee, I hit several shots from deep rough into deeper rough and wound up, finally, with a four-foot putt for an eight. "I need to make this," I told Terry, who was unlucky enough to be my partner. "People will laugh at me if I make a nine."

I missed the putt, signed for a ninety-three, and plodded up the stairs to the Spike Bar, where Gary used the ten euros he had just won to buy me a lunch of brown bread and vegetable soup.

Gary, I soon discovered, was not your typical Irishman. "I'm from Hoylake in Cheshire," he told me as we ate—that is, he was English. And not just English, to paraphrase Shaw, but of golfing blood. "My grandfather was a good golfer—good enough that he toyed with the idea of turning pro. But in the 1920s there wasn't much money in it."

"I'm sure there wasn't," I said.

"But I suppose golf is in my blood. There's four brothers and myself, and we all play golf." Hoylake, he didn't have to add, was the home of the Royal Liverpool Golf Club, a venerable links that has hosted eleven British Open Championships.

"So you're a blow-in, too."

He nodded. "I did landscaping in England—residential, hospitals, factories. Then I married a girl from here, and we came back when her father got sick. We lived in Ballina for a couple of years in the '80s. I went fishing and cutting turf, anything to make a living. My wife's father had a small farm about three kilometers toward Blacksod, just a little bit past George Geraghty's place." He picked up a slice of bread. "So Gary's now a farmer!"

I blew on a spoonful of soup and pondered life's uncertainties, almost forgetting my nine on the eighteenth.

A couple of days later, I rose before dawn and drove up the coast to the Enniscrone Golf Club at the invitation of another Terry—Terry Mc-Sweeney, the former sportswriter and longtime publications director for the PGA of America. McSweeney was a blow-in who spent his summers in Mayo helping his Irish wife run the four-star Stella Maris Hotel. He wintered in Florida, presumably playing golf when he wasn't fashioning prose for the PGA. He was an overseas life member of both Carne and Enniscrone. He had invited me up for a round at the latter.

Enniscrone was shrouded in fog as we walked to the first tee, but our warm-up swings caused the sky to lift. Like Carne, Enniscrone is a challenging links course on dramatic dunesland, but it is tamer in some respects. The fairways are greener, the mowed rough more clearly defined, the putting surfaces smoother and more uniform. "The arrival of Carne forced Enniscrone to improve," McSweeney told me as we walked up the first fairway.

"The holes that Eddie Hackett built in the dunes were always stunning, but the first few holes were dead flat, featureless. A few years ago they got permission to build six new holes along the sea. They hired Donald Steele to come in, and he brought it up a notch or two."

McSweeney was tall and slender, a snappy dresser. He had a big shock of crème-colored hair and a narrow, aristocratic face. He was originally from Boston, and if I'd had to guess I would have assigned him an address in suburban Brookline, somewhere near the famous Country Club. But I would have been wrong. "My father was a Boston cop," he said, "so we had to live within the city limits."

I asked McSweeney to tell me about his first round at Carne.

"It was in ninety-five or ninety-six," he said. "My wife Francis has a sister Maureen, who is a Sisters of Mercy nun, and for twenty-five years she was headmistress of the school in Belmullet. We were down there, driving around, and Maureen said, 'Up there on that hill is a new golf course. You should go play it.' But there was nothing to see, the clubhouse was still being built.

"When we did play it, I didn't know what to think at first. The second hole, the par 3, we couldn't see the hole. I'm thinking, 'You can't have a blind par 3. This is dumb.' There were so many blind shots like that, I was ready to walk off the course. And it was so hilly. I was a smoker then, a package of Marlboros a day, so climbing up the eighteenth I thought I was going to die."

"I can relate," I said, the memory of my Sunday collapse still fresh.

"Of course, Carne was still being built. It had very sharp edges to it. You could go through a half dozen balls in nine holes. But I'll never forget that Kodak moment when we walked onto the eleventh tee for the first time and saw that incredible view. And as the weeks passed, Eamon Mangan and Eddie Hackett smoothed the course out. Carne just kept getting better and better. And now I love it. Francis gave me the overseas life membership for my fiftieth birthday, and it was the greatest present."

Enniscrone wasn't a bad package either, but I had some difficulty getting it open. I'd drive a few yards off the fairway and find my ball sitting reasonably well in the first cut. I'd look for a distance marker in the fairway, perform the meters-to-yards calculations in my head, pull the appropriate

club, and take aim over some dune or hillock. I'd hit the shot. But when I
came over the crest of the hill, the ball was never on the green. The ball was
somewhere in that wild hollow of thistle and thorn that fronted the green,
or in that hidden ravine accessible only to Special Forces units with rappel-
ling gear. "Don't look for it," I kept telling McSweeney, "I'll take a drop."
And once I was on a green, I'd three-putt it. (My first putt, which at first
glance seemed to be downhill, would prove to be uphill, leaving me eight
feet short of the hole. My second putt, benefiting from knowledge gleaned
from the first, would power-lip out of the hole. I was reminded of Rex
Lardner Jr.'s cogent description of the putter as "a club designed to hit the
ball halfway to the hole.")

"Must be the weather," I joked. The sun had come out, and the few
remaining clouds seemed to be nailed to the sky.

"I had a great time," I told McSweeney as we walked off the eighteenth
green. And I wasn't lying. But I wondered if keeping score wasn't dragging
my game back to the depths of the early nineties, when I was trying to recover from my golf-school traumas.

"Give it to me straight," I asked him at the car.

He frowned over the scorecard, rocking his head and closing his eyes
whenever he had to carry a number. Finally, he penciled in my total and
looked up. "I'm afraid . . ."

I started to laugh, because it was a parody of the doctor delivering bad
news.

"You had a 103," McSweeney said.

I absorbed the news without reeling. Or retching. But I did slump
against the car.

"Well," I said with a sigh. "Now I've got a handicap."

I submitted my Enniscrone scorecard that very afternoon, and a few
days later I got a call from Terry Swinson telling me that Carne's handicap
chairman, John Hanley, had awarded me a handicap of fifteen.

"It's too high," Terry said. "You're better than that."

I wasn't so sure, but I didn't argue the point. The important thing was,
I had made it through Q-School and I was ready to take on Carne's worst
in the Sunday competitions.

CHAPTER 16

You may be surprised, as I once was, to learn that, for all practical purposes, the game in Ireland is about the same age as it is in the United States. America's first club, the St. Andrew's Golf Club in Yonkers, New York, was formed in 1888. Ireland's oldest golf club, Royal Belfast, preceded it by just seven years. . . . The fact is that, for much of the first 400 years of its existence, the game was confined to Scotland.

—from James W. Finegan's *Emerald Fairways and Foam-Flecked Seas*

Three cars and a red VW van were in the Carne parking lot. The morning sky was gray. The orange windsock was flapping, and the dune grasses lay down with every gust. A young, pretty blonde hopped out of one of the cars. Men in jeans and hooded sweatshirts unloaded video equipment from the red van.

The principals were already gathered upstairs in the Spike Bar, where coffee and bagels had been set out. Eamon Mangan had on a maroon sweater with the four-swans logo. Three other civic leaders fidgeted in coats and ties, giving the room a funeral-visitation vibe. I knew all three men. Seamus Cafferky was the owner of Cafferky's on Main. Brendan Padden was a prominent realtor. Mícheál McGarry was a retired schoolteacher. All were on the board of Erris Tourism, Ltd.

"You know what the story is? What we're doing?"

The Erris men broke off their murmured conversation to face Bob Corkey, a wiry, balding man in jeans and a blue Oxford shirt with rolled up sleeves. He had on black bowling shoes with white laces.

"It's a new award show called *Gradam Gnó na Gaeltachta*," Corkey continued, "and we've basically drawn up a short list of twenty Irish enterprises that have had a significant impact on a region. We're doing little five- or six-minute profiles of these companies, and the last week of November there will be five half hour programs on TG4. Then, on Sunday, it's the big night, a bit like the Oscars. The nominees are announced, we open the envelope, 'The Oscar goes to . . .' " He grinned. "So now you've got the story."

Corkey was a television director.

A few feet away, a young woman handed out release forms to be filled in by those who would appear on camera. She delivered her explanations in Gaelic, but for my benefit she switched to English, informing me that the twenty nominees were in four categories, and there would be a top award in each of the four. "They're all different businesses," she said. "Fish, pottery, jewelry. . . ."

"There's only one other nominee in Mayo," Corkey interjected.

On the other side of the swinging door, the crew was running cables and setting up lights. Corkey planned to interview the Belmullet men, one by one, in the Hackett Lounge. Afterward, he said, he'd lead his cameramen out on the course, where Aoigení Thuarise—the blonde I had correctly identified as the presenter—would interview some golfers.

"Ah, you're one of the famous Mangan brothers!"

I turned to see Bob shaking hands with Eamon, and I was reminded of my own first meeting with "Mr. Carne" in the summer of 2003, when I was on assignment for *SI*. It took place in the cozy manager's office on the ground floor. James O'Hara, a man of middle years with a gray mustache and a soothing manner, sat behind his cluttered desk, sipping coffee and giving me a quick history of the Belmullet Golf Club. Founded in 1925, he said. Sustained through wars, depressions and population losses. The original nine-hole links had been right there at Carne on the gently sloping land to the leeward side of the dunes. A more recent nine-holer—"the one you saw in 1989"—was just down the road at Cross. Laid out on land owned by three farmers, that course had cattle roaming the fairways and wire fences around the greens.

"Ahh, here's Eamon!" The door opened, and in walked the cofounder and leading light of Erris Tourism Ltd.: a slight, bespectacled man with thin gray hair combed over a bald spot. A soft-spoken, smiling man. An unhurried man.

"Eamon can tell you better than me how the course came to be built," James said.

I stood and reached for the hand that had shaken Eddie Hackett's hand.

"People are trapped in history," James Baldwin wrote, "and history is trapped in them." So I was surprised how easy it was to get members of the Belmullet Golf Club to tell how they had come to be tenants on a world-class golf course. It was simply a case, they said, of God sending Eddie Hackett to look at their land.

No one, however, could tell me much about the club's early years. The above-mentioned James O'Hara, who served thirteen years as honorary secretary and several years as Carne's club manager before leaving to work at an electronics company, knew as much—or as little—as anybody. He showed me a tattered memo book with pen and pencil notes scribbled on lined pages. Entries for 1929 had been torn out, and other pages were covered with doodles of leaves, ships, and a duck. Under the earliest date, "16 April 1926," someone had jotted down thirteen names. Was it the club roster? Were they entrants in an early club competition? James couldn't say. (There were no Geraghtys on the list, but there was a McGarity. I carefully wrote the name down in my notebook.) James let me examine several other items, including a handwritten receipt for "One pound, eleven shillings and sixpence," a 1932 roster (again, no Geraghtys) and a penned version of a 1926 club constitution. "It has been folded in fours, as you can see," James said, "but I'm not so sure it's the original." One line on the parchment document caught my eye: THE SUBSCRIPTION SHALL BE ONE GUINEA.

The first Mullet links, my tutors told me, had occupied a relatively level stretch of land on the Blacksod Bay side of the Carne Banks. That land had also served as a race course, which is why today's seventh hole is called *Árd na Gaoithe* ("The Grandstand"). "I remember very well when they had the races there at Carne," Seamus Cafferky said. "It would be the Ascot or the Irish Derby of Mayo, that's the kind of day it was. The town would close a half day, and everybody went to the races. And there would be horses from all over Ireland taking part in it, maybe seven to eight races. You had the beer tent along the side of the course, and somewhere up where the seventh green is now, on that huge sand dune, that's where people would stand and look down at the course. It was like a grandstand." Now golfers climbed the dune to reach the green of one of Carne's quirkier holes, a par 3 of 177 yards with a tee down on the flat.

That first course had been abandoned a long time ago. It was replaced by the Emlybeg/Cross nine, a simple layout in a cow pasture south of the Carne banks. Pat and I got a car-window glimpse of it in 1989. I remember a coal gray sky, a roadside fence, a prefab starter's shed, stone tee markers, caddies warming their hands over a barrel fire, and three or four golfers with muttonchop whiskers, tam-o'-shanters, wool jackets, and hickory-shafted baffing spoons. The years have somehow conflated the Cross nine with some vaguely remembered painting of golfers in nineteenth-century Scotland.

James O'Hara gave me a tour of the Cross nine one afternoon—or, rather, of the cow pasture where golf had once been played. I beheld a placid stretch of knee-high grass with views of a crescent beach. A few cows grazed close to the shore. "It's striped now, three pieces of land," said James— meaning that the pasture was former commonage that had been deeded to its current owners. "Muredach Reilly, the chemist and my friend, we'd often come down here and play a few holes." James handed me a scorecard with a line-and-circle map on the back. "This is an old card of the course. There was a caravan"—he pointed down to where the road brushed the shore— "and we started down on the flat there and came up here." He nodded to where the first shaggy dunes began to bubble up. "The fairways were marked with white stones, same as they still have in Mulranny and Achill."

A big smile creased his face. "Well, look at this." He led me up to a little three-bar gate suspended between two concrete posts. There was no fence—just the rusted gate, which groaned when he pushed it open. "The greens were fenced, you know, to keep the cattle off. This was the fourth. The greens were pretty much square, I guess." He pulled the gate shut again. "It brings back memories now, all right."

I turned to look back down to the corner of the property, where the road and the fence met another fence at a right angle. "The caravan was down there, was it?" I nodded in the direction of a white farmhouse across the road. "That's where you started?"

"That's right. The first hole ran along the fence line. It was flat and bumpy." I stared, remembering how close the tee had been to the road. I figured the Belmullet Golf Club probably had a lot of slicers on its roster.

James turned and pointed north toward a muffin-shaped mound that didn't look entirely natural. "That mound is some sort of monument," he said. "Some ancient nobleman, he was supposed to have been buried in a chair. And there's a stone chair there in the dune." He then pointed beyond the mound to the northern fence line, where a terraced dune rose like a parapet by the shore. I recognized it as the dune to the right of Carne's fourteenth green, pictured on the jacket of this book.

"Sometimes I'd go walking in the banks," he said, "all the way up to the high ground. It was so beautiful, you had to rub your eyes. But when talk started of building a new golf course there, I couldn't see how they'd do it. The valleys were so deep that you'd get lost in them."

I smiled, remembering a story that Seamus told about his aunt Molly Lavelle. The old woman had broken the silence on the way to her husband's funeral to ridicule the notion that a golf course could be built in the Carne banks. "I think you're mad in the head," she had told Seamus. "How in the name of God are you going to level all those humps and hills?"

Back at the car, James reached into a plastic bag and pulled out a sleeve of Top-Flite XL golf balls. "You might like to have these," he said, emptying the sleeve into his hand. I took one of the balls and examined it. There was a legend in red: BELMULLET GOLF CLUB 1925–2000.

There was something that Pat and I didn't know in eighty-nine: the Mangan brothers were back in town.

There were five Mangan brothers—Michael being the oldest and Eamon the youngest—all born in Doohoma, a hamlet some fifteen miles south of Belmullet on the eastern shore of Blacksod Bay. Michael emigrated to England in 1948, when he was sixteen. The others followed. Like most male immigrants, Michael started out as a field hand, hoeing beets. He then became a construction worker. "It didn't matter your color or your creed," Michael told me one morning at Carne. "If you were capable of doing the job, you had the opportunity in England. Here it was only the hierarchy that could get jobs—the clergy, the politicians. If you wanted a job in those days, you'd have to see a parish priest and make a case for yourself. Thank God, those days are gone!" Michael, it seemed, was not as sentimental about the Catholic Church as the Irishmen in Hollywood films. "Anywhere the Church dominates," he said dismissively, "the people are the poorest on the planet."

The five brothers, to continue the story, saved enough money to start a company, Mangan Bros. Ltd., that built and opened petrol stations for corporate clients. The business grew, and the Mangan brothers were a fixture in Southern England until 2002, when they sold the company. In the intervening years they invested in various enterprises in Western Ireland. One of their ventures was the Palm Court Ballroom, a wildly successful dance hall in Belmullet.

All of which is preface to this one pertinent fact: In 1981, Michael Mangan bought a house on the Mullet.

Carne House.

When Michael bought it, Carne House was a five-thousand-square-foot manor house with a small orchard on sixty acres overlooking Belmullet town. In its heyday, the house was the command center for a five-hundred-acre estate owned by the Nash family, one of the Mullet's most powerful English landlords. "Thirty-two people worked here, living in old stone sheds," Michael told me on a tour of the grounds. "All these walls would have been built by slave labor." Michael moved his family into the house, but he rented the pasturage to a farmer, whose cattle grazed in the big dunes behind the property. "I was here two years before I even knew where the banks were," Michael said, indulging in some Irish hyperbole. "I had no interest in them. All I knew was that I had a share in the commonage."

One night, a farmer came to Michael's door and told him that the Carne banks were going to be striped. Seventeen shares, each amounting to fifteen acres, would be selected by drawing lots. The new owner of each plot would then be given an eleven-hundred-pound grant to fence his private strip—thus "striping" the land.

The draw meeting was held at the old vocational school near the stone pier on Shore Road. There were two boxes. One box had seventeen numbers in it, to determine the order of draw. The other box contained seventeen numbered tags. Michael reached into the first box and drew number thirteen. Then, with the thirteenth pick—cue the ESPN analysts—he reached into the second box and drew number fifteen. "Plot fifteen," he told me, "is where the fourth and fifth fairway are now."

The next morning, Michael got a neighbor to show him the acreage that had fallen into his lap. You could see it from Carne House—a bumpy stretch of feedland, shaggy mounds and blowouts. His curiosity piqued, Michael got in his car and drove up a farm road to the north end of the banks. It was a windy day, but he decided to go for a walk. For four and a half hours he wandered around in the dunes. He descended into inky vales and scaled the grassy heights, half the time lost, half the time awed by the ocean views. He walked past yellow flowers that reached his shoulders. He hiked through patches of primrose, buttercups, vetch, milkwort and bird's-foot trefoil. He trekked into canyons of sand and marron grass that narrowed down to nothing, so narrow that he had to turn around and walk back out.

By the time he got back to his car, Michael Mangan had reached two conclusions about the Carne banks. The first was that "it would be a mortal sin to see it divided into seventeen portions and fenced off." The second was that, to his eye—the eye of an avid golfer who had played at Enniscrone and Rosses Point—it was *golfing* ground.

Said Michael, "I was looking at 260 acres of prime linksland."

I'm sitting in the manager's office at Carne. It's a rainy day in July, 2003, and I've scooted my chair back to make room for the chairman of Turasóireacht Iorrais. *Tournament schedules and travel brochures cover a corkboard. File folders, documents and a tea tray take up most of the manager's desk.*

"Eamon can tell you better than me," says James O'Hara, and Eamon proves equal to the task—although, like James, he seems almost too amiable for his position. Eamon explains that he, his brother Michael and some friends started the nonprofit Erris Tourism Ltd. in 1984 because they thought the rural west desperately needed the stimulus of tourism. Numerous ideas had been floated—walking trails, fishing lodges, an amusement park—but the notion that took hold was that of a golf course on the Carne banks. The land they wanted, 260 acres of commonage shared by seventeen farmers, was about to be striped. To keep that from happening, the Erris group had mounted a campaign to acquire the seventeen plots. "There was a real need to embrace the tourist traffic," Eamon says, "and we thought a golf course might answer that need."

He adds, "It was a difficult argument to make. We had been bypassed for decades."

Mayo, you see, was an impoverished county. Belmullet was a dying town. "Thirty percent of the houses were empty," Michael Mangan told me one morning at Carne. "The streets were dark. Grass was growing up around the windows. It was sheer dereliction."

The good news: Land was cheap. The Erris group offered the seventeen land owners 500 Irish pounds per acre—a not unreasonable amount for unfarmable land at the edge of a cruel sea. "Myself and another guy, we worked on the farmers," Michael recalled. "We met with them and told them the land would be used for recreation, and one by one they threw their hats in." In fact, ten of the farmers promptly agreed to terms. Michael made eleven. But six owners refused to budge. One of them was an enthusiastic promoter of the striping scheme, but he died, and his widow said she didn't want the land. "So she threw her lot in," Michael said. "*Five* people to contend with."

And so it went for a year and a half. The final meeting with the farmers was held in an upstairs room at the Western Strands Hotel. "It's all or nothing," Michael told the holdouts. "We need every parcel of land to build the course." Telling me the story more than two decades later, Michael shook his head. "And there was *one* that held out."

"One?" I pictured a grizzled old coot in a worn sweater, corduroy pants and muddy Wellingtons, his jaw set and his arms crossed in defiance.

"Just the one. He offered to exchange his land for fifty acres on the perimeter, but we couldn't do that. So he said he wasn't going to sell, and we left the meeting that night with everything canceled. It was a terrible, terrible outcome after all the work we had put in." Michael shook his head.

"But the next day, you know, he came up to me in a shop, and it was a remarkable thing. He said I had put him under pressure the previous night, but he had gone and had a long talk with his brother. And he said to me, 'I want to live in peace and harmony in the village. I don't want to be the odd man out.'"

"So he agreed to sell?"

"He did," Michael said, "and the minute he walked out the door I was on the phone to the solicitor to draw up seventeen contracts."

Two nights later, the would-be land barons booked two upstairs rooms at the Western Strands. One by one, the farmers drifted in, walked down the dark corridor to the back of the building, and climbed the squeaky stairs to meet with the solicitors. "A few were late," Michael recalled, "but they all signed. And as they say, 'Drinks all around.' That was how it started. That was the beginning of the Carne Golf Links."

He nodded thoughtfully. "It was just promises, of course. We hadn't any money."

It's all right to laugh. If we're to believe Michael Mangan, Erris Tourism had only thirty punts in the kitty on the night he and his gang agreed to pay 130,000 Irish pounds for the Carne banks. But as the actress Ruth Gordon once said, "A little money helps, but what really gets it right is to never, I repeat, *never* under any conditions face the facts." It was in that spirit—and always stressing the contribution that a championship golf course could make to the Gaeltacht economy—that Erris Tourism submitted grant applications to everyone from *Bord Fáilte* (the Irish Tourist Board) to the EEC (European Economic Community). It took three years, but through *Údarás na Gaeltachta* they finally landed a government-backed loan of IEP 130,000 with a seven-year moratorium on repayments. At that point they were able to cut checks for the farmers and take title to the seventeen parcels. And that, as Eamon explained to me years later, left them with just one minor obstacle to overcome.

"We had secured the land," he said with a smile, "but we didn't have any money to build the course."

CHAPTER 17

More and more people became aware of the Belmullet course when in November 2005 it was placed at 28th in the Golf World *Top 100 Golf Courses. The Erris gem was sandwiched between Royal St. George's in 27th place and The TPC at Scottsdale in 29th, with Royal Troon, Carnoustie, Royal Portrush, The Belfry, Mount Juliet and Royal Birkdale numbered among the courses trailing in Carne's wake. . . . Many would have taken the acclaim and had a little smug smile for themselves, but not the Erris people.*
—from the Western People *Archives*

A t that point," said Brendan Padden, "we called a priest."

Bob Corkey, who was waiting for his technicians to finish setting up, cocked his head and smiled. He wanted to hear more. So did I, although I knew the story by heart. It was the story that Jim Engh had started in the car in Colorado, the story that began, "Carne? It's in this godforsaken out-of-the-way place that nobody ever heard of."

Brendan, who was an "auctioneer"—a realtor in American parlance—was telling the part about Father Peter Waldron, the golfing priest from Clifden, County Connemara, a hundred miles to the south. Brendan explained that Connemara already had a golf course of some repute, an eighteen-hole links by the legendary Irish golf architect, Eddie Hackett. Waldron was widely credited for getting Hackett, soon to become famous for his work on the Waterville Golf Links in County Kerry, to design Connemara on a shoestring.

"So we invited the priest up to get his opinion of our property," Brendan said.

As always when I heard this story, I pictured Father Waldron, in full vestments, mounting a dune and beholding Carne: this great swath of heaving godland crying out to have eighteen red flags planted on it.

"He was staggered by what he saw," Eamon interjected. "He promised to help us."

The priest's help had come in the salutary form of prayer and in the more practical form of a phone call to Hackett at his home in Dublin. Hackett was seventy-six at the time, but the old pro couldn't resist the lure of linksland. He agreed to make the four-hour train trip to Ballina, where he would be met by Michael and Eamon Mangan. "We had 260 acres and a lot of ideas," Eamon said, "but we would have gotten nowhere without Eddie Hackett. He was one of nature's true gentlemen."

From my spot at the end of the bar I had only to peer through the porthole in the swinging door to see the portrait that hung over the fireplace in the Hackett Lounge. In the painting, the true gentleman—a kind-looking white-haired man—stood on a staked-out stretch of plowed ground under a blue sky. He wore an oilskin jacket over a shirt and tie, and he had a long scarf draped around his neck. He clutched a folded course routing to his chest—a drawing as crimped and creased as an old road map.

"He didn't drive anymore, he always took the train," Eamon continued. "We picked him up in Ballina and brought him down to take a look at the banks. And he was overwhelmed. When he saw the undulating nature of the dunes, he said, 'It took nature thousands of years to create this. We must not let the bulldozers destroy it.'"

"Did he say how much it would cost?" It was my question, asked on Corkey's behalf.

"No, he wouldn't talk about money. I believe the total we paid him over seven years was less than ten thousand pounds. We had to beg him to send the bill for travel expenses."

Seamus nodded vigorously. "Eddie Hackett was nature's gentleman, as far as I was concerned. He always said about Carne"—Seamus pronounced it *CARE-en*—"he always said, 'That's the last piece of great ground that's left in this country for a real golf course.' And that gave us encouragement. I remember one of the first meetings we had with Eddie, and it was during the time of eighty-six, and I happened to be captain of the local golf club at the time, down at Cross and Binghamstown. He would address me as 'Mr. Captain,' you know, and I wasn't used to this."

Seamus had to pause as Corkey, apologizing, stepped aside to answer a question from a member of his crew.

The draper turned to me. "I remember saying, 'Eddie, we appreciate you giving us your time. We'd love to have you, but there's no point in putting dogs on windows, the possibility is that we cannot afford you.' And Eddie Hackett sat back in the chair, and he folded his arms, and he said, 'Mr. Captain,' he said, 'if that's all that's bothering you, let's do the work first, and we'll talk about money afterward.' "

The others nodded and Seamus beamed. "To people sitting there that night, I suppose we got lifted about six inches off the chair with excitement. And I suppose that was the one night that really started the move on Carne. Eddie Hackett was a man of vision. He was a man of character. It wasn't for the money, it was for the love of golf and the love of good design and the love of good ground. What he's left us here at Carne is a legacy that will be here forever and ever."

Seamus was near tears.

"All," he added, "at a very, very nominal fee."

Catching the tail end of Seamus' recital, Corkey said, "Build it and they will come?" He rubbed his hands together. "What was the name of the movie? *Field of Dreams*? Anyway, we're ready for Mícheál McGarry."

The chairman of Erris Tourism started for the door, a confident smile on his face. Eamon said, "If you don't come out, we'll know what happened."

While their friend answered questions under the hot lights, the others continued to talk about the man whose portrait hung in the next room. "I've put together a file of Eddie Hackett's letters for John," Eamon said, nodding in my direction. "You'll see from his reports that he was hugely encouraging. He never said the mountain was too big to climb. And he had a wonderful, sharp memory. I'd contact him on the phone, I'd say, 'I have a little problem on the left of the seventh green.' He'd picture it perfectly, even though he was working on several courses. The whole eighteen holes were installed in his memory."

"A very patient man," Brendan interjected.

"Time didn't matter. He was in his seventies, but he was never anxious to speed it up so he could see the end product. He just made a *huge* contribution here and a huge contribution to golf architecture in Ireland."

"Do you have any film or tapes of Eddie Hackett?" I wanted a better sense of the man.

Eamon, looking sad, shook his head. "The night of the official opening he spoke for three quarters of an hour, a fantastic speech. But it wasn't recorded. I regret that."

My mobile rang in my pocket, so I stepped into the upstairs corridor to take the call. As I left, the Erris men surrounded a tray of fancy breakfast rolls, staring with undisguised longing but fearful that a crumb or a dusting of sugar might spoil their presentation. When I returned, they had turned their backs to the tray and were discussing Gaelic football in solemn tones. A few seconds later, the door opened and Mícheál McGarry emerged.

"Did you get any tough questions?" Eamon asked.

"No, no," the chairman said with a smile. "Actually, they were quite easy. They direct you." He turned to the bar for a cup of coffee.

I stepped over to the window. Two golfers were visible in the distance, tiny figures walking in erratic loops at the foot of a dune.

I'm studying a framed picture on the wall. It's an aerial photograph of the Carne Golf Links. Or maybe not. The yellow-green terrain is vaguely lunar.

I look across the desk at James O'Hara, who responds with a sardonic smile. "I used to go for a walk on the banks," the club manager says. "It was all wild. I thought, how can you build a golf course on those big valleys and sand dunes? How could you physically walk it?"

Understand, I'm a golf writer. I know how golf courses are built. A man named Nicklaus or Dye or Jones arrives with an army of workers, truckloads of sand, gravel, plastic pipe and sod, and enough earth-moving equipment to level a mountain. Nine months and a few million dollars later, you've got a golf course.

But not on the Mullet.

"Construction on the first nine started in 1987," Eamon says, "and it was a very slow process. The work fell to a couple of dozen farmers, most of whom had been drawing down some form of dole. They were paid under a state-financed labor scheme, a half week at a time, so they could tend their own farms. They built the course with spades and shovels, and Eddie Hackett was quite happy with that. It made the course natural."

I look up from my notebook. "Hand tools? How long did that take?"

"Six years."

Seeing my jaw drop, Eamon adds, "The back nine took another year, and we had to rent bulldozers for a few days." Not wanting to mislead me, he mentions a few other applications of modern technology: jeeps, dump trucks, weather reports, radios. "On the third fairway," he says, "we used a tractor with rolling treads that crushed and smoothed, but didn't shape."

I picture the third hole: a dead-straight par 4 with an elevated tee, a two-tiered green, and a fairway as restless as windblown silk.

"We created very few mounds," Eamon continues. "If Eddie's plan called for one, we simply tipped a load of white sand and left it alone for a few months. The wind and rain took care of the rest."

I lift my eyes to the photo on the wall. I see nature's sandbox.

W hen I first came to Belmullet," I said to Seamus, "it was bleak. It felt like a ghost town."

"That would be very correct indeed." The clothier peered through the porthole to see how his friend Brendan was faring under the lights. Eamon had joined Mícheál McGarry at the bar.

"Around nineteen ninety or ninety-one they did a survey," Seamus said, "and we had thirty-six derelict buildings. Which was huge for a town of this size." He straightened and turned away from the door. "There was no opportunity here. In my trade, the draper's trade, come the month of March

I made sure to have a stack of suitcases for people who were emigrating. I would sell all those suitcases by May, because those were the months when people went off for the farm work in England."

I asked how many derelict buildings Belmullet had today.

"Two!" He beamed. "Credit the council and the county manager for this, because I always like to give credit where credit is due. And I suppose the fact that we were in the Celtic Tiger. But that said, he never really galloped an awful lot to this north Mayo region."

"It must have seemed risky," I said, "building a course here." I was thinking of a comment that Eamon had made—something about there being fewer than a hundred members of the Belmullet Golf Club at any given time.

"It was," Seamus said, sitting on an upholstered bench by the window. "The nine-hole course was a low-budget operation. Three hundred pounds for a mower to cut the grass, that was a major undertaking."

Eamon, overhearing, chimed in. "All we had was squatters rights, because three farmers owned the land. There was no clubhouse. Two years before we moved here, we splashed out on a caravan for two hundred pounds."

"So, to take on an enterprise like this . . ." Seamus gave a sideways nod toward the course.

Eamon finished the thought: "It was daunting."

There was a moment's silence as the Erris men remembered the endless meetings, the weekends spent writing grant proposals, the personal loans made to keep the project moving, the lotteries, the benefit shows and bake sales.

"It took a lot of hard work, a lot of late nights," Seamus went on, "and some aggro here and there. There were weeks we wondered where Friday's wages were going to come from. But you had everybody singing off the same hymn sheet, you had everybody willing to put in the effort, because we felt a golf course that was a cut above the rest was the one thing that would be a great boost to our area."

He turned to look out the window. "That's not to say that Carne is the be-all and end-all. The angling club has been here for years. There's freshwater fishing at Bangor, and you've got the festivals and all that. But if you were to imagine Belmullet and Erris without Carne, I'd say it would be a doomsday situation. Carne brought us tourists. Carne brought prosperity. It brought employment. The spring off has been phenomenal."

The door opened and Brendan came out, saying, "They want you now, Seamus."

The draper stood, gave the lapels of his suit coat a straightening tug, and walked through the door toward the bright lights.

I didn't stay for the rest of the shoot, but I arranged with Eamon to return in the afternoon for a course walk. I wanted to hear about his collaboration with Hackett, and I thought a stroll in the dunes without clubs, caddies, or playing partners would stimulate his memory.

"I'll bring the Hackett file," he said.

On the way to my car, I walked past a van from the Broadhaven Bay Hotel as its driver unloaded golf bags for four men and two women. The golfers wore sweaters and logoed ball caps, and from the way they kept looking around—staring one moment at the clubhouse and the next at the steel-gray quilt of clouds over Blacksod Bay—I guessed that they had come some distance to play.

So, I reminded myself, had I.

CHAPTER 18

I fell in love with Carne in 2002. Certainly, the massive and wild dunesland was a factor and the fact that the holes were borderline silly made it interesting. Carne had individual hole character through many different types of landforms. Some holes went through the valleys formed by the dunes and others were in the "flats" with wildly undulating fairway contours. I greatly preferred the Carne experience to that of Royal Portrush, a fabulous course on really beautiful coastal links land. Certainly, this idea of individual hole character is a major factor informing my core beliefs.

— from *An Interview with Jim Engh*, GolfClubAtlas.com

I used the hours before my appointment with Eamon to inspect the ceiling of my apartment from the vantage point of the couch. I may even have dozed. When indolence became unbearable, I sat up to watch a black-and-white rerun of *The Virginian*, one of the many shows from my American youth that had somehow found their way to twenty-first-century Mayo. The television, which sat on a plastic patio table, was tethered to the wall by a cable that provided a thin trickle of programming, mostly from the BBC. Irish content was limited to national news, Gaelic Games, and the high-minded offerings of the aforementioned TG4, the Irish-language channel.

During a commercial break, I opened a copy of *Western People* and read MAN SMASHED GIRLFRIEND'S PHONE WITH A HAMMER.

It was late afternoon when I met Eamon back at the club. The wind had strengthened, and clouds formed an undifferentiated ceiling of gray. Eamon and I wore similar outfits of a sweater and rain jacket, and we each had a wool cap pulled down over the ears. (Brimmed hats tend to leave Carne of their own volition when the wind picks up.) We climbed the timber steps onto the tenth tee, which Eamon said was pretty close to the spot where he and Eddie Hackett had begun their initial exploration of the banks, two decades before.

"Eddie spent three days here on that first visit," Eamon began, practically shouting over the wind. "He always wore his oilskin coat and Wellingtons. And he insisted on walking. He said, 'I want to feel the ground!' He was old school."

"Is it true that he went under fences like a rabbit?" I had read that Hackett didn't mind getting dirty in the pursuit of a good routing.

Eamon nodded. "We'd come to a fence with seven strands of barbed wire, and Eddie would lie flat on the ground and roll himself underneath. I'd take the aerial route, but he was always on the other side before I was."

Eamon took a slow look around, remembering what the banks had looked like in 1986. I followed his gaze, mentally erasing the clubhouse, the mowed fairways, and the two visible greens. "How did he orient himself?" I pointed toward the big dunes in the distance. "I walk in there, and I'm lost."

"So would most of us be. We didn't have topographical maps or aerial photographs. All we had was an ordinance survey map, and it wasn't to scale. But Eddie was making his sketches, and after a few days he had a mental picture."

A mental picture, I realized with a degree of sadness, was all I would ever have of Eddie Hackett. Unknown outside Ireland, the former head pro of Portmarnock Golf Club designed or remodeled dozens of courses on the Emerald Isle, including a number of notable links courses; and he did so for far less money, in toto, than Tiger Woods received from the sheikhs of Dubai for his very first design effort, Al Ruwaya. "Half the people playing golf in Ireland are doing so because of Eddie Hackett," the golf writer and course designer Pat Ruddy once said. But Hackett, who died in 1996 at the age of eighty-six, lived a life of humility and religious observance, spending more time kneeling in church pews than any man outside a monastery.

"His rough drawings were certainly not to scale," Eamon said, interrupting my reverie. "He took them to a draftsman in Dublin, and the plans came out of that."

The wind was annoying, so we took the stairs from the tee and circled past the eighteenth green and on down into the eighteenth fairway. The deep valley took the sting out of the gale and made normal conversation possible. Starting up the eighteenth fairway—emphasis on *up*, as the eighteenth has slopes as steep as a roller coaster's—Eamon said, "That first day, he didn't walk into the center of the property. He wanted to walk the boundaries and the high ground. From up there"—he pointed ahead to the eighteenth tee—"we had a 360-degree view of the whole property."

The wind battered us again when we reached the tee, but I felt my usual exhilaration. We had the sullen sea on one side of us and the frothy bay on the other, with Belmullet's rooftops and spires straddling the isthmus where the two harbors conjoined.

"After a few hours of walking around, we sat here for a while," Eamon continued. "I was getting hungry, so I suggested we go into town to get something to eat. But he wanted to stay and sketch. He said, 'Bring me out a sandwich.'"

"How did he visualize a hole?" I turned the above-mentioned 360 degrees, taking in the bewildering mosaic of ridges and ravines. "Did he simply stand on a dune and say 'This is a tee. There's the fairway. Over there is a green'?"

"He was a great man for finding green sites and then working backward. He'd put a stake in the middle of a green site and then walk backwards to find a tee. He'd put a stake there, and finally he'd put a stake in the middle of a fairway, two hundred to 225 yards out."

"That's pretty much the way Old Tom Morris worked," I said, pretending to know the design philosophy of the four-time British Open champion who, among other achievements, had laid out the classic Irish links of Lahinch, Rosapenna, and Royal County Down.

"Exactly." Eamon tilted his head toward the timber steps, which I interpreted as a suggestion that we get out of the wind. "It was a real learning experience for me. I was almost thirty when I took up golf, so I didn't know what made a good golf hole."

"But Eddie taught you?"

"Well, he tried. He was very generous with his knowledge." Eamon paused at the bottom of the steps. "I suppose, in hindsight, that he must have been concerned. We had a plot of ground with so much potential, but that was about all we had. We didn't have the funds to engage engineers or the sort of team you would associate with golf course development. But he was very patient with us."

Patient, I was thinking, as in *seven years*—the time it took the men of the Mullet to sculpt a golf course in the rugged Carne banks.

The thing about Eamon was that he never seemed to be in a hurry, and yet he got more done in a day than most men accomplish in a week. The chairman of Erris Tourism returned phone calls. He arranged meetings. He popped up at Carne as you were making the turn, just to make sure that your needs were being met. "He's getting everything done on the day," said Martina Mills, Carne's bookkeeper. "The hours, the *years* he's spent on this place, you can't imagine. If not for Eamon, there wouldn't be a Carne."

There was certainly no aspect of the golf operation that the Doohoma man didn't know as well as his wife's face. Following Eddie Hackett's direction, Eamon had served as Carne's project manager and design apprentice. He had supervised the labor-scheme farmers as they whittled away at the dunes with their shovels and rakes. He had drawn up contracts and met payrolls. He had hired staff. He had overseen construction of the clubhouse. If an employee called in sick, it was probably Eamon Mangan who took your one-euro deposit for a trolley handle and gave you a smiling sendoff to the first tee. "He's an inspiration," Mary Walsh told me. "I can ring Eamon at eleven o'clock at night. He never says to me, 'It's not a good time' or 'Can I ring you back?' He's always accommodating, always polite." When I pointed out that everyone at Carne seemed accommodating and polite, Mary blushed with pleasure. "That's what we aim for here. And if that means biting your tongue on occasion or being nice to someone who isn't as nice back, so be it. But that's Eamon's way."

Michael Mangan, who could fairly say that the Carne Golf Links would not exist if he hadn't vowed to save the banks from striping, gave all the credit to his brother. "I'm the one who contacted Eddie Hackett," Michael said, "but after I brought him in, Eamon was the liaison. He and Eddie worked together on everything—the grasses, the shaping, the drainage, all the little details of construction and design." It was Eamon, he said, who had made Carne the inviting place that it was—a destination links with none of the fussiness or formality of a country club or resort course. Michael liked to tell the story of the holiday player who stormed into the golf shop after a pint or two in the Spike Bar to report that his clubs had been stolen. Promising to get to the bottom of it, Eamon had studied the CCTV tapes. Seeing that a tour company had picked up the golfer's bag by mistake, Eamon drove up the coast to Enniscrone to recover the bag. He then drove an additional forty miles to Rosses Point so the golfer would have his clubs in time for the next day's round. "That's dedication," Michael said. "Eamon has gone to the ends of the earth for Carne, and he's never taken a penny for petrol or expenses."

Over a number of visits to Belmullet, I had coaxed a few autobiographical details out of Eamon. The youngest of nine children, he emigrated to England in 1964, when he was eighteen. "All my brothers were over there, developing filling stations for Shell, Total and all the different oil companies," he told me. "I worked for my brother John for a year until I got confident, and then I'd be given a particular station—mostly out of London because I was single and it involved staying out for five nights a week. We weren't running petrol stations, but we handled the whole development from greenfield site to completion." Mangan Bros. Ltd. was so successful that the brothers began to plan a return to Western Ireland. In 1969, Michael and John purchased a 4½-acre site on the Ballina Road, two miles out of Belmullet, and secured planning approval for a dance hall and a forty-bedroom hotel. The hotel was never built, but the Palm Court Ballroom was, and Eamon was sent home to run it.

"Twenty-three years I operated a night club," Eamon said. "The Palm Court opened on 11 April, 1971, and it was such a big business from the start that I never returned to London." In peak times the Palm Court averaged seventy-five dances a year, sometimes three in a week, and to this day you find married couples from Westport to Ballina who say they met their spouses at the Mangans' ballroom. "I had somebody in Castlebar booking acts—generally Irish show bands and some overseas groups. For the first fifteen years it was primarily country and western, which is still very popular here, particularly in the border counties." Eamon met Katherine a few years into the Palm Court era, and they eventually married and settled into a house on Blacksod Bay with an unobstructed view, over the water, of the distant, jagged profile of the Carne banks.

The mid-eighties saw the rise of disco and the end of the Irish dance hall craze, so the Mangans—who operated in Ireland as MBD, which stands for Mangan Brothers Doohoma—began to dabble in wholesaling, retailing and investment properties. They sold the Palm Court and opened a furniture store and a pub on the Belmullet town square, putting Eamon in charge.

MBD prospered, but the Belmullet of the 1980s was a sad, lonely little town. At eleven o'clock on a cold night, Michael remembered, the streets were empty and the windows shuttered. "Nobody had any cash," he told me while motoring up the Blacksod Road. "There might be a few bicycles outside a house, but no cars. Taxes were high, employment was low, and nobody was staying in town. People were raising their youngsters, and then they'd all go away. It was 99 percent emigration out of the place." And it wasn't just the impoverished West that suffered; it was the entire Republic. "In the mid-eighties," he said, "we had an actual emigration of about fifty-three thousand a year."

But along came the so-called Celtic Tiger of the 1990s, a period of reform and rapid economic growth that transformed the Irish Republic from a stagnant backwater into one of Europe's richest countries. "Whatever they're saying about Bertie Ahern," Michael said, referring to the scandal-ridden Irish prime minister of the moment, "himself and his party have transformed the whole country. In 2005–2006 we had forty-seven thousand immigrants from the UK alone and eighty-six thousand total, counting Europe. That's *immigrants*," he repeated for my benefit. "By 2012, we'll be looking for seventy-five thousand or eighty thousand a year to augment the Irish work force. That's a big transformation."

For the rural west, however, the Celtic Tiger did not mean an automatic infusion of capital and high-paying jobs. Towns and villages had to look for Celtic Kittens, projects that could attract foreign investment, state-supported industries or—if you were stuck on a remote Atlantic peninsula with a vast stretch of bogland frustrating your efforts—*tourism*. And that, everyone told me, was why the Carne Golf Links usually got credit for the revival of Belmullet. "It was the Celtic Tiger, too," Michael said, "but the golf course put us on the map. It gave people a reason to visit." Carne also gave expatriates a reason to return to the Mullet—as evidenced by the thirty or so upscale houses and holiday homes that had gone up in or near Belmullet. "My brother Paddy is coming back next year after fifty years in London," said Michael, putting a face on the Carne phenomenon. "He's building on Shore Road, and he's a life member of the golf course. Paddy will play a lot of golf here."

Granted, there was no way to prove that an old man was leaving London and moving to Mayo because Eddie Hackett and Eamon Mangan had gone for a walk on the Carne banks twenty years before. Paddy Mangan's return could be explained by the laws of probability, the vagaries of fate, or the famous "butterfly effect," which says that a butterfly flapping its wings in China can send a perfectly hit shot spinning out of control on a golf course in Ireland. But one thing was certain: Carne was the reason that a sixty-year-old Missourian, a great-grandson of Erin, was out walking on the banks in a gale.

"Tell me about the seventeenth hole," I shouted over the wind, following Eamon down the trail.

CHAPTER 19

"Bloody Sunday (Irish: Domhnach na Fola*) is the term used to describe an incident in Derry, Northern Ireland, on 30 January 1972 in which 26 civil rights protesters were shot by members of the 1st Battalion of the British Parachute Regiment. Thirteen people, seven of whom were teenagers, died immediately. . . . Five of those wounded were shot in the back."*

—Wikipedia

Ann Geraghty's kitchen was behind the Sheer Elegance hair salon at the end of a dark corridor that ran past the stairs to the second floor. A window over the sink looked out on her garden, and a second door led to the salon. The two doors produced a steady traffic of children, trades people, family and friends.

"Ann is quite well-known in this town," said Inge Sierens, who was stacking dishes on the food-prep island. "Her shop is like a pub for women, a place to go for tea and coffee. It's a business, but it feels like a family." Inge, a young Belgian, was a part-time Belmullet resident. "I work in the seafood restaurant up the street, and I used to work at the Broadhaven Bay Hotel. But I travel a lot. I want to see the world before I settle down."

"Most people who want to see the world," I said, "bypass Belmullet."

She laughed. "I used to work in an Irish place in Belgium, and all the other employees were from Ireland. I'd say I was going to holiday here, and they'd say, 'How in heaven's name did you end up in a place like Belmullet?'" She opened a drawer and pulled out some silverware. "I said, 'You're wrong. It's such a nice spot, and the beaches are gorgeous.' " She nodded toward the residence door. "And the Geraghtys have received me with open arms."

In the doorway, as if on cue, appeared Ann Geraghty—a slender, attractive blonde with a stylish shag cut. A boy with a backpack squeezed past her, making her laugh. "This is my son, Jack," she said. "He's ten." Without my asking, she added, "Ellie is twelve. Kate is fifteen."

I had explained to Ann that I was looking for links to my family's past, and she had already given it some thought. "My dad is a character, he'd have some great stories for you." She shuffled through some papers on the food island. "I'm sure Aunt Annie can help you, and I can call Seamus and Edith Geraghty in Gladree and Martin and Ann Geraghty at Clogher. All these people are on the Mullet. If you find one of them, you'll find them all."

"How many Anns is that?" I started counting on my fingers, not leaving out my father's American cousin, Anne Hughes, and my own niece, Anne Garrity.

"Isn't it terrible? It causes awful confusion."

Conceding that I was one of the awfully confused, I asked Ann to place herself in the constellation of local Geraghtys.

"Well, my dad is Jimmy Geraghty, who owns the garage down past the bridge, and you might talk to him. My mother is Mary." She closed her eyes while tapping the countertop. "My great-great-grandmother worked for one of the landlords, and there's a photograph of her with a bicycle he bought for her. That's a story, there."

Ann's mobile phone chirped, and she excused herself for a moment to take the call. When she came back, she apologized for not knowing more about her family, saying, "I often wish I had written down or recorded the stories my grandfather told." It was a common refrain on both sides of the Atlantic, and I silently congratulated myself for having recorded my dad.

"Are you related to George Geraghty, the greenkeeper?"

"I am," she said. "My father and George are second cousins, and I actually stayed in that house as a child. I have lovely memories of Cross."

The phone chirped again, and she rolled her eyes. "Sorry!"

While she took the call, Inge and I chatted about Carne and the influx of golfers at the ninety-room Broadhaven Bay Hotel. "Jesus," she said, "that golf course is busy." I passed on a well-sourced rumor that the hotel was going to build an entire new wing for golfers, along with a couple of nineteenth-hole lounges. "Well, I wouldn't be surprised," she said. "The wedding parties pack the hotel on weekends. The golfers can't even get in."

"So, yes," Ann said, putting down the phone. "Where was I?"

"George Geraghty," I prompted. "He thinks there may be some Mediterranean blood in the family. Shipwrecked sailors."

"That may be," Ann said. "I'm very fair now, from being indoors, but I have somewhat dark skin. And my dad has dark skin, so we often claim we had something to do with the Spanish Armada. That's our theory, anyway."

She went to the sink and ran some water over a colander full of vegetables. "Our local history has a tragic side, as I'm sure you know. My dad told stories of the hardships his father suffered as a boy. I remember him talking about his younger sister." She turned off the water and turned away from the sink. "His mother died giving birth, and his father was very bitter about that, to the point of blaming the little girl. So when she was eleven, she broke her leg, and they couldn't afford to bring her to a doctor. So eventually she got gangrene. Friends and family rallied for her, they raised money for the doctor, but the old man said, 'She's not good to anyone with one leg,' and he refused their help." Ann paused a beat. "And she eventually died."

She took the colander and gave it a shake over the sink. "I was horrified to hear that, that he would just let her die." She gave me a sheepish look. "I don't know if my father would want me to tell that. But it says something about the harshness of the times."

More children trooped through the kitchen, and then Ann needed a minute in the hallway to consult with her ex-husband, who said something that made her laugh. When she returned, I said, "Your kitchen is the cross-roads of Belmullet."

"It's rarely quiet," she agreed, picking up her mobile. She thumbed a number and started a conversation with an unidentified Geraghty while I gazed out the window at the gathering gloom. She then called another, and yet another, and within ten minutes I had appointments to visit more Geraghtys than I had met in my lifetime. She said, "They'll be excited to see you."

She wrote the phone numbers and driving directions on a card and handed it to me. "It's family stories you're wanting, is it?"

"No matter how small," I said.

She hesitated. "I can tell you an experience I had, although my grand-father would be rolling in his grave if he heard me tell it."

I leaned forward to express my interest—a move perfected through years of interviewing subjects not half as engaging as Ann Geraghty.

"When we were very young," she began, "we didn't have a lot of money. So whenever the turf would be getting a little low, my granddad would get some bags and take us out to collect the little leftovers. The scraps. This was old Jim Geraghty, my granddad, and he used to drive this green Consul car, and I was only a few years old, so I used to sit in the middle on the armrest in the front. And we were getting some turf—pickin' up clods, as we'd say—and putting them in the bags. And we were coming towards where the mushroom factory would be now, coming into town—that would be down Shanaghy, between Borhauve and Shanaghy—when this heavy fog came down."

Ann's voice dropped. "There was this donkey and a cart with a coffin in it. There was a woman, all dressed in black, and a little boy with sandy hair." Ann paused and put a hand to her mouth. "And there were some men in black walking to the front of it." She took a breath and lowered her hand. "So we slowed down, and we drove behind them for maybe ten minutes, and nobody spoke until we were directly outside the church. And as quickly as the fog happened"—she made a sweeping gesture with her hand—"it disappeared. And so did the woman and the little boy. The funeral just disappeared, and that was it. My granddad said, 'Surely to God, something *terrible* has happened in the world today.' And he didn't say another word all the way home. And when we got there in our house, directly over our kitchen door was a television. And I just remember walking in and seeing everybody looking up at the TV, and Charles Mitchell was reading the news." She paused a beat. "It was Bloody Sunday."

Ann smiled and shrugged. "People say I'm mad, but I saw it. They just appeared, and then they disappeared. That's something I'm one hundred percent sure of."

Her mobile chirped, and just like that the fog of enchantment lifted.

Ann took the call, and Inge opened the fridge.

Ann Geraghty's stories energized me. The ghost aspect was fascinating because for several years I had been writing "Golf Ghost" articles for *Sports Illustrated Golf Plus*. These whimsical tales, inspired by Charles Dickens' *A Christmas Carol*, cast me as a twenty-first-century golf writer visited by spirits dressed in plus-fours, argyle hose, and cashmere sweaters. And while I had never encountered a ghost in real life—and didn't expect to—I spent an inordinate amount of time communing with historical golf figures. When they spoke in my stories, their words were their own, things they had written in books or private correspondence, things they had told the golf writers of their day. But after hearing Ann's Bloody Sunday story, I began to wonder if ghosts and Geraghtys were an established combination.

I was also reminded that what I was looking for in Ireland was not a family tree. I could walk through a hundred Irish cemeteries and search a hundred genealogical Web sites, but to what end? One tombstone was pretty much like the next. Seeing one's name on a nineteenth-century passenger manifest was only marginally better. But a *story* was different, a story *restored*. A little girl, a Geraghty, had died of a broken leg, and another little girl, a Geraghty, had seen ghosts on Bloody Sunday.

I wanted more, so I rang up George Geraghty from my flat and invited myself to his house for an after-dinner chat. I told him I had more questions about his work at Carne, "sand and gravel stuff," and if he didn't mind a few questions about himself . . .

"No, that's no problem," he said. "Come on over."

So I drove out to Cross Lake again, meeting only two or three sets of headlights on the journey. George, wearing jeans and a T-shirt, answered the door with a woman at his side—Bridget, his companion—and the two of them led me to their cozy parlor. They sat on a sofa with their backs to the windows. I sat on a facing armchair. A peat fire smoldered in a little stove.

We talked about the golf course, and I learned some things about links agronomy. Some of Carne's fairways, for example, had been planted with rye grass and barley. ("The barley holds the sand together," George explained, "until the grass takes root.") The new nine, on the other hand, would be seeded with a spray application of mulch, some kind of gel. ("It's a new technology. I don't agree with it.") But after a few minutes, I abruptly changed the subject. I said, "What was life like when you were a boy?"

"Here in Cross?" He rubbed a hand across the dark stubble on his scalp. "We were pretty self-sufficient. We had our own fuel, meat, spuds. We grew everything. You came home from school, threw your school bag on the fence, and went to work. If you were hungry, you pulled a carrot out of the ground and ate it."

"No one's self-sufficient now," Bridget said in a tone of resignation. "They don't know how to milk a cow or pick a potato. If it's not out of a bottle or a packet, they don't know what to do."

George voted for subsistence farming with a nod. "Belmullet was our supply depot," he continued. "Castlebar sometimes. The main road was tar, but all the village roads were gravel with holes in them. We didn't get to Ballina that often. It was a long, hard drive."

"What did you do for entertainment?" I was thinking of Seamus Cafferky's cinema and Eamon Mangan's Palm Court Ballroom.

"We had radios. There was music in Belmullet. Eventually we had televisions. Richer people had them in the fifties. And there was the cinema." He turned to Bridget. "I can't understand why there isn't one now." Noticing me eyeing the flat screen television in the corner of the room, George assured me that he wasn't a satellite subscriber. "Five channels is more than enough for me," he said. "I only put on the television for the news."

I changed the subject again. "What was it like to leave Ireland?"

He leaned forward and rested his folded arms on his thighs. "I went to England in 1965 because there was no work here. There was absolutely nothing. Everybody emigrated. To England. To Australia. To America."

"You found work in England?"

He nodded. "We were picking potatoes there. And it was hard work. We'd all be in the truck on a frosty morning, fifteen bloody miles to the farm. You'd be frozen solid by the time you got there. The drills were a mile on. Break your bloody back from dawn to dusk. Two breaks, at ten and one, and that was it. When the ground was wet, the clay used to stick to it and make your basket half that weight again. Slave work, that's what it was."

He looked at Bridget. "I'll tell you what I was thinking. *What* the *fucking* hell took me over here? Why didn't I stay at home?"

He turned back to me with a little smile. "We slept in a cow barn. The rats were pulling our clothes off in the nighttime. Your only shower was a tap and a bucket in the yard. When you shampooed yourself, another guy had to throw a bucket of water on your head." He looked at the floor and laughed. "It's God's truth. Imagine it in November and October, having ice cold water thrown on you."

I didn't say anything. I was remembering bus rides through the Florida Everglades with my high school basketball team. We shared the two-lane blacktops with truckloads of migrant farm workers returning from the cane fields—dark-skinned Latino men with vacant stares and machetes.

"There was a gang of us," George continued. "Friends. We moved on to construction in the seventies, and that was rough, too. Eight in the morning to six at night. You ate your lunch on the side of the road, and on cold mornings the sandwiches in your box would be frozen solid. And that's the truth."

"What year did you say you went to England?" I was still back in the cow barn with the rats.

"It was 1965."

That was the year, I reflected silently, that I transferred from the University of Missouri to Stanford University. It was about the time I first heard of Cesar Chavez and the United Farm Workers, who were soon to make history with their 340-mile march from Delano to Sacramento. I sympathized with the farm workers, went to their rallies and honored their five-year boycott of table grapes. How lucky I was, I thought, to come from a family that, while often broke, was never desperate.

"You're how old?"

"Fifty-six," George said.

Four years younger than I.

We talked for another hour. Afterward, I drove back to Belmullet under a gibbous moon. The quay was quiet when I parked beneath my balcony. The Chinese restaurant was closed. The windows in my neighbors' apartments were dark. I walked out to the boat ramp and looked up at the stars, trying to imagine an Ireland—a *recent* Ireland—with so little promise, so little hope.

Golf never crossed my mind.

CHAPTER 20

Construction of the access to the forward 17th tee, around the side of the very high dune,
will be a risky job for the men and an adventure for the players—I am sure you will
make a great job of it. The site for the 17th green is a "natural" and its development, as
we arranged, will provide a very attractive green and an inviting target for members to
aim at.

—from Eddie Hackett's letter to Eamon Mangan, 31 July 1991

I had to clear space on the dining table for the Eddie Hackett materials.
There was a file folder filled with typewritten reports, most of them bearing the salutation "Dear Mr. Mangan" and beginning, "I refer to my visit
to Belmullet" on such-and-such dates. These letters, posted from Dublin
and written over a span of seven years, tended to be arcane and technical
("The costly Triplex mowers should be power hosed after every mowing. . . ."), but they were invariably encouraging. ("I am delighted, but not
surprised, that work is going so well.") There were also a couple of pre-
liminary course routings, which covered half the table when unfolded.

"Number ten is a par 4 on this one," Eamon had told me, running his
finger over the indentations and creases on one of the old drawings. "And

eleven actually didn't exist yet. You walked off to the right of the tenth green, and then you played a par 3." When I asked about an area marked "Cottages and Tennis," Eamon explained that Erris Tourism had originally planned to put in a trailer park. "Or, as you would call it, a caravan park. We wanted to let people know that we weren't just about golf. We had plans for other things, as well."

Hackett's letters and drawings fascinated me, and I wished that my brother had gotten a chance to see them. Tommy had taken a stab at golf course design in his thirties, and if the economic recession of the mid-seventies hadn't shut down virtually every golf project in the U.S., he might have pursued that dream to fruition. (Unlike most pros and ex-pros with design ambitions, who merely lent their names to projects, Tommy had quit his corporate sales job and enrolled at the University of Florida, where he earned a degree in landscape architecture.) My own design experience was limited to the planning and construction of Kansas City's Crestwood National, a nine-hole coffee-can course that I sweated over with a push mower when I was twelve.

I pored over the Hackett material for several hours, stopping now and then to look out the windows. The tide was on the rise, brown water inching up each time I turned until it lapped at the wheels of a red pickup parked on the boat ramp.

I grew sleepy. Did I sleep?

I'm holding an old book. The title is Fore! *The name on the spine is Charles E. Van Loan.*

"This is the book that got you started, right?"

My father nods. He's sitting on my new couch, his reading glasses, water glass and a bag of gum drops within easy reach. His sand wedge is by his side. I'm on the matching love seat in front of a large window that looks out on a covered porch and a leafy neighborhood of shirtwaist and Victorian houses. It's 1979. Dad—an engaging septuagenarian with impaired hearing and unimpaired garrulousness—has moved into an upstairs bedroom.

"Charlie Van Loan was a hell of a writer," he says. "I got the book for Christmas when I was twelve or thirteen, and I was fascinated. Then Father Fallon came to town, and they built a little golf course at Bass Lake, about seven

miles southwest of New Richmond. A Scotchman came in, supposed to be very knowledgeable, the son of a bitch." Dad laughs. "He built six holes. Sand greens, of course. And there were mounds. They called them 'chocolate drops,' and there'd be seven or eight of these goddamn mounds about so high around the greens"— he raises his right hand above the table—"and there was no way to get onto the greens! If you were to fly one over the mounds, which nobody could do in those years, your ball would bounce like on pavement and go a mile. So what you'd do is, you'd hit a shot to get close to the chocolate drops, and then you'd try to find the opening with any kind of club, and eventually you'd make a five or six."

I've never heard Dad mention a Father Fallon. He must be the priest in all those jokes that begin, "A priest and a rabbi go out to play golf. . . ."

"Did you play at Bass Lake?" I lean forward to check that my clunky cassette recorder is operating properly.

"Well, my cousin Jamie got interested in golf, and he used to take me down there occasionally. This was around 1916 or 1917. I was only ten or twelve. He said, 'John, you have to understand. You won't be able to play. You'll just have to caddie.' But eventually they let me play." He clears his throat and reaches for the water. "Jamie only had about two or three clubs."

"In a bag?"

"No, no, just held in your hand. And a ball or two in your pocket."

I wait for him to go on.

"And then they built the course in New Richmond, Johnny, when I was in about eighth grade. They had a contractor there, I've forgotten his name." Dad frowns again. "I should remember, because I worked on the course, and they gave me a lifetime membership. In any case, this contractor built concrete tees. Nine of them. And the course we built looked like this. . . ."

Dad leans forward and starts drawing on the coffee table with his finger. "No clubhouse, not even a tent. They had a barrel of ice or something. But here's the first tee"—he slides his finger—"and four hundred yards away is the green. Down the right side is a fence and a cornfield. Here's the second tee"—he slides his finger left at a right angle—"and four hundred yards away is another green. Fence and cornfield, same thing. Third tee"—another hard left with the finger— "and here's the Soo Line railroad tracks. All the way around"—his finger completes the square—"another fence, another cornfield. Well, nobody had played *golf before, Johnny, and here's the tee and right here's the fence. And no idiot is going to aim at the cornfield. You're going to aim left, like this." He turns his shoulders to simulate an open stance.*

"Well, you know what happened. There were 207 members of the New Richmond Golf Club, and except for the Quinlans, who were left-handed, everyone developed the most god-awful slice you ever saw. They cut every damn shot." He chuckles. "Well, I've told the story many times, but some years later I came back from the University of Minnesota, and they had changed the course completely." He leans over the table again. "Here's the first tee, here's the green"— he points—"it's completely clockwise now. Well, you can imagine what happened. Everybody in the whole damned club, except the Quinlans, hooked the ball."

Dad laughs heartily. "I told that story to Buster Bishop, the golf coach down at the University of Florida, and he said it was the best description of a hook and slice that he'd ever heard."

The Reversed Nine is one of my father's favorite stories, and it has changed over the years in only one respect: the number of club members. ("There were exactly forty-three members," he used to say, "and forty-one of them couldn't hit a hook if their lives depended on it.")

"Where was I?" He looks to the ceiling for inspiration. "Oh, yeah, you asked about the first golf club I owned. I sold my bicycle, Johnny, and rode the blinds over to St. Paul, which was thirty-six miles. . . ."

"When you say blinds . . ."

"The blinds were those accordion-pleated closures between passenger and Pullman cars. You see, the Soo Line trains used to come through east and west"— he draws on the table again—"and we kids would hop on as the train was pulling away from the New Richmond water tower. They'd stop to take on coal and water, and you could just step on." I'm about to ask about the infamous "railroad bulls," the hired cops who beat and killed hoboes during the Great Depression—but that was apparently outside Dad's experience. "They were friendly people," he says. "The railroad dicks didn't bother you at all in a town like that."

"What about at the other end?"

"St. Paul? It wasn't too bad getting off in the railroad yards, but they had those little signal lights and switching lights, and you could break your ass if you

dropped off when the train was moving too fast. As a matter of fact, when Ellis Borkman and I came home after our first year at North Dakota State in Fargo, he stepped off at a turntable on the Northern Pacific and stepped right into one of those goddamn things. Elly went ass over applecart." Dads looks amused. "I thought he was killed. But riding the blinds, you could save eight or ten dollars. I used to take my clubs and ride the blinds over to St. Paul and Minneapolis."

"Are these the clubs . . . ?"

"Jesus Christ, how I wander." He laughs again. "So, after reading Fore!*, I took the blinds over to St. Paul and walked to the Spalding Brothers store. I didn't have much money, Johnny, but I bought a hickory-shafted cleek with a leather grip for ninety cents, four golf balls for sixty cents and a book, Spalding's* How to Play Golf, *for twenty-five cents."*

"Another book?"

"Well, that's not surprising. I read everything I could get my hands on."

"So, you rode back . . ."

"Back to New Richmond on the blinds, and I rushed right over to a cow pasture near our house. I propped the instruction book up against a fence post, and I tried to hit balls. I worked at it for days, Johnny, but I didn't have much success. And then one day Gus Williams came over. He was rich at the time, and he'd actually played some golf in California. Gus climbed over the fence and hit some shots with my club. And Johnny"—Dad's expression turns earnest—"he hit it so straight and long." He pauses, giving me time to picture an old Haskell ball soaring over a field of dreams.

"Those shots were a revelation," he goes on. "When it was my turn again, I must have employed the imitative technique that youngsters seem to be born with, because I also hit an incredible shot. It was like magic."

Dad picks up the sand wedge and grips it with the shaft pointed at the ceiling. He studies his hands, checking to see where the V's between his thumbs and forefingers are pointing and how many knuckles of his left hand are visible.

"Who designed your course?"

Dad lowers the club and leans it against a sofa cushion. "We hired a Saturday-afternoon architect, one of those self-promoting quacks who designed sand-green courses for small towns. He charged practically nothing, and that's about what he was worth. He just walked around and stuck a stake in the ground for a tee and another stake for a green until there were eighteen stakes, and then he said, 'That'll be fifty dollars.' A clown like that could design three or four courses over a weekend."

It occurs to me that the clown in question could have been Spalding's Tom Bendelow, the so-called "Johnny Appleseed of American Golf." Bendelow laid out hundreds of small-town courses between 1900 and 1917, many of them for a twenty-five-dollar fee. Then again, Dad would certainly remember if the New Richmond course had been launched by the man who designed the three courses at Chicago's Medinah Country Club, including the No. 3 course that has become a U.S. Open and PGA Championship venue.

"The fairways and rough were pasture grass," Dad continues, "and our mowers were the four-legged kind—cattle and sheep. When you lost a ball, Johnny, you rolled around on the ground until you felt a poke in the shoulder blades. Even our lady players were not above rolling around in the grass. A Silver King golf ball cost a dollar, and that was a lot of money in those days."

"No clubhouse?"

"No clubhouse, and no sanitary facilities to speak of. There was an outhouse in the adjacent pasture."

"What if you wanted a snack?"

"Well, we'd be out there all day, so we brought sandwiches and cookies, as I recall. There was an artesian well with a winch, a rope, a bucket and a dipper. We'd play seven or eight rounds on a Sunday. We'd play until it was too dark to see."

"Concrete tees?"

He nods. "We had concrete tees, wooden tee boxes and hard sand greens, because they were cheap to build and maintain."

The tee boxes Dad refers to are not the teeing areas on a modern golf course. They were literally boxes filled with sand—a pinch of which was used to make a perch for the ball before the invention of wooden tees. Dad gets apoplectic when he hears Ken Venturi or one of the other TV commentators say that a player is "walking onto the tee box."

"The typical green, Johnny, was just a circle, twenty feet in diameter, with a hard macadam base. We topped that with oil-treated sand, which you could smooth by dragging a burlap sweep over it. The cup was always cut in the center of the green, so the longest putt was about ten feet and absolutely straight.

All you had to do was aim the putter, and you could one-putt damn near every green."

Dad executes one of his nimble transitions: "But we were talking about riding the blinds. One time I went to Minneapolis to see my first exhibition match, George Duncan and Abe Mitchell. And it was on a real golf course, Interlachen, which had grass greens. Anyway, Duncan and Mitchell played Jack Burke Sr.—that's Jackie Burke's father—and Willie Kidd, who was the pro at Interlachen for a couple of hundred years."

I recognize Kidd's name. He was the Scottish-born pro credited with the late-forties grass-greens renovation of New Richmond's nine-hole course. George Duncan, I will learn in time, was a Scot who won the 1920 British Open. Abe Mitchell, an English golf star of the period, served as seed-merchant Samuel Ryder's personal golf tutor and survives as the gold-plated figure atop the Ryder Cup.

"I was only ten or eleven years old," Dad says, an assertion that will not withstand a fact check. "In those days an exhibition match was thirty-six holes, so I rode the blinds to Minneapolis and then took the streetcar from the Great Northern Station. I think the street car was a nickel or a dime then, and it didn't quite get me to Interlachen, but it got me within a mile. So I walked a mile and picked up the match at the third hole. And it was the damnedest thing I ever saw, Johnny. Abe Mitchell had the reputation of being one of the longest drivers in the world, and Kidd was long, too. They hit the ball out of sight, I couldn't even see the goddamn thing. And then to see them come into the par-3 holes—150, 160, 170 yards. Grass greens, and they had the ribbed clubs in those years. They'd hit into those greens, and the ball would back up! Remarkable."

"Do you remember what a ticket cost?"

Dad laughs. "Not a damn cent. They didn't charge admission for exhibition matches. And I didn't know that there were lunch facilities, so when they broke at noon I walked all the way back to the streetcar stop, where there was a place to eat, and then walked all the way back to Interlachen. So I spent the entire day at the club and didn't spend a goddamn cent." He reaches for his water glass. "But I rode the blinds back and forth many times to play Como Park, Phalen Park, St. Paul and some of the others in Minneapolis. We all did that." He takes a sip, smacks his lips, and takes another.

"Did you ever get to play Interlachen?"

I wait for an answer.
"Dad, did you eve . . . ?"
Something is ringing.
"Did . . . ?"

"Hello?"
       "John, it's Valerie in Travel."

"Yes?" Blinking, I rolled into a sitting position on the couch. The Belmullet flat was dark, the sky outside a purple curtain. In New York, of course, it was midday.

"I know it's late there, but I wanted to catch you. Do you want me to ticket you to Glasgow, or are you holding off?"

"No," I said, feigning alertness. "I mean, yes. The trip is on."

"Fine, I'll get right on it. And just so you know, it looks like Aer Lingus may charge you a fee for your golf clubs."

"Really?" I pictured my dad playing with three or four clubs at Bass Lake. "What if I carry them under my arm?"

"And just to confirm," she went on, "do you want this charged to your personal Amex instead of the corporate card?"

Outside, the headlights of a truck swept across the quay, briefly illuminating a tiny red-and-white boat anchored a few yards out. With its pristine deck and cracker-box cabin, it looked like a bathtub toy.

"That's right," I said. "This trip's personal."

CHAPTER 21

The first patent for golf balls in Great Britain was to Captain Duncan Stewart in 1876.
Patent #3228 combined gutta percha with ground cork and metal filings.

—from Beachgolff's *History of Golf Balls*

A few weeks into my sabbatical, I locked up the Belmullet flat, drove to Knock, and caught the once-a-day Aer Arann flight to Edinburgh, Scotland. "I've got a nine a.m. tee time at Aunt Mary's old course," I told Pat during our evening video chat. I had the camera angled so that she could see the sumptuous drapes and furnishings of my room at the Dalmahoy Hotel and Country Club, site of the 1992 Solheim Cup. Pat and I had spent a couple of nights at Dalmahoy in 1999, when I was researching a *Sports Illustrated* feature about Scottish town courses.

"Who?" She didn't get the Stuart reference.

"Aunt Mary. The Queen."

"Oh, right." She didn't look up from the stack of mail in her lap. "Do you want to renew your subscription to *Golf World?*"

"I already did. They just keep sending reminders."

"It says it's absolutely your last opportunity to renew at the golf-professional courtesy discount rate."

"I'm not a golf professional."

"It's a good rate."

I gave it a moment's thought. "You could figure out my life expectancy and sign me up for that many years minus one."

"Moving on." She dropped the offer in the wastebasket by my desk.

"Papa, look!" Maddie, my four-year-old granddaughter, leaned into the camera, her blond bangs and blue eyes filling the screen. "Look what I drew!" She held up a piece of notepaper covered with thick green squiggles and brown lines laid out like upended railroad ties.

"It's a golf course!" I gushed.

"No, it's not!" She yanked her creation back and studied it solemnly. Before she could offer an alternative interpretation, six-year-old Jack muscled her aside with a triumphant, "Look, Papa, a tiger!" My screen filled with an orange-and-black-striped blob with whiskers and stick legs that resembled hickory-shafted baffing spoons.

"Nana!" Maddie wailed, slapping at Jack's masterpiece.

I uttered a few calming words from Edinburgh while Pat separated the combatants in Kansas City, and within seconds the kids were kneeling on chairs at the glass-top table in our sun room, happily starting new drawings.

Had Steve Jobs been there, I would have hugged him.

A few words about Scotland.

It's where golf began, give or take an historian's quibble. It's where shepherds allegedly smacked stones into rabbit burrows, switching to a lofted crook when they needed more backspin. It's where the first wooden-shafted clubs and feathery balls were fashioned. It's where the rules of the game were formulated, where the first competitions were staged, and where the words "Ne'er up, ne'er in" were first uttered.

So, having learned some years before that my no-longer-golfing mother carried the golf gene, I was finally giving my Scottish heritage some attention. And I knew just where to go: Musselburgh (pronounced *Mussel-burrow*), and Machrihanish.

The Musselburgh Links is a nine-hole course that has been around for a long, long time. In fact, it is advertised as the "oldest playing golf course in the world." But you wouldn't know that to look at it now. The flatness of the land is relieved by the occasional grassy bump or revetted bunker, and there are bands of rough with tall, wispy stalks bearing seed heads. Otherwise, the course is as featureless as a racetrack infield—which, in fact, is what it is. Since 1816 the linksland has known the thunder of equine hooves, and the golfers now share their riverside meadow with the track and grandstands of the Musselburgh Racecourse.

My playing partner and guide at the Musselburgh Links was Alan Minto, a still-young-and-fit former tournament pro from Musselburgh who has found his niche promoting tourism in the golf-rich environs of East Lothian. "I actually learned to play here at the racecourse," he told me on the first tee. "I've played in a couple of hickory tournaments."

He was being modest. During our quick spin around the links, I learned that Alan was a regular participant in the World Hickory Open Championship, a competition that had started as a lark and grown into a fifty-pro event with a purse of 17,500 pounds. "We play with the modern ball, but with pre-1935 hickory clubs," Alan said, "and we hit the ball 275 yards. Which proves that the ball is the biggest advancement in golf technology." The Hickory Open was a successor to the British Golf Collectors Society Championship, which Minto won in 1989 on his first try. "I borrowed five hickory clubs," he recalled, "and shot sixty-four for eighteen holes, or two loops of nine. The course record was sixty-seven with any kind of clubs, so I broke the course record by three shots." He shrugged. "It was just one of those days. I think the record has been broken again, but it still stands as the professional record."

Alan interrupted his story to show me what he could do with a modern, steel-shafted 5 iron. With just the quickest glance at his target, he punched a shot that bored through a stiff headwind, the ball hopping twice on the green before snuggling up to the flagstick. "The funny thing was," he continued as he shouldered his carry bag, "I had just signed with MacGregor when I won here. I was tempted to throw my new clubs away and stick with my five hickories."

Young as he appeared to be, Alan knew his Musselburgh history—

enough, at least, to suggest that he read more than greens. He told me that it was a nineteenth-century Musselburgh greenkeeper who introduced the hole cutter and set the hole size at today's standard 4½ inches. He told me how the first-ever ladies' tournament, a competition for fishwives, was played at Musselburgh. He told me that the brassie was invented at Musselburgh in 1885. He told me that a Musselburgh member, the whiskered Bob Ferguson, once beat Old Tom Morris in six straight challenge matches. There was so much golf history in East Lothian, Alan said, that you could hardly take a stroll without stumbling upon some artifact. He, for example, owned Old Tom Morris' walking stick—a bamboo cane with an ornamental handle and a silver plate engraved with the words OLD TOM MORRIS' STAFF. PRESENTED AFTER HIS DEATH TO HIS CLOSE FRIEND JAMES JAMISON. "My great-aunt inherited it from a cousin who was an antiques collector. He wasn't a golfer, so we can't see the connection, but there was a James Jamison in St. Andrews who had a lodging house on Pilmore Links. He was two doors from the New Club's clubhouse, where Old Tom spent most of his later days. They were probably drinking buddies."

When we finished our whirlwind round, Alan invited me across the street to the Musselburgh Old Course Golf Club, a stone building with a frieze honoring the five local golfers who, between 1860 and 1889, won ten Open titles: Bob Ferguson, Mungo Park, Willie Park Sr., Willie Park Jr., and David Brown. The facade also bore the club crest and a one-word legend: HONESTAS.

Inside, we were lucky enough—at least I think it was luck—to run into the club secretary, Robin McGregor. He showed us around, stopping to point out treasures like the 1890 John Smart painting of two golfers in the Pandy Bunker, a vast sand pit shored up with timbers. ("It's a euphemism for pandemonium," Robin explained.) Further on, he showed us a copy of the original rules of golf set down by the Honourable Company of Edinburgh Golfers in 1744, when that club played at the nearby Leith Links, before their move to Musselburgh Links in 1836. "We had thirty years of Open Championships," Robin said, "all played under local rules."

Alan, who knew all this stuff by heart, teed one up for Robin with a question about the challenge matches.

"Yes, well," Robin said, flashing a collegial smile. "The early pros, the

Parks and Morrises, they made their money taking advertisements in the papers asking other golfers to challenge them. Tom Morris Sr. and Old Willie Park played one such challenge here for a hundred pounds, but Old Tom went into a pub and refused to complete the match because the crowd was so partisan that it was unfair." Noting my look of surprise, Robin said, "It wasn't the nice polite crowds you see today. It was more like a football match."

Confident that Robin was a man who knew his history, I asked if he could confirm what I had read, that my ancestor, Mary, Queen of Scots, had played at Musselburgh Links.

"It's not absolutely certain," he said, "but it's assumed she would have played here. She stayed at Seton House, just a few miles down the road. Do you know the story?"

"About Lord Darnley's murder and the Earl of Bothwell?" I congratulated myself for remembering both names.

Robin gave me an approving nod. "It's written that she was seen playing golf at Seton after her husband's death, which was a bit of a scandal. Now, King James VI—her son—he was a nasty piece of work, too. He definitely played here. And he bet at golf. There's a diary at the Royal Museum in Edinburgh in which he recorded that he lost two pounds, six shillings in a match."

I made a mental note to visit that museum someday. I wanted to see if James' diary recorded the name of the man bold enough to demand payment of a golf wager from a king at a time when kings, if irked, sent the royal executioner to sharpen his ax.

Alan, having volunteered to help me track down the Stuart golfers, led our two-car procession east along the Firth of Forth to Gullane, a village with three eighteen-hole golf courses that climb up and over an immense hillside of heather before returning to town a few miles shy of Muirfield, which has a pretty decent course of its own. We were met outside the visitors' clubhouse by a short, ruddy-faced character named Archie Baird, who unlocked an outside door, reached inside to turn on the lights, and led us into a room packed with golf artifacts.

"Welcome to the Heritage of Golf Museum," said Archie, who was dressed for golf in slacks and a navy wind shirt. He immediately turned toward a picture display and launched into a practiced dismissal of Scotland's claim to have invented golf, crediting the Dutch instead. To make his point, he *pointed*—in this instance to framed etchings of Renaissance types using long sticks to bat balls through gates and around windmills. "There's no argument about this," he said, so I didn't try to make one.

Archie continued his delightful monologue, rattling on as if there were forty of us instead of two, but my eyes landed on a framed engraving hanging on an adjacent wall. In the picture, three white-gowned angels—two of them holding baffing spoons and another with a golf ball in one hand and a big key in the other—fluttered over the heads of a ceremonial party. The center of attention was a woman in a brocaded dress and big ruffled collar. She had a wooden golf club in her left hand, which helped me to recognize her as Mary, Queen of Scots. Standing at Aunt Mary's side was an elegant gentleman—Lord Darnley in better times?—and next to him a drummer boy, and behind the drummer boy a factotum holding a silver golf club with attached "captains' balls," the traditional prize awarded to captains of ancient golf clubs.

"It's the opening of Muirfield," Archie said, noticing my interest. Indeed, I recognized the famous stone clubhouse in the background. I had been there not two months earlier, covering Tom Watson's victory in the Senior British Open. I doubted, however, that Mary Stuart and Darnley had been able to make it to Muirfield's opening, which occurred in 1889.

"They're on the first hole, obviously," Archie said, misinterpreting my puzzlement. "That was Tom Morris' layout." Archie promptly debunked another bit of conventional wisdom: that Old Tom was the first to design two loops of nine holes ending at the clubhouse. "That's horseshit," Archie said with a snort. "Harry Colt was the first."

But I needn't have worried that Archie would whiff on Aunt Mary. He said that the Queen's golf outing, six days after Darnley's assassination, had prompted John Knox, the famous Presbyterian minister, to denounce her from the pulpit of Edinburgh's St. Giles Cathedral. Said Archie, "He did not think six days was a decent interval. It should have been at least a week."

Alan and I laughed.

"Anyway," Archie said, "she played golf on the other side of Aberlady Bay, at Seton House. And maybe at Musselburgh."

"Musselburgh is cagey about that," Alan said.

"Golf aside," I interjected, "the House of Stuart seems to have had some bad actors."

Archie gave a philosophical shrug. "Bad behavior was very common in those days. There were a lot of hooligans. If they took a dislike to somebody, they attempted to murder them."

On that cheerful note, Archie resumed his counterclockwise stroll around the room, stopping here to comment on a top hat filled with feathers (the amount packed into a leather casing by early ball makers), stopping there to hammer on a gutta percha ball to show how hard it was. My favorite exhibit was a standing golf bag from 1897. It was a narrow plank with two wood legs and a leather enclosure at the bottom. A wood handle was attached with pivoting metal rods, and there was a leather ball pouch at the top. It looked like a big insect. "These disappeared for one hundred years," Archie said of the stand-up bags. "Didn't reappear until 1997."

When I told Archie he had a wonderful collection, he said, "It's only the bottom of the pyramid. I've got the good stuff at home." He added that he had been a veterinarian in Edinburgh for many years, and he probably wouldn't have become a golf collector if he hadn't married the great-granddaughter of Willie Park, Sr., winner in 1860 of the very first Open Championship. "We had a big basement flat which was used as an air raid shelter during the war," Archie said. "To spruce it up I went to sales of old stuff, and at one sale I found an old golf bag with clubs sticking out. I rubbed the dirt off a club, and it said, 'W. Park, Musselburgh.' " He looked around, his gaze taking in the little room's anachronistic clutter. "That started my obsession." In time, Archie had sold his practice and his home in Edinburgh, and in 1980 he opened the museum at Gullane. Ben Crenshaw, the PGA Tour star, attended the opening ceremony.

"Getting back to the Stuarts," I said. "Anything here I should know about?"

"Well, you've heard of the club maker."

I gave him a blank stare.

He looked exasperated. "You're just starting!"

I nodded sheepishly.

"Well, there was an early cleek maker from St. Andrews named Thomas Stewart with a 'W.' I don't know when they divided the spelling, but Stewart was one of the great cleek makers in the gutta ball period. Most of his clubs don't have his name on them, just his cleek mark—a little clay pipe." Archie rummaged around in a bag of old clubs and pulled out a stainless-steel putter from the 1930s. On the back of the blade, slightly worn, was the clay pipe logo. There was also a white sticker identifying the putter as the work of Alec Aitken of Gullen.

"Aitken assembled clubs from component parts," Archie explained. "He'd write off to the cleek maker, 'Send me two dozen putter heads, two dozen mashie heads, two dozen niblicks.' Then he would put shafts in them and sell them. But the cleek mark gives you the original maker." Archie pointed at some strips of leather hanging on a rack. Stamped on the strips were the cleek marks of other tradesmen: a star, a hand, a diamond, a shamrock, an anchor, a hand clutching a pint glass. "I tend not to collect St. Andrews clubs," Archie said, betraying his East Lothian loyalties. "But Stewart was a very important man in early club making. He produced iron heads for most of the top club makers and players, including Old Tom himself."

Archie raised a finger, as if a thought had just occurred to him. "Get the book by Jeffery Ellis, *The Clubmaker's Art*. There's pages and pages on Stewart."

I was going to say something, but my eyes fell on a bulky item propped against the back wall: an antique push mower. Above it was a sign: EARLY GRASS CUTTER. NOTE MAKER'S NAME—SHANKS! I was absorbing that when I realized that Archie had somehow moved on to the subject of rabbits and golf. "The rabbits were very important," he was telling Alan, "because they invented the hole. The head buck rabbit would scrape an area out and urinate on it to mark his spot. The golfers would then use that hole, but they had a better way of marking the spot—a feather on a stick!"

Archie reached into the corner for what appeared to be a cane. "Now this is a 'Sunday club'. . . ."

I gave up trying to steer the conversation. Archie was at the wheel, and he didn't need advice from a backseat driver.

CHAPTER 22

The Blackheath pair were Captain Stewart and George Glennie; they went through the field like a devouring flame and Blackheath made them life members for "Constituting this Club the Champion Golf Club of the World." I am sure Mr. Glennie did his full share, but for me Captain Stewart will always remain the heroic figure. They used to lay two to one on Allan [Robertson] against him. I should incontinently have taken the bet.

—from Bernard Darwin's *British Golf*

The road to Machrihanish, if you're a Stuart, goes through Linlithgow, a medieval town some fifteen miles west of Edinburgh. You round a bend on the A803, and there it is, the family manse—a massive stone redoubt on a hill overlooking a public garden and a tree-lined loch. You lose sight of it as you negotiate the narrow, twisting streets of the old town, but a cobblestone lane takes you up a narrow drive and through a stone gate to a small car park. There's an old stone church—the Church of St. Michael of Linlithgow—and a surrounding graveyard littered with eighteenth- and nineteenth-century headstones. The main attraction, though, is the castle, Linlithgow Palace—summer home to the golfing Stuarts from roughly

1424, when King James I started reconstruction of a manor house destroyed by fire, until 1746, when the Duke of Cumberland's army torched it. In its penultimate year, Bonnie Prince Charlie used Linlithgow as a halfway house on his march to England.

A gray sky and intermittent drizzle prevailed on the morning of my visit, forcing me to pop open my pocket umbrella as I toured the fountain courtyard, royal apartments and Great Hall. (The palace roof was gone, along with the royal furnishings, kitchenware and armory.) Spiral staircases led to stone chambers with spectacular views of the ancient town and the mist-shrouded loch, upon which pairs of sport fishermen in rowboats posed as if for a painting, their rods looking like pen scratches against the pond. Looking down from that great height, I could easily picture James VI or Charles I batting a feathery along the lakeshore, accompanied by the royal caddie, royal club maker and royal swing coach.

That's not to say that I felt a deep connection with the former residents of the palace. The male monarchs, as pictured on museum-style displays scattered throughout the castle, looked nothing like Mel Gibson in *Braveheart*. With their long, flowing hair, black beards and lace cravats, they resembled the *villains* in Gibson's epic—cold, treacherous effetes who'd sooner cut your throat than concede a two-foot putt. I also had to balance any pride in my ancestors' golfing accomplishments against the undisputed fact that it was a Stuart king, James II of Scotland, who in 1457 had banned the playing of "gowf" on Sundays because his soldiers were skipping archery practice to try out the new game. (The golf ban was lifted in 1502 upon the signing of the Treaty of Glasgow, which promised eternal peace with the English. James IV promptly made the first recorded purchase of golf equipment—a set of clubs from a bow maker in Perth.)

Still, I couldn't suppress a surge of pride when I stepped into the Great Hall. A walk-in fireplace as big as a three-car garage hinted at the room's former grandeur. During the Stuarts' heyday, the high stone walls were covered with rich tapestries and the wood ceiling was painted in decorator hues. "Furniture would have consisted of long tables and benches with rushes strewn on the floor," I read in the tour notes. The king and his most important guests ate in front of the fireplace at the "high table." And when I say ate, I don't mean sandwiches. A Saturday menu from the Stuart household accounts, dated December 19, 1528, had the king's party consuming ninety-five loaves of bread, twenty-three gallons of ale, forty white fish, forty codlings, two hundred herrings, four salted salmon, one halibut, two pike, and "unspecified quantities" of scallops, eels, cuttlefish, butter, cheese, eggs and apples. The next day's repast, heavier on meat and fowl, included "2 quarters of salt beef, 5¾ sheep, 13 capons, 1 fat capon, five fat geese, 6 chickens, 8 other fowl, 1 partridge and 2 woodcocks." A golf historian might reasonably conclude that James V, although only sixteen at the time, had invented the pro-am party.

If that was the case, the party was long over. Linlithgow Palace was an impressive ruin, but it was just that—a ruin. Somewhere along the line the Stuarts had fallen on hard times—or, in some cases, on sharp swords—and had gotten out of the royalty game. Some of the Stuarts, including my mother's Francophile ancestors, emigrated to Canada, and some of their descendants would later push on to the United States. One Stewart, after moving to California, changed his name to Charles S. Howard (to disavow a millionaire father implicated in a Canadian land swindle), made his own millions selling Model A Fords, and eventually found fame as the owner of a racehorse named Seabiscuit. Another Stuart, my wonderful aunt Lorry, married a sweet guy named Francis Hubbard, owner of the Hubbard Lawn Sprinkler Company of Minneapolis (and brother of the Twin Cities' television tycoon, Stanley Hubbard). And yet another Stewart, famous for his classic golf swing and buckled-below-the-knee trousers, rode the golf gene out of Springfield, Missouri, and onto the PGA Tour, where he won eleven tournaments between 1982 and 1999, including two U.S. Open Championships and a PGA Championship.

I could only guess at the intrigues and political machinations behind the Stuart diaspora. Leaving Linlithgow Palace and continuing my drive to Machrihanish, I pictured a family tree rooted in medieval Scotland and spreading over the centuries, its thick limbs sprouting more and more branches until it practically covered the globe. Then I imagined a similar tree representing the history of golf, and it, too, was rooted in medieval Scotland with branches covering the globe. Was it so improbable that the two trees would occasionally share branches?

The example of my fellow Missourian, Payne Stewart, came to mind.

Payne's path and mine crossed several times in the 1990s. I particularly recall an encounter in Chicago, where he petulantly blew off a promised interview after a bad round at the 1993 Western Open. Had I told him my middle name was Stuart, maybe he would have collected himself and chatted. As it was, he called my given name as I was leaving the locker room and sheepishly pleaded that I not punish him in print. (His exact words were, "Be kind to me.") I recall, as well, the 1998 U.S. Open at the Olympic Club in San Francisco, where Payne handled the disappointment of a runner-up finish with surprising grace. I then covered his redemptive victory over Phil Mickelson in the 1999 U.S. Open at Pinehurst No. 2 in North Carolina. On the latter occasion I phoned Payne's mother from the press tent to ask about a perceived softening of his demeanor. "I gave him an attitude adjustment," Bee Stewart answered with a laugh. "He's learned you can't go around being rude to everyone." When I pressed for a more serious explanation, Bee cited her son's religious awakening. "Payne talks more with God. He is a different man, a better son." A year later, at yet another U.S. Open, I was on the scene when Payne's peers gathered on the Pebble Beach Golf Links to mourn his untimely death in an aviation accident.

There was also the example of former *SI* staff photographer Lane Stewart. I met Lane while on assignment in Scotland during my first year as a golf writer. The magazine wanted an opening photo spread for a story I was writing on the Royal and Ancient Golf Club of St. Andrews, so they called on Lane, a Texan who had moved to England and adapted the wardrobe and manners of a Londoner. I don't recall if Lane and I talked about our Stuart heritage, but I remember him trying to photograph the R&A clubhouse from the Old Course. Lane wanted the warm colors of late afternoon or sunset, but the forecast called for days of cloud and rain. Undeterred, he went out every afternoon and set up his tripod on the northwest bank of the Swilcan Burn, where golf's most famous ditch crosses the first and eighteenth fairways. He then sat on the edge of the burn, his feet dangling above the water, and read a book. "I'm a patient person," he said. And sure enough, on the third evening the clouds broke and sunlight bathed the links and the old stone clubhouse in an amber glow. *SI*'s photo editors later sent me a Cibachrome print of Lane's R&A photo. I framed it and hung it over the desk in my home office.

But it was neither Payne nor Lane who dominated my thoughts as I drove west through a variable landscape of forest, farm and loch. Rather it was the Stuart who began life as the pampered daughter of an American utility executive, the Stuart who learned the game on the tree-lined fairways of Interlachen Country Club in suburban Minneapolis, the Stuart who could play a Chopin étude on the piano and then repair to the kitchen to perform a variation on a recipe by Escoffier.

My mother.

I have already mentioned that I was surprised, years ago, to learn that my mother, the former Grace Helen Stuart, had played golf as a young wife. Mother had never spoken of it, and neither of my older siblings had filled me in. But surprise turned to astonishment, on the eve of my Machrihanish trip, when my sister divulged during a phone interrogation that our grandfather, Charles Stuart, had been an Interlachen member.

"You didn't know that?" Terry was puzzled by my gasping reaction. "Mother and Aunt Lorry practically grew up at Interlachen. Uncle Francis was a member, too."

Uncle Fran? I remembered him as a good-humored, bespectacled businessman and his two daughters, my cousins Ginny and Francie, as spirited tomboys who babysat me when we visited Minneapolis. But again, none of these treasured in-laws had bothered to tell the Garrity brat that they belonged to a blueblood private club that had hosted, or would host, a U.S. Open, a U.S. Women's Amateur, a U.S. Senior Amateur, a Walker Cup, a Solheim Cup and a U.S. Women's Open.

"I thought you knew," Terry repeated. "Mother took Daddy to Interlachen when they were dating, and he was very impressed. Golf was one of their bonds in the beginning."

"Interlachen," I repeated, stupefied.

Thinking about it later, I decided my reaction was overblown because I had worked two international tournaments at Interlachen, the 1993 Walker Cup and the 2002 Solheim Cup. On both occasions I had felt an almost palpable nostalgia while touring the old Georgian clubhouse or walking on the Donald Ross-designed course. I replayed my dad's stories in my head: his tales of train-hopping to Interlachen, the remembered shots by Abe Mitchell and Walter Hagen, Bobby Jones winning the third leg of the Grand Slam, the fabled lily pad shot, Glenna Collett Vare winning the 1935 U.S. Women's Amateur. To Dad, Interlachen had been a shrine. So it was *his* ghost I saw in the deep shade of Interlachen's maples and spruces, *his* spirit that whispered on the breeze. Or so I had thought.

"Mother went to tournaments, too," Terry said. "She remembered seeing Patty Berg play there."

I peppered my sister with questions. "Was Mother a good player?" ("She was straight down the fairway.") "Did you ever play together?" ("No, but I saw her play in Kansas City. I think it was in Swope Park.") And finally, the big one: "If she was so into golf, why did she quit?"

The line was silent for a few seconds. "I think . . ." Terry hesitated. "I think she got really tired of hearing about golf all the time."

I smiled at that. I remembered how Dad and Tommy could go on for hours about Hogan and Snead, Seminole and Shinnecock, Titanic Thompson and Doc Yawkey, the pronated wrist versus the pause at the top, the punch shot, the cut shot, the lob and the bellied wedge, the Spalding Dot ball versus the Wilson Staff ball, the famous pro who was thought to cheat, the merits and demerits of the interlocking grip. . . .

"And as we got poorer," Terry added, "it was probably too expensive for her to play." She paused again. "I don't know what happened to her golf clubs."

I had an idea. "Hocked them, probably."

It was not these late-life revelations, however, that had put me on the road to Machrihanish. That particular journey started a year earlier, in New Jersey. I was in the library at the Far Hills headquarters of the United States Golf Association, researching one of my Golf Ghost stories, when yet another Stuart leaped out of a quaint and curious volume of golfing lore. The book *The Spirit of St. Andrews* was by Alister MacKenzie, the Scottish-born designer of Augusta National, Royal Melbourne, Cypress Point, and dozens of other acclaimed golf courses. MacKenzie was an accomplished writer with a gift for description and anecdote, and he had written of a visit to Machrihanish, a links course begun by the Prestwick greenkeeper and golf professional Charles Hunter, and extended to eighteen holes in 1879 by Old Tom Morris.

"As the years go by, Machrihanish is steadily deteriorating," MacKenzie wrote. "The rabbits have been destroyed on the clubhouse side of the burn, and as a consequence the beautiful velvety turf has been replaced by rich agricultural grasses, daisies and weeds, whilst on the other side of the burn, where there are millions of rabbits, the old character of the turf still remains. As the club accumulates more funds, however, they are used to destroy the gorgeous natural features."

MacKenzie's words went to that warren in my brain devoted to remote, mystical golf links. Machrihanish, out near the tip of Scotland's southwestern peninsula of Kintyre, is the ultimate destination in *To the Linksland*, Michael Bamberger's compelling tale of a 1991 golf odyssey. "Machrihanish was an unknown," Michael wrote after a nine-day visit. "Nobody I knew had set cleated foot there. It never came up in conversation; it never came up in reading; it never came up." Nevertheless, Michael would find Machrihanish to be "a golfing Nirvana. If I were allowed to play only one course for the rest of my life, Machrihanish would be the place."

So you can imagine the explosion of synapses when I read in MacKenzie's book that "the founder of Machrihanish" was a man named Stuart—a man of such incontrovertible authority that he traveled under the honorific "Commander" instead of his given name. Even more intriguing was the author's assertion that my ancestor had given Tom Morris Sr. the opportunity to gush about the site's natural attributes in the manner of all golf architects to follow. Wrote MacKenzie, "Commander Stuart told me that when he and Old Tom first saw Machrihanish they stood on 'yonder hillock' and Old Tom looked round in a spirit of deep reverence and said, 'Eh, Mon! The Almichty had Golf in hes e'e when he made this place!' "

If that wasn't enough to land Machrihanish on my must-visit list, MacKenzie all but nominated Commander Stuart for golf sainthood in a passage dedicated to a 1905 patent infringement lawsuit. The case, aired in a London court, involved the so-called "Haskell ball," a rubber-cored, filament-wound golf ball named for its American coinventor, Coburn Haskell. The Haskell ball, I remembered from a long-ago tour of the R&A's museum in St. Andrews, had replaced the molded gutta-percha ball in use since 1848. The watershed event was Alex "Sandy" Herd's one-stroke victory over Harry Vardon and James Braid in the 1902 Open Championship at Royal Liverpool. Herd, a young pro from St. Andrews, was the only player in the field to play what would soon be known as a "bounding billy."

MacKenzie, in his posthumously published book, had nothing to say about Herd. But he weighed in on the side of the British defendants in *Haskell v. U.K. Ball Manufacturers*, pushing the argument that certain Scotsmen were years, if not decades, ahead of Coburn Haskell in the rubber ball department. "Stuart," he wrote, "was called on to give evidence in the case of the Haskell ball patent, and proved that he and Old Tom Morris manufactured a rubber covered ball long before the 'Haskell' had been invented. He told me that he had conceived the idea from seeing strings of elastic protruding from ladies' elastic-sided boots. He thought that if similar elastic strands were strung tightly round a central core and covered with gutta percha, a ball of great resiliency could be made. During his evidence, so he told me, the judge asked him, 'Can you tell me, Commander Stuart, of any man except you and Tom Morris who played with your rubber cored balls in those days?' 'Yes,' he replied, 'your own father, sir.' This clinched the case against the Haskell people."

Thanks to my putative cousin, in other words, the honor of Scottish ball makers had been defended against Yankee expropriators, and a Stuart had emerged as the genius behind the wound-ball technology that would dominate golf ball manufacture for a century.

But who was this Machrihanish man? When I checked out MacKenzie's story, I found a couple of minor discrepancies. Contemporaneous accounts credited the key defense testimony to one Duncan Stewart, and the gentleman's title was Captain, not Commander.

"The only way I can clear this up," I told my wife after the New Jersey trip, "is by going to Machrihanish."

"Will you take your clubs?" she asked.

"Should I?" I responded.

CHAPTER 23

The founder of Machrihanish was another remarkable man. His name was Stuart and he held the rank of Commander in the Navy. The story ran that he had been kicked out of the service for knocking down an Admiral.

—from Alister MacKenzie's *The Spirit of St. Andrews*

A Sunday morning in September. Dark clouds whipped up like licorice-flavored cotton candy. Pelting rain. I stood at the dining room windows in the Machrihanish clubhouse and took in the dismal prospect. Beyond the car park, on the other side of a two-lane road, a modest, solitary structure with a peaked roof took the brunt of the gale. The first tee, described by Bamberger and others as perhaps the most dramatic first tee in golf, looked like a place to avoid at all costs. Wrapped around the far corner of the golf shop and raked by wind and rain, it presented as a sodden shelf cantilevered over a crescent of rocks, sand, and pounding surf.

A man emerged from the golf shop and crossed the road in my direction, his umbrella shaking in the wind. I turned and walked through the dining room and past the bar to meet him at the door.

"Horrible day," he said, parking the dripping umbrella in the hallway.

We didn't shake hands because I had met Ken Campbell earlier that morning in his pro shop. Decked out in a windbreaker and golf slacks, he was a big, affable man with a healthy shock of golden red hair. He had been the head pro at the Machrihanish Golf Club for a mere twenty years, which made him, by his own admission, something less than an expert on the club's history. He said, "You've probably done more research on the club than I have."

I doubted that, but Campbell didn't give me time to argue. He led me into a narrow corridor lined with bulletin boards, old photographs and a shelf bearing a touch-screen handicap computer similar to the one in the Carne changing room. He breezed past those attractions and ushered me into the empty dining room.

"Here we are, here's the boy." Campbell pointed at a framed assemblage of old Machrihanish captains. Leaning in, I saw that his finger was on the fifth portrait from the left on the top row. My eyes darted down to the caption—1880 COMMANDER STEWART OF KNOCKRIOCH—and then up again. Looking out from the depths of history was a balding gent with a dark, curly beard and muttonchop sideburns. He wore a buttoned up jacket and a foulard tie gathered with what looked like a napkin ring.

"That's a strong face," I said, noting the big, arched nose and heavy-lidded eyes.

"But then there's this fellow." Campbell pointed to the first captain on the top row: a gray-bearded man, balder than the Commander, but with the same big nose. This captain was pictured standing. He wore an unbuttoned topcoat over a waistcoat with a watch chain showing; his tie was knotted loosely over an open collar. And I loved this: he was wearing loud, checked trousers—a heavy woolen version of the polyester pants that touring pros would wear a century later.

I read the caption: 1876 COLONEL J. L. STEWART OF COLL.

"Another Stewart?" I looked to Campbell. "Were they brothers? Father and son?"

He shrugged. "I couldn't say."

The tour was over that quickly, but Campbell invited me to sit by the window for a chat. On the way, he ducked behind the bar and grabbed a shabby vinyl scrapbook that was secured with a rubber band. He put the book on an adjoining chair as we sat on opposite sides of the table. Outside, the storm raged on; rain splattered on our window with every gust of wind.

"I hope I haven't put you out," I said, worried that my Stewart inquiries might seem to be of no public relations value to Campbell's club.

"No, no, I understand. I'm from Lanark, which is near Edinburgh, but I'm a Campbell, so I always had an attraction to Campbeltown."

Campbeltown, six miles up the peninsula from Machrihanish, is a minor seaport with a handful of tourist attractions, my favorite being the Scottish Owl Center. ("OWLS FROM AROUND THE WORLD—INTERACTIVE FLYING DISPLAY.") If you go to Machrihanish by car, you have to drive through Campbeltown or disembark at Campbeltown from the Caledonian car ferry.

"But I'd never visited here," Campbell continued. "It seemed a long way from Edinburgh. You couldn't possibly drive four hours just to play golf." Besides, his duties as an apprentice pro at the Lanark Golf Club hadn't given him many travel opportunities. "It was a fairly old course, put together in 1851. It was on moorland. The early golfers played on links and moors, you know, because the grass doesn't grow as much." He drummed his fingers on the table. "Anyway, this job came open in the spring of eighty-eight, and Sandy Jones, who was secretary of the Scottish region, thought I would be suitable." The corners of Campbell's mouth turned up in a wry smile. "He thought I had the right sense of humor and probably would fit in here."

Remembering my first visit to a then-somnolent Belmullet, I tried to picture Machrihanish as a tiny outpost of pickled postwar sensibilities. Which wasn't difficult to do, because that's how it looked in the twenty-first century.

"What was your initial impression of Machrihanish?"

"I couldn't really believe it. It was a day like today." He looked out the rain-streaked window. "My father came on that interview, and we both loved the place. Everybody had a very laid-back and relaxed attitude. I don't want to be too romantic about it, but it was the charm. Even Campbeltown, which is a bit run down, but charming." He added, "I never actually played the course until I got the job."

Thinking again of Belmullet, I asked if Machrihanish had changed much in his twenty years as head pro.

"There's a lot more members. I think it was four hundred when I arrived, and now there's fourteen hundred. We've got members from all over Scotland, and there are a lot of Americans. But it's still very, very quiet. You've still got to make a commitment to get here." Giving it some thought, he added, "The members who have been here a long time think we're overrun."

A certain percentage of the new business, I ventured, had to be foreign golfers in search of a transforming experience, literate types looking for Shivas Irons or Michael Bamberger behind every dune and gorse bush. "Do you get the *Golf in the Kingdom* and *To the Linksland* disciples?"

He nodded. "Mostly the latter, since Bamberger's book was partly set here."

"You get pilgrims?"

"We do. They come all different ways, even by bus." He shook his head in wonder. "I have a good friend who invited me to San Francisco on a golf holiday a few years ago, and on the last day of the trip he gave me a signed copy of *Golf in the Kingdom*. And for the life of me, I couldn't get through it. It just doesn't fit my personality."

"But you're the head pro at *Mach-ri-han-ish*." I drew the name out to suggest that, at the very least, he ought to have a few baffling aphorisms he could recite for pilgrims, perhaps with a thick burr added to his Lothian accent. "You could have cards printed. 'Golf Taught. Life Mysteries Explained.' "

He gave me a blithe shrug. "The romanticism, the mystique, really doesn't exist in my practical world. But there are a lot of people for whom it does, and I respect that."

Campbell reached for the scrapbook and placed it on the table. "I have to go for a while, but I thought you might find this useful." I thanked him, we shook hands and, a minute or so later, I watched him cross the car park with his shoulders hunched and his umbrella tilted against the wind.

The scrapbook was a dime-store album with a broken spine held together with green tape. On the front cover someone had painted a bird standing on one leg in a puddle. It was the oyster-catcher logo of the Machrihanish Golf Club.

I slid the rubber band off, opened the scrapbook, and began turning pages. It was a disorganized mess. There were newspaper clippings from the 1950s. There were old photographs, the most interesting being an oft-reprinted image of golfers putting on the eighteenth green in front of a prior clubhouse, a caddy shed, and the long-defunct Ugadale Arms Hotel. There was a roster from 1887–88, when the club was still known as the Kintyre Golf Club. Five Stewarts (or Stuarts) were on the list, including "Captain Duncan Stewart of Knockrioch." There was also a Reverend Stuart and a Professor Stuart, giving me the impression that my Scottish ancestors wouldn't lift a finger unless a title went with the job.

While I was going through the scrapbook, the barman approached my table with a framed object. "This has mention of a Stewart," he said, handing me the frame. He lingered while I studied the artifact. It was a reproduction of a poem "The Golfers," taken from "*Memories of Kintyre* by James McMurchy, 1887." There were numerous quatrains, the first of which began: "Doon amang the beaty knowes / O' far-famed Machrihanish shore. . . ." I read straight through, reciting when I got to quatrain four:

> *Captain Stewart begins the game*
> *Wi' sturdy stroke and steady aim;*
> *Out o'er the heights his ba' does bang*
> *Hard followed up by Mr. Strang*

I interrupted my reading and looked up. "Wow! Sturdy stroke and steady aim!"

There was no other mention of the brave captain, but out of respect for the poet I recited the final quatrain:

> *So thus they play wi' pleasure keen*
> *Alang the grassy sward sae green'*
> *They view swee Machrihanish tide*
> *Where health and happiness abide*

The barman and I shared a moment of respectful silence. He then returned to his post, leaving the poem behind so I could copy it into my notebook.

I resumed my study of the scrapbook, vaguely aware that someone had switched on the wall-mounted television. But then I turned a mildewed page, leaned in for a closer look . . . and blinked in wonder. I was staring at a two-page master score sheet from a tournament at Machrihanish dated April 11, 1894. The scores for two rounds of play were set down in black ink and pencil on heavy, red-lined ledger paper. But it was the names that made me whistle. I counted five Open champions in the field of pros and amateurs: W. Ferne of Dumfries; A. Simpson of Carnoustie; H. Kirkaldy and W. Auchterlonie of St. Andrews; and Alex Herd of Huddersfield. The winner, with a score of 78–76—154, had been Herd, who collected twenty pounds for his efforts. Willie Auchterlonie, who on the date in question would have been the reigning Open champ (and whose brother Laurie would win the 1902 U.S. Open), had won a single pound for finishing sixth.

It was a document that belonged in a museum, and it was secured with Scotch tape.

"Would you like something to drink?" asked the barman, approaching the table again.

"I think so," I said. "Something stronger than 7-Up."

The wind continued to blow, but the rain softened to a drizzle and then stopped altogether. Pale sunbeams filtered through the clouds. I left the scrapbook with the barman and hustled out to the car park to get my clubs.

The first at Machrihanish, I am pleased to report, is as wonderful as advertised. You stand on a tee that is practically floating in the Atlantic Ocean, and you aim across as much sand and surf as you think you can carry to a flat fairway angled diagonally from right to left. When gathering players and pro-shop dandies are watching, any golfer prone to first-tee jitters must tremble and quake. I, fortunately, had the tee to myself, and after a few warm-up swings I smacked a solid drive that rode the wind over the cove and landed deep into the fairway. My 8-iron approach, played to the accompaniment of flapping pants legs, reached the lower tier of the green. I then rolled my long putt to within a foot of the cup, giving me a tap-in par on the hole that George Peper, in *The 500 World's Greatest Golf Holes*, called "the best No. 1 hole in all of golf."

That was the highlight of my round, because the rain returned as I was walking to the second green. I crouched behind my bag and tried to hold my old golf umbrella steady against the powerful gusts of wind. Three or four minutes later, the onslaught ended and the sun popped out again. That was the pattern for an hour or so—one squall after another, each followed by a brightening. And while the bad weather did nothing to spoil my enjoyment of the round, it prevented the calm assessment of individual holes that golf writers are expected to provide. I came off the course, a few hours later, with generic impressions of gentle dunes and sun-splashed fairways, with the odd geezer and geezette pulling trollies up some distant ridge.

I was surprised, given its reputation, that Machrihanish was so . . . What's the word? Civilized? The fairways, roughs and fringes were clearly defined, the greens were uniformly green, and the sand bunkers were perfect ovals with crisp edges—punched out, it appeared, by some giant wielding a mammoth cookie cutter. It was nothing like wild, disheveled Carne, where you got the impression that the features were on loan for golf and might be erased by the next Atlantic storm. That said, I could see why Bamberger or anyone else might choose Machrihanish as their course for a lifetime. It was open to the passerby's eye and imagination in a way that Carne was not, and I could picture myself as an old man on a bench by the road, watching the young golfers play the eighteenth on a summer evening against a background of green hills and sparkling sea.

After my round, I ducked into the clubhouse to wash up, stopping in the central corridor to examine the handicap sheets. There were three Stewarts on the 233 player list; their handicaps were eleven, fourteen, and twenty-eight.

"I'm heading into Campbeltown," I told the barman, "but I'll be back for dinner." First, though, I planned to stop for a change of clothes at East Drumlemble Farm, my farmhouse B and B.

It was midafternoon, and the sky had cleared. I cruised up the road in my rented van, taking in the bucolic scenery. It was flat pastureland on either side, but humpy landforms blocked any view of the sea. Grazing cows, farmhouses and dairy barns slid by. I was mentally replaying the eighteenth hole as I approached a village crossroads. There was a little red general store on the right, and there was a farm road that branched off toward some distant houses. I wouldn't have noticed them at all if I hadn't caught the flash of a pole sign in my peripheral vision.

Braking gently, I pulled to a halt and looked back over my shoulder. The road was clear in both directions. The farm road was also empty. I threw the van in reverse and backed up slowly, watching the dark side of the sign grow in the hatch window. And then I was past the sign, and I could read it through the windshield:

STEWARTON

\]

After Machrihanish it had been my plan to spend a few days at Askernish Old, a ghost course in the Outer Hebrides, before flying back to Ireland. My itinerary changed when Ralph Thompson, the manager at Askernish (or "liar in chief," as he liked to call himself), asked if my Stuart studies would take me to Inverness.

"Why Inverness?" I had been to the Highlands capital one time, with Pat, and the only family connection I recalled was a statue of Bonnie Prince Charlie in the city center.

"Castle Stuart," he said. "It's a new golf course that's soon to open." Ralph knew about it because his recently restored Askernish course—an eighteen-hole links designed by Old Tom Morris in 1892 but later abandoned—was going to join Castle Stuart, Nairn, Royal Dornoch and a few other Scottish gems in a "Highlands and Islands" golf promotion. "I'll call Chris Haspell," he said, pulling out his BlackBerry. "I don't think Castle Stuart is ready for play, but I'm sure he'll be happy to show you around. He might even want to put your face on the club logo, but you can negotiate that."

I had a plane to catch out of Glasgow, but I figured I could spare a couple of hours for Castle Stuart if I took the morning car ferry from North Uist to Uig, on the Isle of Skye, and then barreled through the Highlands and along the scenic banks of Loch Ness to Inverness, home of the annual Highland Games. "Maybe I'll meet a real live Stuart," I told Pat in a phone call. "Maybe I'll be invited into the castle."

On the day, leaky clouds followed me until I drove across the Skye Bridge, and then the sun broke out. I had a compilation of piano jazz in the CD player, a package of shortbread fingers on the passenger seat, and a bunch of scattered thoughts for company. I reflected on the Stuarts, who had once owned castles and led armies. That led to some poignant musings about my mother, whose share of the family swag amounted to a couple of pieces of furniture, some silverware, a green glass decanter, and an old set of Booths china. She might have inherited more had she not married Jack Garrity, but my prosperous, Presbyterian grandfather and his Interlachen clubmates had little use for an Irish Catholic orphan from rural Wisconsin, even if he could beat them at golf and make their daughters laugh.

Would things have turned out differently if my dad had finished the course work for his law degree at the University of Minnesota? Would the golf gene have gone somewhere else if my mother had not shopped like an heiress in her freshman year at Smith College and been called home by her angry dad? I don't know. But by marrying when the shadow of the Great Depression was sweeping across America, my go-it-alone parents pretty much guaranteed that they would live in genteel poverty.

Understand, I'm not knocking genteel poverty; it made me the half-baked dilettante I am today. But it took me years to figure out where I belonged on the social continuum. Other kids called their parents "Mom and Dad." I addressed mine as "Daddy" (sweetly infantile) and "Mother" (strangely formal). I went to grade school and junior high in the millionaire's playground of Palm Beach—body-surfing in the Atlantic, playing with friends in the courtyards of the Brazilian Court Hotel, racing bicycles through the boutique-lined arcades off Worth Avenue—while dealing with the gradual dawning that I was practically the only latchkey child on the island. ("We always had good addresses," my sister, Terry, told me. "The fact that they were falling down didn't matter.") My summers in Kansas City only added to the confusion. Dad's fortunes rose and fell with his little scaffolding business. He had one salaried employee, a Johnny Cash look-alike who worked in the warehouse when he wasn't under the hood of the stock car he raced on weekends. Dad answered his own phone and banged out all the invoices on a portable typewriter. But profits from the good years bank-rolled a four-bedroom Colonial in the leafy Crestwood subdivision and a membership at a second-tier country club.

Then came the bad years. Two periods of labor strife shut down local construction for months at a time, crippling the scaffolding business. Dad and my stepmother divorced. They sold the house in Crestwood. Dad ended up in a studio apartment in a red brick building on Volker Boulevard, just down the hill from the limestone parapets of the old Paseo High School. He kept the Buick, his clothes and his books, and I'm sure he would have gotten around to buying furniture if business had improved. But at the end of the month, after paying his rent, utilities and golf club dues, Dad had nothing left for curtains, armchairs, bed frames, area rugs or end tables. He slept on the wheeled half of an old trundle bed, the top mattress of which went on the floor for me to sleep on during my summer stays. There was a couch with broken springs, and Dad spent his evenings reading Marquand or Maugham with his rear end practically on the floor and a pack of Camels, an ashtray and a glass of bourbon at his feet. "It's not the Palmer House," he'd say, looking over the top of his reading glasses, "but the food is good."

And the food *was* good. Dad made regular trips to the butcher for pork chops and porterhouse steaks; to the A&P for watermelons, marshmallow "circus peanuts" and five-pound boxes of jumbo shrimp; and to Allen's Smokehouse for smoked briskets and slabs of ribs, which he bought three or four at a time. We consumed these staples at a chipped Formica break-fast table, using *The Kansas City Star* for a tablecloth and bath towels for napkins—towels, I might add, bearing the HILLCREST C. C. monogram.

Both parents worried constantly—and unnecessarily—that they were failing me. When I was a fifth grader, my mother sat me down for one of those "Santa's bag will be a little light this year" briefings, in which she ex-plained, through gathering tears, that there was not much cash in the cookie jar and our Christmas celebration would have to be modest. As she spoke, I looked to the left, past our grand piano (bought on an installment plan), and out the French doors to a reflecting pool and fountain surrounded by palm trees and a tall hedge. Then I looked to the right, through the big west windows, past a bigger circular fountain and an expansive lawn to the marina across the street, where big white yachts were docked. We were broke, but we lived in the central hall of a mansion.

Mother called it "our castle apartment."

Inverness had changed since my last visit. There were baffling round-abouts, ambiguous road signs, a freeway on stilts, and rush-hour traffic to rival that of Glasgow and Edinburgh. I got lost crossing to the east side and had to negotiate the same streets two or three times. So it was five o'clock when I finally broke free of the vans and lorries and sped into the countryside on the A964. I had no trouble finding the right exit; there was a CASTLE STUART sign. I had no trouble finding the castle, either. Constructed of black stone, it stood all by itself in a small grove of shade trees—a seventeenth-century Tower House with battlement views of pastureland and the picturesque Moray Firth. It was by no means a large castle, and it was clearly not a tourist attraction. A short lane led to a stone wall and a closed gate.

I drove on, looking for the Castle Stuart golf development. The road curved this way and that, through farm and copse and along the boundary of an airport, but there was no sign of a golf course in any stage of development. What's worse, there was no sign of a *sign*. When I arrived at a T-junction that led to Nairn, I concluded that I had missed the turnoff. I made a U-turn and drove back on the lightly traveled road, looking for any clue that golfing ground was nearby. There was none.

Castle Stuart was on my right when I cruised by it a second time. I pulled off the road, grabbed my mobile, and thumbed the number for Chris Haspell. Nothing happened. I hit the redial button. Nothing.

I turned in my seat and looked back toward Castle Stuart. The opening song from Brigadoon ran through my mind: *Once in the Highlands, the Highlands of Scotland / Two weary strangers lost their way*. Then I thought of the horror flicks of my childhood, in which the lost travelers abandon their car in a violent storm and seek shelter at a darkened castle.

Dismissing the potential danger with a snort, I wheeled the car around, drove back to the castle, and turned in at the lane, stopping at the big iron gate. I reached out the window and pressed the button on a wall-mounted box.

There was a long wait before I got an answer. "Yes?" It was a bureau-cratic male voice with a note of wariness.

"Sorry to bother you," I said. "I'm looking for the Castle Stuart golf course."

There was a long pause. "The what?"

"The Castle Stuart golf course. Or Chris Haspell. I drove up the road, but I didn't see a sign or anything." I waited, picturing a black-suited butler toggling a downstairs intercom. "He's expecting me," I added lamely.

There was another long pause. "I don't know anything about a golf course," the voice finally said. "This is a private residence."

"Uhhh . . ." I rubbed my forehead. "Can you think of anybody nearby who would know?"

"I'm afraid not," said the voice. "This is a private residence."

I sighed and put my hand on the shift lever. "Okay, sorry to bother you."

"Sorry," echoed the voice.

I backed out of the lane and pulled onto the road. This time I drove at a snail's pace, stopping at every farm gate or dirt road that disappeared into the trees. I detoured into the airport grounds, spun around the parking lot, and came back out on the original road. I drove until I reached the Nairn road for the second time; stopped and tried the phone again; got nothing. I sighed and sat, watching birds glide over the golden fields.

Tossing the phone aside, I made another U-turn and sped up the road. I raced by Castle Stuart without a backward glance, took the ramp onto the motorway, and headed back into Inverness.

I had a plane to catch.

CHAPTER 24

It's an X-ray of the soul, this game o' gowf. I knew a married fellow from London who kept a girl goin' here in town, a real captain's paradise. Well, damned if he didn't keep two scorecards for a round, one for the first nine and one for the second. And changed his balls for the second nine, too, just like he did in real life. I wonder which scorecard he showed to his wife?

—Peter McNaughton in *Golf in the Kingdom*

It was good to be home. I gave the Belmullet flat a brisk dusting. I bought tomatoes at Centra, broilers at Londis, and buffalo mozzarella at the Eurospar. I stopped by the O'Naillin Fishing Tackle Shop, just off the square, and paid twenty euros to top off my mobile phone. And when all my chores were done, I wrestled my clubs out of the travel bag and drove out to Carne.

The sun was out, and birds were in flight. I joined up with another single on the first tee, a sinewy young Austrian who said he had driven down from Enniscrone to squeeze in another 18 before dinner. I hit a big drive and opened with a birdie 3. I bogeyed the par-3 second. I pulled my drive into the long grass on No. 3 and made another bogey. Then I three-putted the par-5 fourth for yet another bogey.

"Look at your score," the Austrian said, tapping his scorecard with his pencil. "You've gone 3, 4, 5, 6. It's a progression."

"Are you a numbers man?" I stood by his shoulder and peered at the card. He was keeping his score in one column, my score (on his own initiative) in another, and he was filling the others with digits and symbols that probably tracked putts taken, fairways and greens hit in regulation, and his score, plus or minus, in relation to bogey.

"I *am* a numbers man," he said. "I'm very American that way."

Touché.

Numerology," Michael Murphy once said, "is the bargain basement of the sciences. It's a notch below astrology."

The *Golf in the Kingdom* author dropped this gem on me some years ago after a round at the Pebble Beach Golf Links. The occasion was a metaphysical golf retreat called the Shivas Irons Games of the Links. It was a spin-off from Murphy's engaging novel about a seeker of truth named "Michael Murphy," who tries too hard, and a Scottish pro named Shivas Irons, who gives lessons in golf and life out of a shadowy ravine at a course called Burningbush Links.

Numerology was on Murphy's mind that day because of a curious thing that had happened during our round. On the seventh hole, Pebble's famous oceanside par 3, our foursome had registered a hole-in-one (by magazine executive Andy Nusbaum), a birdie (by me), a par (by the Pebble Beach Company's marketing director, Steve Wille), and a bogey (by Murphy). The sequence of 1, 2, 3, 4 was of interest to Murphy, who said, "There is a peculiar play of numbers that Jung called 'synchronicity'. . . ."

Murphy's tone was facetious, but weeks later, when I recalled his ironic tone, he said, "That's it! That's the way I am. Obviously, a lot of this stuff is just silly, but . . . *but!*" He laughed at the emphasis. "But there's this realm of the mystical that intervenes in our lives, and I've gotten so many reports from sober people—lawyers, doctors, judges, REPUBLICANS! . . . people to be trusted, telling me these stories. I would have to be a complete ostrich with my head in the sand to deny these things."

And yet, Murphy went on to say, it was unlikely that the truth-seeking golfer would find enlightenment at the sharp end of a pencil. "I don't keep a conventional score anymore," he confessed. "I just try to see how many pars and birdies I can make."

The wise man had thrown me a line.

Carne sometimes pulled me into Murphy's realm. I was on the eighth hole, late one afternoon, when the sun disappeared during my backswing. A dense clammy fog had drifted over the course, and a profound silence had settled in. Putting on the eighth green, which is almost completely walled in by dunes, I felt like a character in a Conan Doyle mystery. I was lost on the shrouded moor.

Another time, while playing in a Sunday competition, I hit a shot that bordered on the supernatural. Stuck in rough on a steep upslope behind a dune on the par-4 fifteenth, I had 190 uphill yards that could only be covered with a sweeping hook over a deep defile. Choking up on a 6 iron, I settled over the ball, only to be momentarily distracted by a vision of my brother hitting from that same spot during the last round of his life. I saw Tommy in my mind as clearly as you'd see an actor in a film, saw him in his white cable-knit sweater and tan ball cap, saw him choke down on an iron, settle into a crouch with his left leg braced against the hill, saw him work his hands onto the club with a couple of gentle squeezes, saw him start his takeaway . . . and my swing was suddenly in synch with his. I felt the solid, satisfying pulse of impact run up the shaft and watched the ball whistle away on its sweet, flat trajectory, hooking over the defile and disappearing beyond the fairway's brow.

Young Damien Murphy, watching from the top of a dune up ahead, yelled, "Great shot!" A few minutes later, I walked up and found my ball at the back of the green, fifteen feet from the hole. A couple of minutes after that, I holed the putt for a birdie. "That's amazing," I said as we walked up the hill to the next tee. "I don't have that shot."

I didn't mention the vision.

Others were not so reticent. "Have you seen Shivas Irons at Carne?" Terry McSweeney asked me one day.

"Not yet," I said. "Will I?"

The Bostonian smiled and shrugged. "There's something mystical on that golf course when there's a fog. I've always thought that the left side of seventeen is where Shivas might live."

The locals encouraged such speculation. They were eager to point out that the four swans in the Carne logo were the Children of Lir—Fionnuala, Aodh, Fiachra, and Conn—who were turned into swans by the spell of a jealous queen and sentenced to nine hundred years of swandom, the last three hundred on the island of Inishglora—which, they would always add, "you can see from the back nine on a clear day." Some club members could even quote lines from one version or another of *Liannai Lir*. My favorite was *Out with you upon the wild waves, Children of the King! Henceforth your cries shall be with the flocks of birds!*

Others tried to raise goose bumps by pointing out that the Gaelic name for Carne's par-5 eighteenth hole (*Log 'a Fola*, or Bloody Hollow) was not a golfer's curse. Depending on who was telling the story, a cattle thief (or thieves) had been killed (or buried) in the hollow (or dunes) beside (or in) the eighteenth fairway, either recently or 1,800 years ago. If the latter, the name commemorated the massacre of an army of Munstermen who invaded Erris during the Bronze Age. Many of those slain, the legend went, were buried alive. For centuries to follow, superstitious passersby remembered the invaders with this cheery stanza:

> *May you have wet bottoms*
> *Munster scum, evil rogues,*
> *Without benefit of sun,*
> *Or bee or flower,*
> *In a lonely hollow,*
> *Without cerements in misery,*
> *May the hordes of hell follow you*
> *Round and round forever and ever*

Then there was No. 8, where I had encountered the fog. The eighth was called *Log 'a Si*, or Fairy Hollow, and according to legend it belonged to the fairies and little people.

"Leprechauns, if you like," Chris Birrane told me. "So I had a couple here—" He took a breath. "They were both on their second marriage. Just been married, on their honeymoon. They would have been in their late forties or fifties, lovely couple. And I caddied for the two of them. They'd never been here before, and they were interested in the local folklore. So I said, 'This is called the fairy hollow. Please don't swear when you get down to the green, that's bad luck. You're on your honeymoon, you don't want any bad luck.'

" 'Absolutely,' said the gentleman.

"So we got on the green, and I said, 'Please, folks, just mind your language here, this is a hallowed area.'

"They played out the hole, and I said, 'Have you made a wish?' He said, 'No. Is that regular?' I said, 'Have you heard of the Blarney Stone? Well, this is something like that. You can make a wish every time you're here, but the first time is the most important.' So he said, 'Okay, come here, honey.' And the two of them stood in the middle of the green. It's a big green, maybe fifty yards by thirty yards. So he's in the middle of the green, holding his wife's hands, and both of them have their heads down and their eyes closed, making a wish.

"Now, I meant *make a wish*. Like 'I want to be healthy' or 'I'd like to be rich,' and you walk off." Chris snorted. "They spent the best part of ten minutes on the green, and I was up on the hill and looking down, saying what's he wishing for? Are they wishing in tandem? They eventually finished and walked off the green, and he said, 'I feel great. I absolutely feel great.' I said, 'Yeah, this particular hole does that for you.' He said, 'Do you make a wish when you come around here?' I said, 'Yes, every time.' He said, 'What do you wish for, can you tell?' I said, 'Absolutely. It's the exact same thing every time.' He said, 'What would that be?'

Chris smiled. "I said, 'A better back nine.' "

I too was falling under the sway of numbers. This was a departure for me, as I have explained. I followed the advice of Shivas Irons, who said, "Dona worry about the score so much. It's not the important thing." If you searched my golf bag, you would not have found a single scorecard with my name on it. If you searched my *house* you would not have found such an artifact—not even a card from my childhood summers, when I got excited over a nine-hole score in the fifties.

But since my Sunday competition results were now the property of the Belmullet Golf Club, I had to fall in line. Handed my scorecard at the end of a round, I signed at the bottom and muttered the usual disclaimers. ("Hard to play with all those sheep bleating.") I then went to the changing room, entered my club PIN into the handicap computer, and tapped out my hole-by-hole scores on the touch screen. When I was finished, I dropped my card in the slot.

The Seventeenth Hole Challenge required a more sophisticated score-keeping system, one that could chronicle the daily variables of wind direction, cloud cover, temperature and hole locations, while providing Shotlink-style summaries of fairways and greens, distances to the hole in yards, putts taken, and, when appropriate, what club was used to extract my ball from which hellhole. I settled on a compact analog system that was flexible, easy-to-use and—best of all—free. (I had a whole box of business cards and, like most golf writers, I never run out of Marriott pens.) The system's only shortcoming was capacity. At two inches by 3½ inches, the cards required brevity and tiny, tiny handwriting.

Here, for example, is a line from a card dated "Oct 2 2007":

1. 4(5')—5—7 (2 IN F)

Translation: "On my first three balls I hit two in the fairway and fin-ished par, bogey, and triple-bogey, holing a 5-foot putt for the par."

Another card, dated "Sept 26 2007," provides a bit more detail:

4. 4(2P25')—5—8(3P15'YK3') (1R, 1L, DWD, INT FD)
B3 OFF E, FKD, 2 TO F, 2M TO G B1 D-6-IRON FLG RNBW

Translation: "On my fourth set, driving downwind, I hit one left, one in the fairway and one way right into two-shots-back-to-the-fairway land. I parred ball one with a 6 iron that covered the flag, taking two putts from twenty-five feet. Ball two, driven off the cliff to the left, led to a routine bogey. Ball 3 turned into a snowman when I three-putted from fifteen feet, pulling my second putt, a three-footer. And when I was finished, I looked up and saw a rainbow."

My Sunday cards and my seventeenth-hole cards were very different. The former were third-party affidavits submitted to unseen authorities for the purposes of evaluation and ranking. The latter supported a private database that I could use to measure my progress toward the goal of shooting 90. The former disappeared down the slot. The latter accumulated in tidy piles on the dining table in my bayside flat.

The Sunday cards hung my scores out on the clothesline for the neighbors to see. This bothered me more than I cared to admit. A handicap, once posted, calls out for improvement, and my 15 handicap—a product, I was sure, of bookkeeping error, if not outright malice on the part of the handicap chairman—took a little of the snap out of my stride. (It took all the discipline I could muster to avoid Carne's practice field and putting green.) But when I shot an 82 in my second club event, the Vice-Captain's Competition, I felt like a sandbagger.

"Check the club's Web site," Terry Swinson told me after the eighty-two. "You finished second."

Sure enough, when I tapped belmulletgolfclub.ie into my laptop I got the four-swans logo and a button labeled "Fixtures." Under a column headed "Prize" there were cells for first, second, third, Cat1, Cat2, F9 and B9. Some fellow of no importance had won with a net 67, and I was second with a net 68. However, my name also appeared as the winner of "Cat1."

"What's Cat1?" I asked Terry the next time I saw him. "Is that the blow-ins flight?"

"No," he said, "it's for players with handicaps up to eighteen. Category 2 is for nineteen up to twenty-six."

"Fair enough. Did I win something?"

"Oh, Jesus, you did, surely. You'll get a big lamp or something you don't want." He added, "And your handicap will go down."

My handicap did go down—a half stroke, to 14.5.

To be honest, I was surprised that my Irish friends, who had the souls of poets, spent so much time worrying about their handicaps. According to conventional wisdom—which I have spread in various articles—Scottish and Irish golfers consider stroke play to be an abomination. "Your American golfer," we're told by the weathered gent with the Highlands burr, "marks and cleans his ball when he's two feet from the hole, takes five hours to play a round, and cries like a baby when his ball lands in a pot bunker he couldn't see from the tee. He's not playing golf, he's playing *score!*"

I now believe that this argument is a sly ploy, a way to throw American visitors off their games. Either that, or those who swear that match play is the norm in Britain and Ireland are golf burnouts like myself and Michael Murphy—men and women of a certain age who are happy to pick up a ball hit into the gorse and start anew on the next hole, conscience clean and spirit light.

Some members of the Belmullet Golf Club did, in fact, complain about the frequency of stroke-play events, which made up roughly a third of the Sunday competitions. Their preferred format was Stableford, a scoring system that awards points to a player for his score on each hole. (5 points for an eagle, 4 for a birdie, 3 for a par, 2 for a bogey, and 1 for a double-bogey.) The player with the highest score is the winner under the Stableford system, so I had to get used to members who brooded over a twenty-eight or bought a round of drinks after a forty-two. But no matter what the format, the Irish golfer still has to submit an eighteen-hole score for handicap purposes.

The Seventeenth-Hole Club, of which I was the sole member, was as strict as the BGC in some respects. No mulligans. No gimmees. No preferred lies. I did establish a couple of "local rules" for the sake of practicality. I deemed a ball to be lost if I couldn't find it after a minute or so, and instead of walking all the way back to the tee under the stroke-and-distance rule, I took a penalty stroke and dropped a replacement ball. "This is fair," I told the rules chairman—me again—"because the rough is deep and I don't have anybody helping me find the ball." Another local rule permitted "the golfer, upon finding a ball that has, at one time or another, belonged to him or her—even if it is not the ball that he or she is currently playing—to call off the search and play the found ball without penalty." This was a good rule because I often scuffed around in Friday's rough and found the ball I had lost in Wednesday's rough. It was such a good rule, in fact, that by October I broadened it to include *any* golf ball I found, as long as it was in my search area.

I didn't have to post my seventeenth-hole scores, thank God, but sometimes Pat noticed me looking off camera during a video chat. "Sorry," I'd say, holding up a business card. "It rained, and the ink is smeared. I can't tell if I shot ninety-four"—I'd hold the card close to my nose and squint—"or seventy-three."

I didn't keep a log, either, but when I lined the cards up on the dining table they showed a favorable progression. The ninety-sixes and ninety-sevens of August became the ninety-fours and ninety-fives of September. On October second, when the planets were favorably aligned, I made five pars in eighteen balls and finished 4-4-5 for a personal best of ninety-two.

"I had no chance at ninety," I told Terry Swinson, who expressed an ongoing interest in my efforts. "But I hit twelve fairways, and I had three birdie putts of twenty feet or less."

God help me, I had become a numbers man.

CHAPTER 25

The crowd was thick around the practice green at Carnoustie last Saturday morning, which should've been a tip-off that something was up. Yet Rory McIlroy of Northern Ireland, a slight 18-year-old whose freckled, cherubic cheeks make him look more like 14, eased past a pair of security guards and onto the practice area with the confidence of a veteran pro, dropped a couple of balls, then casually began stroking putts toward a cup near the one being used by Tiger Woods.

—Gary Van Sickle in *Sports Illustrated*

My brother, the touring pro, drove a metallic blue fifty-nine Mercury. It was a huge, boxy sedan with a long, flat expanse of hood and four big doors that swung out like palace gates. Dad had found the Merc on a new-car lot in Independence, Missouri, and it would have been way beyond Tommy's means if the dealer's inventory hadn't been pelted by a summer hailstorm. "Mechanically, it's sound as a dollar," Dad said of the car. "Drives like a million bucks. And nobody gives a damn what it looks like."

Well, Tommy cared a little. The Mercury looked good from a distance, but when you got close you could see that the hood, roof and trunk were as dimpled as a golf ball. "It kind of stands out in a country club parking lot," he said, making light of the situation. "I park as far from the clubhouse as I can."

"At least you've got a car," I told him. "Mother and I have bicycles."

*I*t's December 1960, and the Mercury is parked across the street from our Palm Beach apartment. My mother and I now live on the ground floor of a carriage house behind a stucco mansion designed by Addison Mizner, the Flagler-era architect who built holiday palazzos for tycoons and heiresses. The address, 247 Royal Palm Way, is a long block from the ocean and two long blocks from the Intracoastal Waterway on a boulevard lined with the eponymous palms, which grow as straight as light poles on trunks that resemble poured concrete.

Tommy is in town for the West Palm Beach Open, which is a fixture on the PGA's winter schedule. He's missed the thirty-six-hole cut at Mobile, Alabama, shooting nervous rounds of 74–76 in his first tour start. So he's driven all night to save the expense of a cheap motel. When I get up on Saturday morning, I find him sleeping on sofa cushions on the terrazzo floor of our living room.

"Don't wake him," Mother whispers from the tiny kitchen. "He's exhausted." She makes me a stack of cinnamon toast and then pours a tall mug of milk, standing in the kitchen door to make sure I drink it. I chug it down without taking a breath and then make a sour face, erasing the milk mustache with the back of my hand.

Minutes later, I slip out the kitchen door, cross a flagstone patio shaded by a banyan tree, and hop on my bike for the short ride to the outdoor basketball court at Palm Beach Junior High, where I am a ninth-grader. Mother, after some hurried attention to her makeup and wardrobe, is out the same door and up the street to the bus stop for her hour-long commute to Riviera Beach, where she works as a sales clerk in an antique store.

The tour pro on the floor sleeps until noon.

*T*hat's how I remember it, anyway. My tales of Palm Beach at the turn of the sixties are no more and no less reliable than my father's recollections of sand-greens golf in New Richmond. And even Dad sometimes questioned his almost photographic recall of distant events. "They say as you get older your memories of days long gone gets sharper," he wrote in his seventy-fourth year. "True, you do seem to recall with perfect clarity events of sixty years ago. But you learn that your recollections, along with your appearance, can get a little moldy over time." Dad remembered practically every detail, for instance, of Tom Creavy's victory in the 1931 PGA Championship at Wannamoisett Country Club in Rumford, Rhode Island. Which was remarkable, because Dad had never been to Rumford, "wherever the hell that is." What he really remembered was the 1932 PGA at the Keller Golf Club in St. Paul, Minnesota, won by Olin Dutra. "I can't imagine how one's memory could possibly play such tricks on an old man," Dad wrote, "as I practically grew up on the Keller course and spent the entire week following Dutra." On the other hand, when Dad went to the record books to check his recall of the 1935 Women's Amateur Championship at Interlachen, he found that his recall was spot on: five-time champion Glenna Collett Vare had, indeed, defeated sixteen-year-old Patty Berg in the finals, closing her out on the sixteenth hole.

"So now I can be quoted as a reliable source," Dad wrote. "But again memory plays tricks. I recall the scene as if it were yesterday, but the details escape me entirely. With one exception: the last putt, where the great Glenna closed out the youngster and the gallery closed in on the two.

"So to hell with details," Dad concluded. "It was a great moment in golfing history, and I was there."

I take a similar position when I try to reconstruct my brother's Palm Beach visit. One memory—of a morning spent drop-line fishing on a charter boat—is so sharp that I asked Tommy about it forty-six years later, when we were driving across Ireland.

"I have this memory," I said. "Before the tournament started—did you take me deep-sea fishing?"

"Oh, yeah." He gave me the throaty chuckle of misadventure. "We drove over to the marina in West Palm and bought tickets for one of those charter boats. You got seasick and spent most of the cruise with your eyes closed. The rest of us stood at the rail for three hours and caught nothing. I mean, *nothing*. The captain kept saying 'This was a great spot yesterday.' And nobody caught anything. So he'd spin the wheel and chug over to another spot and cut the engine, and he'd say, 'The mullet were practically jumping into the boat yesterday.' And it got to the point where I said, 'Could you show us some of the fish from *yesterday*?'" Tommy tilted his head slightly to emphasize the word "yesterday." "Because it was pretty clear that he had no *clue* where the fish were. And then"—he laughed again—"we got back to the marina with no fish, and as we're stepping onto the dock there's a boat right next to us that's just come in, and they're unloading fish. And they're *weighing* fish, and they're taking *pictures* of each other with the fish they've caught. And our captain just ducks out of sight. He doesn't wanna talk about it."

I laughed, but I was amazed that Tommy had such a clear memory of the fishing trip. And I was no less confused. "Why wasn't I in school? It had to have been a Tuesday or a Wednesday."

"Did you play hooky?" Tommy thought about it for a moment before remembering that he had driven overnight from Mobile. "It might have been Sunday morning. I'd have spent the rest of the weekend hiring a caddie and practicing."

I kept my eyes on the road. "Okay, another memory. Did you come to my basketball game?"

He hesitated. "Well, I'd say yes to that, too. I saw you play in that little cracker-box gym at the junior high. You kept running back and forth along the baseline until you got the ball, and then you'd shoot from the corner. You were a *real* good shooter." He gave me a sideways glance. "A one-handed set shot with plenty of arc, right? You put it up in the rafters."

"Wow," I said. "How do you remember that?"

"I don't know." He looked out the car window. "Dad always remembered those things."

So, I remember.

It's Thursday afternoon. Somebody picks me up at school, drives me past the old-money mansions on South Ocean Boulevard and then over the Southern Boulevard Bridge to the mainland, dropping me off at the West Palm Beach Country Club. Looking around, I spot Tommy's hail-dented Mercury near the clubhouse, its front bumper nuzzling a white sign that says CONTESTANT. Other big cars are parked on either side of his—big cars from Detroit with winglike tail fins and hunks of chrome. Cars belonging to Sam Snead, Tommy Bolt, Dow Finsterwald and Cary Middlecoff.

Looking for my brother, I stop at a scoreboard to watch a man with *calligraphy pens fill in boxes on the big cardboard score sheets. I search anxiously for the name that matters and then breathe a sigh of relief. TOM GARRITY, it says in medieval script, has shot a one-under-par seventy-one.*

Now I'm standing under a coconut palm as three golfers come off the eighteenth green, their spikes clacking on the cart path, their caddies toting big leather staff bags. One of the golfers is George Bayer, the PGA's long-drive king. A burly man with a crew cut, Bayer stops for a moment to check something on his scorecard and then walks on, his spikes going clack-clack-clack.

*S*ame day? *Cool shadows flood Royal Palm Way as the beach traffic heads toward the setting sun. A white-haired man in canary yellow slacks and a lime green jacket stands on the sidewalk outside Alfredo's restaurant, checking his watch every so often.*

Tommy and I are out on the landscaped median, playing football between the rows of sentry palms. I get down in a three-point stance. He barks, "Hut-one! Hut-two!" and on two he takes a pretend snap and drops back. I come out of my crouch and run a slant pattern. When I look back over my shoulder the ball is already in the air, a perfect spiral thrown by my brother, the tour player.

*W*ind, *lots of wind, and dark, nasty clouds. Palm fronds waving, fairways littered with pine branches and coconut husks. The man with the colored pens is at his post, but one of the score sheets has thrown a tack and is flapping at the corner. The man calls for a roll of tape and a hammer.*

"Garrity did good," someone says. "That's one hell of a score under these conditions."

Fade to black.

*I*roll *out of bed early on day three, excited. Tommy is already shaved and dressed in pleated slacks and a Lacoste alligator shirt. (He's got boxes of clothes in the trunk of the Merc, free stuff from Izod and Wilson.) Now he's folding sheets and putting the sofa cushions back in place. The aroma of fried eggs and bacon comes from the tiny kitchen, where Mother is pouring orange juice.*

"I'll get the paper," Tommy says. He goes out the front door and disappears up the driveway.

Mother and I are eager to read the Saturday sports page. There is sure to be something about Tommy in it, something like FORMER WILDCAT IMPRESSIVE IN WIND, OR PBHS GRAD TRAILS SNEAD BY FOUR AFTER SECOND 71. Tommy's interest is more practical. Like most tour players, he needs to check the morning paper for his tee time.

Tommy has a section of the paper open when he returns. "Holy cow," he says, standing in the doorway.

"What? What?" I'm in a wicker chair at the glass-top table where we eat our meals.

Tommy looks up. One of his eyebrows is raised doubtfully, as if someone has just offered him a million dollars for his car.

"It's my pairing," he says. "I'm playing with Arnold Palmer."

There's a crash of silverware in the kitchen.

A sky so blue, a sun so bright. A first hole lined with spectators from tee to green. Palm trees shaking in the wind. A Southern voice: "Next on the tee . . . from Kansas City, Missouri . . . Tom Garrity!" Cheers and applause, followed by a hush so profound that I fancy I can hear the sound of my brother's tee penetrating the ground.

His nervousness doesn't show. He takes an easy practice swing, just brushing the grass with his driver. His eyes are shaded by a white visor, and he has on his golf glasses. He's such a handsome guy. There are women in the gallery who, if they can't have the charismatic Palmer, will happily settle for Garrity.

He addresses the ball, takes a couple of waggles, and smacks a passable draw down the right side. The gallery claps, somebody yells, "Go get 'em, Tom!" I let out a sigh of relief.

"Next on the tee . . . from Pocono Manor, Pennsylvania . . . Art Wall Jr.!"

U p steps a man of such bland presentation that his peers have nicknamed him "The Ribbon Clerk." He's slight and gray and so subdued that you might find yourself looking away as he starts his backswing—which is folly, because Art Wall, at thirty-six, is a force. He won four times last season, most memorably at the Masters, where he birdied five of the last six holes to deny Palmer a second straight green jacket. Wall also won the fifty-nine money title, the Vardon Trophy for best scoring average, and Player of the Year honors.

Wall tees it up, settles over his ball, and hits it. To a smattering of applause, the ball goes somewhere.

N*ext on the tee, from Latrobe, Pennsylvania . . . the 1960 Masters and U.S. Open champion . . . Arnold Palmer!"*
The crowd cheers so loudly that the woman in front of me covers her ears with her hands.

Why do they call him the King? Palmer has the forearms of a stevedore, the red neck of a farmer, and the backcombed forelock of a drugstore lothario. He's a greenkeeper's son, not a prince. His is the change-a-tire, catch-a-marlin manliness of a John Wayne or a Ted Williams. I find myself staring at his hands, wondering if his handshake makes other men wince.

Palmer acknowledges his so-called army with a nod and a smile. At address, he presses his lips together, cocks his head to the right, and takes a ferocious swipe, finishing in a crouching, hands-low-and-left posture. His fans erupt at impact. They surge into the fairway while his ball is still in the air.

T*he ribbon clerk again. He has a tricky little shot from the right rough that he has to thread between some palms. I don't get to see the shot because I'm caught in a line of spectators stretched four- and five-deep across the fairway. But I hear the shot—a muted* thwump—*and guess from the polite applause that the ribbon clerk has either found the green with his second or knocked it within chipping distance.*

My brother pulls an iron from his big leather bag, which has WILSON *in red on the side. His caddie lifts the bag by the collar and steps away. Palmer, whose ball is a good twenty yards farther up the fairway, waits at the edge of the left rough, the glowing end of his cigarette stoked by the wind.*

My brother swings and pinches one off the turf. The ball whistles away on a low trajectory and then starts to climb. He holds his finish until the ball lands, but he is not happy with the shot. Too much spin? Wrong club? He steps toward his caddie, but—rookie mistake—forgets to look both ways.

"After I hit the shot I started to reach for my golf bag to get a cigarette," Tommy *will tell me years later. "I almost lost my right hand as the crowd stampeded past me to get behind Palmer."*

My brother will laugh. "That's when I learned that there are golfers . . . and there are Arnold Palmers."

*T*ommy watches Palmer. Not as a fan, but as a student of the game. Palmer hits one hard and high into the wind. Why? Palmer doesn't try to cut the dogleg on the short par 4. Why? Palmer hits a greenside bunker shot with a square clubface and hook spin. Why? Palmer, Palmer, Palmer.

I can't deny that Palmer cuts a compelling figure. I'm right behind him as he argues with his caddie over what club to use for an approach shot. He rests one hand on the head of an iron in his bag. Lifts the other hand to his lips and takes a drag off the cigarette. Shakes off the caddie's suggestion. Studies the waving fronds of the palms. Bends over for a pinch of grass, flings the blades in the air, and watches them drift away. He finally nods, pulls the club, and flicks away the cigarette. He swings again, that violent slash, sending a huge divot down the fairway.

Something is wrong. Palmer tips his head to the side and groans. Palmer barks out an oath. When the shot lands short and left, he turns, tight-lipped, and slams his iron into the bag. The club rebounds a good foot in the air before falling back with a rattle.

That bouncing club will stick in my mind for a half century.

I remember these few things, but I remember little else about the 1960 West Palm Beach Open. Fortunately my father, forced to follow Tommy's career from Kansas City, had subscribed to *Golf World*. He kept all the back issues, with his underlinings and marginal notes, in a file drawer at the scaffolding company. I inherited the magazines upon his death, and I took several of them with me to Ireland. (At sixteen pages, they weighed a couple of ounces.) The issue of December 9, 1960, has a story headlined POTT ROILS SNEAD, and from this article you learn that Johnny Pott, a four-year tour veteran out of Louisiana State University, made up three strokes on Sam Snead in the final round to notch his second tour victory. You learn that George Bayer was the first-round leader with a sixty-five; that in round two Snead drove to within thirty yards of the green on the 380-yard seventeenth hole; that two-time U.S. Open champ Cary Middlecoff missed the cut with rounds of 81–79; that Julius Boros withdrew after three rounds due to "a broken toe suffered when he fell off a couch"—*what the hell?*—that songwriter Hoagy Carmichael, one of seven amateurs in the field, shot a final-round seventy-five; that Snead, playing behind Pott, was annoyed by the winner's slow play ("The Slammer grumbled on the tee all day while waiting for the green in front to be cleared"); that Art Wall finished third and Palmer fifth ("Fans of Palmer were waiting for the usual Palmer kick over the final round, but it never came"); that Pott got $2,000 for his victory; and that Tom Garrity, with scores of 71–71–77–74—293, finished tied for twenty-second and won $160.00.

There is no mention of a hero-worshipping thirteen-year-old following his brother around the course for two days.

Or was it one day? "I have no independent recollection of the final round," I told Pat on a long-ago trip to Florida with the kids. "I don't remember who Tommy was paired with. I don't remember a great up-and-down or an eagle putt that lipped out. I don't even remember my mother being there. How could that be? She was very proud of us, and she hadn't seen Tommy play since the divorce, as far as I know. Maybe she saw him play on Sunday—that would have been her day off."

"What I *do* remember," I rattled on, "is the first hole with Palmer—but not the putts—and then the second hole, a par-5. Tommy birdied the second hole from the left rough." Pat gave me a look that said *You can't possibly remember that,* and I said, "You're right. I can't possibly remember that. How do I remember that?"

On a very sad day in the spring of 2006, I found the answer in an old chest in an upstairs bedroom. It was a typewritten letter, dated December 5, 1960, from a thirteen-year-old boy to his father. "Dear Daddy," it began.

Hi! Am enclosing clippings from the local newspaper. Tommy got good coverage. After his two 71s, he was paired with Arnold Palmer and Art Wall! He couldn't play his own game with them there. He had very large galleries. Tommy

sank a beautiful putt on number two. The paper
calls it his best hole of the day. I don't
agree. He pulled his drive off to the left into
the chickweed, blasted a 1 iron over a bunker
into a trap and out again, and left a wedge
way short. He then holed the putt. Art Wall
turned out to be a terrific player and a darn
nice guy. Palmer was too. Tommy played with
Don Fairfield on Sunday. He played beautiful
golf, hitting almost every green, but I could
have putted better than he did. He missed four
birdie putts in the first five holes. He ended
up with a 74 and a 293. It was good for $160
and his first pro money.

Palmer said Tommy was good and Art Wall
thought Tommy was good. Tony Penna of Mac-
Gregor has been trying to get Tommy to sign
up. Tommy hasn't said yes to anybody. He looked
good to me and should do fine in Coral Gables.

Be sure to write.

Love, Johnny

I had no memory of writing the letter, and I had no memory of finding
it among my dad's possessions after his death. "It explains why I always
remembered Tommy making birdie on the second hole," I told Pat, "and it
confirms my memories of Palmer and Wall."

The letter was spooky, in a golf-ghost kind of way. I dated my
golf-writing career to the mid-eighties, and I was fairly certain that the
first tournament I ever covered was the 1986 NCAA Championship
at Winston-Salem, North Carolina, won by Scott Verplank. Now I was
staring at my own reporting of a PGA tournament from twenty-five years
earlier.

"The scary thing," I told a circle of mourners at my brother's wake, "is that if you throw out the misspellings and a couple of exclamation points, it's pretty much how I write today."

They were too quick to agree that it was.

The morning after. The sun hangs over the Atlantic. The palm fronds are barely moving. Mother and I watch from the sidewalk as my brother, the tour player, leans across the car seat to give us a final smile and a wave. "I'll write!"

He shifts into drive, checks the rearview mirror, waves again, and steers the big blue Merc into the flow of Caddies and Lincolns heading toward the bridge and the world beyond. "There he goes," I say.

I would give anything to be going with him.

CHAPTER 26

This is one race of people for whom psychoanalysis is of no use whatsoever.
—Sigmund Freud on the Irish

October brought shorter days, but no discernible change of season. If anything, the weather improved. There were fewer mornings of wild wind and rain and more occasions when the rising sun made Broadhaven Bay shine like aluminum. From my balcony I watched the new apartments on either side of me go up, their rafters and ridge beams hammered into place by carpenters in yellow vests. On the unpaved portion of the quay, a crew laid pipe and conduit and poured new sidewalks as part of a docks beautification project.

Sometimes I walked along the canal that connected the two bays, crossed the little bridge to the Mullet, and went around to the opposite shore. A paved lane twisted uphill through fenced pastures, and from the high ground I could look down on the gray roofs and painted facades of Belmullet, punctuated by communication masts and church steeples. To the south, Blacksod Bay stretched to the Saddle of Achill and the rocky summits of *Sliabh Mór* and Saddle Head.

One morning, on a whim, I gassed up at Geraghty's Texaco and drove up the R313 and N59 to check out Bellacorick's musical bridge. The drive took me across the blanket bog, a bleak expanse of russet prairie dotted with tarp-covered piles of peat. Past the village of Bangor, the road followed the Owenmore River, a rocky stream favored by fly fishermen. Tommy had looked at the Owenmore with longing when we drove along it in '05.

Bellacorick was a ghost town—a cluster of boarded-up buildings on the site of an abandoned power station. At the time of my visit, the old cooling tower was still standing, a 267-foot-high monolith shaped like a laboratory beaker. (Tourists, spotting the mighty profile from a distance, mistook the peat-fueled station for a nuclear facility.) The cooling tower was a landmark, "the gateway to Erris," but it had recently been condemned and was being wired for demolition at 11 a.m. on the following Sunday. I expected, therefore, to see workers on the tower and vehicles raising dust around the plant. But the gates were padlocked, and there was no sign of life in the electrical compound, switch building or main power station.

I parked on the asphalt verge of an abandoned petrol station. The green-and-white panels of the old gas pump were splintered. Corroded parts littered the pavement. A gate in an old stone wall opened onto a field of scrub and wildflowers that sloped down to the river. Across the road, the rusty sign of a locked-up tavern read like a lament: CAROLAN'S MUSICAL BRIDGE INN. There was another sign above the door, LICENSED PREMISES FOR SALE, and a banner over that: SOLD. A white house next to the inn looked as if it had been kept up, but I couldn't tell if it was occupied.

The musical bridge was fifty yards on, past the plant entrance. It was a basic stone bridge, less than a hundred yards long, with lamp posts at the four corners and four arches supporting the roadway. The river gurgled through the arches and spilled over a rocky bed as it crossed under the N59 on its way to Blacksod.

There was no sidewalk, so I had to wait until the road was clear in both directions. The bridge was lined on each side by a three-foot wall topped with six-inch-thick slabs butted together to form rails. I crossed the road and got instant confirmation of the legend: a capstone was missing. That was the stone, according to Eamonn Kelly, that someone had knocked off to end the string of deadly luck that had plagued the bridge during construction.

Three rocks sat on the rail, each about the size of a baseball. I picked one up and turned it in my fingers, but promptly put it back. ("Whatever you do," Kelly had warned, "don't drop the stone!") Checking again to make sure no cars were coming, I ventured out on the bridge. I examined the capstones as I walked, in the manner of a golfer reading a putt. I noticed that the rail had chalklike streaks running the length of the bridge. And when I reached the other end, I found two more stones sitting on the rail.

I stepped onto the shoulder as a couple of cars sped across the bridge, their tires hissing on the wet pavement. I thought about the legend—the old woman and her sons, the pub where they drank, the curse, the worker on his deathbed, his miraculous recovery. "Every legend," James Baldwin wrote, "contains its residuum of truth." I wondered what part of the Bellacorick story was folklore and what part was fact.

When the road was clear, I picked up one of the rocks, pressed it against the first capstone, and started walking. It made a steady scraping noise interrupted by a metallic *ping* or *clunk* whenever it hit a joint. There must have been cavities under the capstones that amplified and colored the percussive tones. I sped up, but the notes didn't coalesce into melody. They merely clicked and pinged at random until I reached the missing capstone at the Bellacorick end.

Was it *musical*? Absolutely. It was a musical bridge.

I left the rock on the rail and walked back to the car.

Driving along the Owenmore under a dismal drip of rain, I thought about the stuff we believe and the stuff we discount. An Irish farmer, for example, finding his dogs dirty and panting in the morning, will tell you that a leprechaun rode them all night. An Irish hairdresser might speak of a phantom funeral party that appeared out of a mist on Bloody Sunday. We are free to believe or disbelieve.

My father had a few tales that crossed the line into pure fantasy. His best bedtime story, borrowed from *The Wizard of Oz*, had the skies over New Richmond turning very dark one summer afternoon. "It was before my time," Dad would say, "but as I understand it, my aunt Jane looked out the window and saw the storm clouds building up, so she handed my cousin Willie an umbrella and told him to run down to the Hughes law office and give it to the old man. And then Willie was supposed to come right home. Willie couldn't have been more than eight or nine, Johnny. But what happened was, William Hughes wanted to get the whole family in the storm cellar, so he locked up the office, grabbed Willie by the hand, and started running for home. And the two of them were running down Main Street, I believe, when the tornado struck. And the damnedest thing"—and here Dad would shake his head—"the funnel tore Willie from his father's grasp and sucked him right up into the clouds. I don't think William Hughes got a scratch—he was the Greek scholar, you'll remember—but they never found Willie. My cousin Jamie was at the funeral, of course. It was pretty hard on my aunt Jane, as you can imagine."

I believed this story until I was old enough to know better.

Then, on a summer day in 1990, I sat down in the New Richmond living room of the retired judge, Joseph Hughes—my father's cousin, once removed, the man who had told me the Garritys came from Belmullet. "There's a story my dad used to tell," I began, embarrassed to even bring it up, "about a little boy dying in a tornado."

Joe, who had emphysema, was breathing oxygen from a tank, but he opened a desk drawer, rifled through some papers, and came up with a newspaper clipping. He handed it to me, and I read, for the first time in my life, about the New Richmond tornado of June 12, 1899. "Clouds were seen to roll together in the southwest," the wife of a New Richmond physician had written in 1900, "as the funnel-shaped mass of blackness took up its deadly line of march across the prairies, bearing down with steady aim upon New Richmond. . . . There were scenes of wild confusion and terror. People ran through the streets, fleeing to places of shelter. Some shouted 'We are doomed!' 'A cyclone is coming!' 'Flee to your cellars!'" A few paragraphs further on, amidst vivid description of the tornado's explosive advance, I stopped on this line: "Some felt their dear ones snatched from their embrace by the howling demon in his mad dance of death."

I was reading about the deadliest tornado in Wisconsin's history: 117 dead, 135 injured, an entire town flattened.

"So it's true," I said.

Joe nodded. "My dad was eight or nine when the storm hit. He was playing with his sister when they heard this incredible roar. Their mother rushed out and dragged them next door to the Casey house. They had just made it to the basement when the whole house went up in the air. When they came out afterward, there wasn't a house left standing."

Later, at the Immaculate Conception cemetery, Joe pointed out a small granite stone set flush with the ground:

Willie Hughes

1886–1899

"Your dad would have grown up with that story," Joe said. "The cyclone was New Richmond's great calamity, and poor Willie was the family's portion of grief."

From that day forward, I didn't take my father's old yarns with a grain of salt.

Or at least I tried not to. My dad, in his later years, had a way of embroidering the facts. Every doctor who treated his geriatric ailments was "considered to be the best in America." The fellow who fixed his muffler was "top-notch" and "probably the only honest auto mechanic in the Midwest." Dad's younger son was so highly regarded by New York book and magazine editors "that they never touch his copy. It goes straight to the printer." (The proud-father discount had to be applied to anything Dad said about his daughter and sons. One time, when a plumber in overalls was lugging his tools up my stairs, Dad met him on the landing with a copy of *Sports Illustrated* and the classic line: "You're probably wondering what my son does for a living.") Some of it was mere hyperbole, as in his assertion that the Kansas City heat wave of 1936 had delivered "thirty-eight days of August temperatures of one hundred ten degrees or more." Other times he simply let his enthusiasm get the better of him. The three-inch steaks became five-inch steaks. The 8 iron that his older boy had hit over a fifty-foot oak to dispatch Ray Watson in a long-forgotten Trans-Mississippi Championship? It became a 6 iron, and the winning putt shrank from five feet to a foot.

No one could blame me, therefore, when I raised a skeptical eyebrow over the *details* of his New Richmond stories. The townspeople he described as "rich as hell" I demoted to "well off." The dead-at-thirty-two Thomas A. Garrity, who had argued a case before the United States Supreme Court, I consigned to the dead-at-thirty-eight bin—and maybe it was the *Minnesota* Supreme Court. The foster parent who was "a professor of English at Dublin University" and "spoke six languages fluently"—well, I had to roll my eyes over that one. My Geraghty ancestors, the people of the Mullet had assured me, would have been illiterate farmers, and the Hugheses would have been no different.

So I disbelieved these details until I was old enough to know better.

That happened on a summer day in 2006, when I sat down in the Minneapolis high-rise apartment of Anne Hughes, the adopted daughter of Jamie and Billie Hughes and sister of Joe. "There's a story my dad used to tell," I began, embarrassed to even bring it up, "about a New Richmond Hughes who was educated in Ireland and taught Greek and Latin."

Anne, a charming and elegant woman who had sparkled as a legal secretary at a top Chicago law firm, opened a folder on her lap. "That would be William Hughes," she said, perusing a two-page, typewritten document. "He was the city clerk for twenty-four years. Your father grew up in his house on Green Street."

She passed me the document and I read, for the first time in my life, the 1916 funeral notice of William Hughes. "A high-minded man," proclaimed the anonymous obit writer. "A book might be written about Mr. H and his life, but space forbids. He was a wonderful man, a widely read man, a man who could speak several languages." I gave Anne the briefest of glances before reading on: "Mr. Hughes was a native of Ireland, having been born in County Mayo, Nov. 20, 1842, and would have been 74 years old his next birthday. He was educated by private tutors in Ireland and afterward graduated from the University of Dublin. Mr. Hughes then taught school in Ireland, England, Germany & Belgium for several years. He came to America in 1870 and settled in New York state, where he taught school, going from there to Pennsylvania. Mr. Hughes then taught for some time in southern states, including Arkansas and Kansas, and in 1875 came to Erin [Wisconsin] where he engaged in teaching again, and continued this, at Erin and Hammond, until 1882. His future wife, Jane Garrity, was one of his pupils." I clucked my tongue, wondering if my dad had known that about his foster parents.

"Mr. H. moved to N.R. in 1882," the notice continued, "forming a

partnership with Col. S. N. Hawkins, which continued until the year previous to the cyclone of 1899. Mr. H. then entered the law business for himself
and continued, with the assistance of his son James and a daughter, Bessie,
up to the time he was forced by ill health to retire, about a year ago." At the
bottom of the first page, under the heading A HIGH-MINDED MAN, I
stopped on these lines: "It is safe to say that his ruling passion in life was
accuracy. To Mr. H. it meant more to get a thing right than to consider the
financial return it might net him."

"So it's true," I said.

Anne nodded. "Later, Grandma Hughes moved in with us. She was
such a nice lady."

From that day forward, I suspended disbelief altogether. Two Hugheses,
fifteen years apart, had corroborated the most implausible of my father's
accounts. So the plausible tales—such as Dad's story about nearly freezing
to death in the blinds of a Soo Line train after switchmen had hosed it off
in 35-degree weather—surely passed the smell test.

But now, as I steered my rental car down a puddled blacktop highway
in Western Ireland, I tweaked my position. The Garrity and Stuart legends,
whether told by my parents or their dwindling kin, could be trusted. It was
the *omissions* that broke the bonds of trust—the scenes performed off-stage,
the characters pushed out of the frame. My dad concealed the fact that his
mother, Mary Byrnes Garrity, had abandoned him and fled to New York.
My mother wouldn't talk about my grandmother Grace, who died in an
asylum; nor would my mother admit that she had been disinherited in favor
of her father's second wife, his former secretary. These were the family
secrets.

Was it an Old World conceit, the family secret? "You know there are no
secrets in America," claimed the poet W. H. Auden. "It's quite different in
England, where people think of a secret as a shared relation between two
people."

The problem with using secrets to define relationships, I was beginning
to understand, was that death erased both. You were left with a few scattered
leaves instead of a family tree. Local history became a cipher of a fairway
disappearing into the windswept banks.

I suddenly realized that I knew more about William Hughes than I knew about all of my grandparents combined. Thanks to the old obit, I knew that he had belonged to the Modern Woodmen of America, that he had served as treasurer of the Catholic Knights of Wisconsin, that he had a summer home at Cedar Lake, Wisconsin, that he died of a stroke at six fifteen on a Thursday evening and that his good friend, Father Gaughan, had arrived on the four o'clock train, just in time to administer the last rites.

What's more, I knew where William Hughes was born. He came from somewhere out there in the rain, somewhere in Erris.

I drove on, a sojourner on the vast, lonely bog.

CHAPTER 27

Among our golfers there was a refreshing lack of distinction as to age, wealth, social position or professional status. Everyone was on a first-name basis, and there was a genuine warmth that only a closely knit, neighborly community can generate. For example, I, a boy of twelve, often played with the finest trial lawyer in the state; a banker who owned much of St. Croix County; an aging grocery clerk; an executive vice president of the Northern Pacific Railroad; an automobile mechanic; a young chemical engineer who was destined to become chairman of the board of one of America's great corporations; and a retired schoolteacher. We were all brought together, once a week, because we shared a love of golf.

—Jack Garrity, *Remarks and Reminiscence on*
the Founding of the New Richmond Golf Club

You don't expect to meet your familiar on the eleventh hole at Carne.
It's a stunning hole, as I have described: a par 4 that plays from a pinnacle tee to a canyon fairway and back up again to a green above a cow pasture that runs down to the beach. Huge terraced dunes line the fairway on either side. If you spray your tee shot you can wind up making an alpine-style ascent to a vertiginous perch to hit your second. There is also an

unusual hazard down the left side, about 220 yards out—a grassy crater in a pulpitlike protrusion above the canyon floor.

"Hold on!" I yelled, watching my drive hook around the biggest dune and disappear from sight.

"Don't know about that," said Gary. "Could be all right."

I looked for a signal from the golfers waiting down below, where the rough tumbled into a gorge. They had interrupted their search for a lost ball to wave us through, but now they were standing as still as the grazing ruminants in the meadow beyond.

"If my ball had cleared the crater, they'd be ducking." I slipped the head cover onto my hybrid 2 and returned the club to my bag.

Once we had all hit our tee shots, the players ahead resumed their search in the heights. They were assembled in the grassy crater when we arrived on the scene. One of them, a dark-haired flatbelly, was stoically appraising his options. His ball was buried in thick green grass on the face of the crater—a lie that Tiger Woods might have been able to negotiate, but no one else. The fellow seemed to understand this, because he worked himself into the only stance available to him—left foot on the rim of the crater, left leg bent, right leg straight as a fence post, right shoulder dipped, left ear aimed at the sky. Wasting no time, he took a healthy hack and staggered backward. The ball sailed out in a spray of grass clippings and looped listlessly toward the little gulch, where another uncharitable lie probably awaited him.

"Good out," I said.

"At least I didn't hurt myself." He shouldered his bag with a smile and descended from the crater with careful steps.

It took another minute or two for Gary to find my ball, and I wasn't too thrilled when he did. It, too, was in the face of the crater, just a few feet to the right of the spot where the previous victim had left his mark. Following his example, I planted my left foot at the level of my belt and swung with gritted teeth. There was a muffled click at impact. My ball popped out of the crater and followed gravity down to the fairway.

It wasn't until we stepped onto the twelfth tee that Terry Swinson said anything. "Did you visit with John Geraghty?" he asked.

"How's that?" I wasn't sure what he was referring to.

"The fellow you were talking to back there. Haven't you met?"

I laughed and shook my head. I had spoken to John Geraghty on the phone recently, having spotted his name near mine on the Belmullet Golf Club roster. He had invited me to his house for a visit as soon as would be mutually convenient. But all I knew about John was that he lived out on the Mullet and he was "a builder"—a description that covered half the adult males in Western Mayo.

"What are the odds," I asked, "that two guys with the same name, who don't know each other and live on opposite sides of the Atlantic, would each hit a golf ball to the same spot, at the same time, on the same day?"

Gary grinned as he bent over to tee up his ball. "If you're talking about that particular spot, I'd say the odds are pretty good."

A couple of nights later, I drove back down the Blacksod Road to Aughleam, which, like most of the hamlets on the peninsula, was little more than a cluster of roadside buildings and a few farmhouses served by a rib road. Following John Geraghty's directions, I turned right at the designated signpost and drove up into the hills toward the ocean. "Look for the house on the left with the lights," he had said on the phone. Sure enough, there was a modern house with a long, straight driveway illuminated by a row of ornamental lamps, like an airport runway. I turned in and eased my way up the hedge-lined drive, wondering it if was the Mullet Peninsula's equivalent of Magnolia Lane.

John opened the front door as I was walking up and extended his hand in greeting. "We meet again." He stepped back to welcome me into a high-ceilinged entry, which was lit by a chandelier. A room to the right was dark, but I could see into a modern kitchen at the back of the house. John steered me left into a tastefully decorated parlor. Elegant curtains framed the windows. A glass corner cabinet housed collectible crystal. Everything was immaculate. It was a room you would expect to find in a high-end hotel or inn.

The picture was completed when John's wife, Kathleen, entered the room. A beautiful brunette, she wore her hair in one of those stylish shag cuts you see on TV presenters and chanteuses. She had on a blue tank top with glittery trim, and from her toned figure I deduced that she either had a home gym or was a regular at the Broadhaven Bay Hotel's state-of-the-art leisure center. She sat next to her handsome, dark-haired husband, and I couldn't help thinking that, as a pair, they were glam enough to crack the cast of the British soap *Footballers' Wives*.

"It's a lovely house," I ventured. "Did you build it yourself?"

"No, no," John said. "I met Kathleen and we moved here in 2001."

"We just got married this year," she volunteered. She slipped off her shoes and drew her legs up under her. "No going back now, I guess." They laughed together.

I asked John about his golf game, and he shrugged. "It's been a quiet year for me, golfwise. We've been finishing up the place on the island."

"The island?"

"Inishkea South." John explained that he had a 5.5-meter RIB, which stood for Rigid Inflatable Boat. It was one of those Zodiac-style outboards that I saw on Broadhaven Bay from time to time. "We launch it in Blacksod and go out to the islands."

"John is a sea fanatic," Kathleen said, "like he's a golf fanatic."

"We stay on the island on weekends," John said. "If you stand on the 14th tee box, you can look out and see us." He looked at his wife. "I don't know which is more peaceful, being on the island or being on the golf course."

I asked for a quick summary of his life in golf, and he readily complied. "I played soccer and Gaelic games," he said, "but the time came when I couldn't. So I took up golf. I used to play with the hurling grip, as we call it, the unorthodox grip." He butted his fists together with no overlapping or interlocking fingers. "I tried to change. I'd go to the local driving range and hit balls with a conventional grip, and the next day I'd have a pain in the shoulder."

"There's a driving range here?"

"No, in Blackrock, north of Dublin. That's where I was living at the time. But six years ago I went to a professional, and he taught me from scratch. I didn't see a golf course for three months." He pointed a thumb back over his shoulder. "I went up to a hill back here where Terry Swinson goes to hit golf balls. It's a big open area, all sand banks, and the grass is short because the animals keep it down. You'd think you were at Carne.

Well, I hit balls there for three whole months until I got confident enough to take it to the course." While making the grip change, he added with a rueful shake of his head, his handicap had soared to twenty-four. "But now it's back to eighteen."

"Which isn't bad at Carne," I said. I was thinking of my own 14.5.

He nodded. "The country members say an eighteen handicapper at Carne will play to a fourteen at any other course in the country, particularly a parkland course. Because Carne is so tough."

Kathleen went to get me a glass of water, and when she came back I had my notebook out. Following up on the Dublin reference, I asked if they were both born and raised on the Mullet. "I'm originally from here," she said. "I'm a Keane." She pronounced it *Kane*. "My family still has a little farm."

"A working farm?"

"Yes. It's nice to keep some traditions going." Her comment gave me the impression that farming on the Mullet was more of a hobby than a living.

"A lot of people who were brought up on the land have gone into building," John explained, "but I'm afraid our economic bubble will soon burst. A lot of those people will come back to work the land." As for his own background, John said he was from the seaside village of Blackrock, County Louth. "But my father was born just up the road here at Barrack."

"Big family?"

He nodded. "Nine in the family, five boys and four girls. My dad did his time in England, worked on the farms and then went to work for a construction firm. Fourteen years he was there, and then he married my mother. They returned to Ireland in seventy-one, the year I was born. They wanted to bring the children up at home, but not all the way to Mayo, because they were afraid we wouldn't finish school here."

I nodded. I remembered my trip in eighty-nine, when a Geraghty at Cross Lake had told me that Mullet emigrants rarely came back, "and why would they? They would want their children to be schooled." Education reforms, everybody now told me, had reversed that dismal trend. The Republic's system of public education was now the envy of most developed countries.

"I'm sorry. Your father's name is . . ." I looked up.

"John Geraghty, Sr. But they call him Jack."

I smiled over my notebook. "That was my dad's name."

"Really?" He didn't look that surprised. The Geraghtys had been recycling about a dozen male names since the time of the famine.

"I grew up in Blackrock," he continued, "but every summer and bank holiday we'd be up here at the family home at Barrack. Then my brother bought a holiday home here in 1999, and I renovated it. Which was my start in the building trade, although I picked up most of what I know from my father." More recently, John said, he and Kathleen had restored an old house on Inishkea South, home of barnacle geese, gray seals, and—for much of its history—illicit whiskey. Jack Geraghty loved the place and made any excuse to visit. "But he's unwell, he recently had a heart bypass. He's only gone seventy, but . . ." John didn't finish the thought. "He still works in his workshop."

I waited for John to go on.

"My dad has tremendous stories," he said. "Like when they used to go to the dances. They'd cycle five miles to a dance in Blacksod, and after the dance they'd cycle back. And if it was a moonlit night they'd go down to the shore to see what had washed up."

"Beachcombing?" I had heard Eamon Mangan talk of the practice.

"Combing, yes. Cargo would be stored on the decks of ships, and sometimes it would be swept away in bad weather. Or they'd cut it loose. Barrels of coffee. Rope for mending nets. Bales of rubber that you could melt down for mats. Barrels of whiskey. Timber being transported on big ships that sank. Big poles."

"They'd use that for fences," Kathleen interjected.

"Anything you could use or sell. My dad remembers nights when the moon was so bright you could see quite clearly where you were going. His mother would make up a pot of tea in a glass bottle and wrap a sock around it. To keep it warm."

John was leaning forward now. I got the feeling that Jack Geraghty was talking directly to me through his son, the way Jack Garrity sometimes talked through me.

"If an item was too heavy to lift," John continued, "they'd try to drag it above the high water mark. Then they'd put a stone on it or tie a bit of rope around it. They'd go home to get a couple of hours sleep and come back in the morning with a donkey or a cart."

"Tell him about the soldiers," Kathleen said.

John nodded. "During World War Two, dead soldiers washed ashore. They brought them in and buried them." I was sure there was more to this story, but John didn't elaborate.

"Did combing die out with your dad's generation?"

"No!" He perked up. "There's stuff that can go in the best houses. Terry has a gorgeous teakwood fireplace in the back of his house. He found a teak stump on the beach and turned it into something beautiful."

I made a mental note to ask Terry about his find.

"We went on the shore tonight," Kathleen said, making me wonder if beachcombing had replaced golf and boating among upwardly mobile Mayoites. "We pick up the timbers and use them for firewood."

John smiled. "It's turned full circle. I'm doing what my dad did in the fifties."

An hour later, on the road to Belmullet, I considered the chronology. John Geraghty's dad had been born in 1937, making him a contemporary not of *my* dad, but of my *brother*, who was also born in 1937. A split screen appeared in my mind's eye. On the one side I saw a twenty-year-old Tommy Garrity tearing up the back nine in a match at the ritzy Kansas City Country Club. On the other I saw a twenty-year-old Jack Geraghty stacking poles in the moonlight on the Mullet coast.

The images merged into John Geraghty—a modern-day Irishman who played golf at the Carne Golf Links and picked up driftwood on the sandy shore.

CHAPTER 28

"Golf is the only art form where the viewers of the art can not only move within the artwork but also compete against it. That does not mean that I will paint the Mona Lisa on the flags to promote art. But I will give great consideration to the human spaces through which the game of golf is played."

—from "An Interview with Jim Engh," GolfClubAtlas.com

Gary Stanley appeared on the second-floor fire escape of the clubhouse one morning as I was walking from my car. I looked up, and before I could shout a greeting, the greenkeeper thrust his arms over the rail. A small bird rose from his hands, flapping frantically and darting off toward the Carne cemetery.

I got the full story from Sheila Tallot, who was polishing glasses in the Spike Bar. "A starling came down the chimney and got caught behind the gas fire," she said, nodding toward the faux fireplace. "He was making so much noise banging around in there, I had this vision of him being a big bird. But he was just a small little fellow. I don't know if it's a nest inside or he just flew in and couldn't get out again."

Gary came in from the upstairs corridor, having washed his hands. "We probably need a cap for the two chimneys," he told Sheila, sliding on to a barstool.

"Is that part of your job?" I asked. "Birding the clubhouse?"

"Not really," he said with a laugh, "but I get called on for things like that." He turned to look out the windows. "Are you ready? Do you want to walk?" I said I was ready, so we waved to Sheila, clattered down the fire stairs, and walked up the twisty path to the course.

The *new* course, that is. Gary had agreed to give me a walking tour of the Jim Engh nine, which was under construction in the big dunes between the Eddie Hackett nines. But as we walked up the first of the new holes—a dogleg-right par 4 that went out between the existing first and tenth holes—I looked in vain for any signs of construction. The first hundred yards or so of bumpy grassland gave way to a stretch of white-mixed-with-dark sand crisscrossed with tire tracks, but there were no obviously graded stretches or phony-looking mounds. So I began by asking about the sand.

"The sand we have here is very fine," Gary said. He squatted and picked up a handful of the white stuff, letting it sift through his fingers. "Looked at under a microscope, it's all tiny round balls."

"So it packs solid?" I knew just enough about links agronomy to guess that packed sand produced the hard, firm conditions that make links golf special.

He nodded. "But when it dries, it's just like flour. That big bank on the eighteenth, if you walk there in the winter wind, you just get sandblasted." He shook the sand off his fingers. "It's very poor sand. To grow new grass on it, you have to put a little layer of black sand on top"—he reached for a handful that looked more like cinnamon sugar—"a layer of organic material that will hold the moisture." The black sand was not a soil amendment trucked in from a nursery, he said, but a natural product found in the banks. "We use it for top dressing greens, but we have to clean it first."

"Clean it?" I gave him a skeptical look.

"Take out all the big roots and screen it."

We walked up to the first green. Only it wasn't exactly a green—just a big patch of stubble on a slope. My eye was drawn off the property to miles of rolling farmland. "It's just been mowed out," Gary explained. "It'll have to be shaped and leveled." He laughed again. "Or not leveled. If I know Jim, he'll leave it like it is." Engh, we both knew, was fond of strong green contours.

The second hole was a dogleg-left par 4. From the prospective yellow tee, which was just a weed-covered mound, we looked out upon a thinly grassed fairway that was all humps and hollows, like the restless fairway of Hackett's third hole. Gary speculated that Jim might move the tee further east, "because this tee brings the fence into play, and there's no need to. It's okay on a calm day, but the prevailing wind will blow you out of bounds."

The next Engh hole was even more unsettled, having been a par 4, then a par 5 curving left, and most recently a par 5 ending on low ground to the right, by the fence line. Gary's crew had put in plastic pipe to drain water away from the high ground on the left, but now the pipe emptied onto the new green site. This was roughly equivalent to a homeowner letting a rainspout empty into the master bedroom. Assuming they relaid the drains, Gary said, Jim was looking at two options for the third green. They could push it up against the big dune on the other side of the barbed-wire fence—which could only be accomplished by purchasing the adjoining pasture—or build up the existing low area with fill and connect two existing dunes to create a parabolic backstop for the green.

The latter plan would require bulldozing, and I got a sense that Carne's purists would sooner shave off their children's hair than let a backhoe loose on the banks. "This was all natural," Gary said, looking around. "We just mowed it."

Three holes into the tour, I was struck by the elasticity of the design. Compared to most modern courses, which are planned with the aid of topographical maps and engineered to precise specifications, Carne's new nine was positively nineteenth-century. If Jim Engh didn't like the way a par 4 was shaping up on Monday, he could turn it into a par 3 on Tuesday. He could look at a desirable green site and imagine golfers approaching it from any point on the compass. And with no trees, streams, rocky outcroppings or permanent structures to contend with, he could treat the banks as a big sand box.

But as we pushed deeper into the dunes, I began to appreciate how difficult the links designer's task could be. Grassy ridges and sandy blowouts closed in on us like the walls of a maze. The views from the dune tops, while spectacular, were no less confusing. Sand hills blocked the sightlines, yielding only a glimpse here and there of an elevated green—which green?—or a stretch of fairway. The task was daunting enough for Hackett, who had to make sense of the tortured terrain with nothing but shoe leather and a sketch pad to assist him. But Engh's challenge was greater. He had to weave his nine holes through the rugged land that Hackett had deemed too severe—oddly shaped parcels that resembled gerrymandered congressional districts. What's more, Jim had to make his nine holes start and terminate at the clubhouse, and he had to deliver a routing with a traditional mix of par 3s, par 4s and par 5s.

"I'm lost," I confessed, turning in a full circle and seeing nothing but primordial dunes. "How did Jim make sense of this?"

Gary shrugged. "He's built mountain courses. He must be used to it."

The next subject was Grasses 101. It was an area of study that had long fascinated my father, who couldn't pass a healthy lawn without bending over and plucking a few blades for examination.

"The grasses that are here naturally are the fescues," Gary began, "and some rye that farmers bring in to feed their cattle. The fescue can grow to a foot or eighteen inches, and the seed blows out to the fairways and germinates naturally. It's all to withstand the sort of winter we get here. Now that stuff up there"—he pointed at the clumpy vegetation on the dunes—"is marron grass, which is not native to the site. It's imported from Scotland. We plant it in the rough and bare areas because white sand has a lot of lime in it. There's about a quarter ton of lime for every ton of sand. It's all seashells that were broken down in the ocean."

I ventured a guess. "Marron grass likes lime?"

"Marron grass *thrives* in it." He reached down and straightened a fairway stake that had toppled.

The par-5 fifth hole, when we got to it, looked familiar. "Hey," I said, "I walk by this spot about six times a day." We were at the narrow end of a gorge to the right of the seventeenth tee, a gorge that widened onto a valley floor covered with pale green fescue seedlings. Gary and I climbed a dune to "the tee," which was just a flattened patch of white sand and unruly weeds.

"We took the top off the hill, pushed it into four corners, and leveled it," he said, demystifying the mechanics of tee construction in fifteen words.

The tee's scrubby appearance puzzled me. "Isn't it ready for grassing?"

"The longer you can leave these tees after you shape them, the better," he said. "The sand settles. In six months, it'll sink a foot."

We scrambled down the face of the dune and walked to the flat, scoured-out area that was the fairway. "The ocean was probably in here at one time," Gary said, looking around.

I wasn't looking around. I was looking ahead. The fairway split around a notched dune, curving low around the left side and climbing steeply on the right. With either route, the shot was blind, but Gary said the bold play was straight over the notch in the dune, which rose about eighty feet above the valley floor. "But you'd better clear it," he said with a chuckle. The green, when we got up on top, was long, narrow, and perched on a shelf. With the addition of imported sand, two weed-filled excavations would become greenside bunkers.

"Wow," I said.

"This hole," Gary said with a grin, "will be quite the conversation starter."

The sixth hole, a short par 4, turned away from the sea and began a three-hole climb that took us up to a grassy ridge overlooking the seventeenth green. "The seventeenth doesn't look any easier from this angle," I said, staring straight down into the greenside pit.

Gary looked back toward the tee, which looked tiny against the breadth of sea and sky. "It's almost an impossible hole. You've got to fade it off the tee—which I can do—but then you've got to draw your second shot, and I can't do that. I think the best time I played it was in a men's club match. I hit a good drive, played short of the green, chipped up and made the putt."

We watched as three golfers struggled to reach the green with fairway metals. One of them half shanked his ball up onto the moguls. The second golfer hit a low screamer that ran into the guarding pot bunker. The third, after topping his ball about a hundred yards, slammed his club angrily on the turf. "It's just an intimidating shot," I said. "I can feel the tension in my forearms when I'm over the ball."

But what I was really feeling as I looked down on the hole from this new perspective was eagerness. Carne's new nine wouldn't be playable for months, maybe even years, but Eddie Hackett's holes were in the robust, adolescent stage of their development. I had only a few weeks left to play them, and, by golly, they deserved to be played.

I couldn't wait to resume the Seventeenth Hole Challenge.

CHAPTER 29

"Then there are some holes of the dog-leg variety which are constantly puzzling, particularly in certain winds. Generally it is a question of whether to attempt a dangerous long straight shot, or to play 'round with the necessary pull or slice."

—James Braid, *Advanced Golf*

After a month or so of trying, I holed a putt on seventeen. It was a fifteen-footer with about a foot of break, and I was so surprised to see the ball curl in on the low side that I dropped my putter and stared at the hole. Had spectators been present, I would have taken one of those Hale Irwin–style, hand-slapping victory laps.

But up to that point, I don't think I had made a putt longer than eight feet on seventeen. "That's not an impressive record," I told Pat during our next video chat. "But if the law of averages is really a *law*, I'm due."

Had I given it some thought, I would have recognized that the law of averages doesn't apply to stubborn golfers. The truth is, I am my father's son when it comes to putting—which is to say, I don't think it has any place in golf. I don't think about putting, I don't dream about putting, and I certainly don't practice putting. Given a choice between cleaning my electric shaver and trying to hole ten consecutive three-footers on the putting clock, I'll take the capful of Klean-All every time.

I can say this now because my first golf-instruction book, *Sports Illustrated: Putting*, is long out of print.

In any event, I didn't make that fifteen-footer entirely by chance. I made it because I had an epiphany the day I stood with Gary Stanley on that highest of dunes overlooking the seventeenth green. From the starboard perspective I could see the prevailing slopes of the putting surface: the short, scary incline from dune wall to cliff's edge, the gentler rise from the tongue-like front tier to the rarely used back lobe, and the spillway transition between the two. More important, I could see them all at the same time—holistically, if you will. It dawned on me that I had been playing seventeen like a truck driver hauling hazardous cargo up a mountain road. Preoccupied with the dangers on either side, I saw the distant green in only two dimensions—a fixed target with a profile no wider than a country lane. I put all my energy into *getting there.*

Once I had three balls on the green, however, I wandered around like a sleepwalker, swatting putts toward the hole with less thought than you'd give to slapping a mosquito on your cheek. My distance control was particularly bad, bringing to mind the great line of the old touring pro Homero Blancas, who, when asked if he'd had any uphill putts in his round, said, "Sure. After each of my downhill putts."

It was time, I decided, to give my putts a little more attention, to give the seventeenth green the respect it deserved. It slowed my play down, and on more than one occasion I had to hustle off the green to let other golfers play through. But it paid off. I began to make putts longer than my two o'clock shadow.

I also benefited from the slow accrual of "local knowledge," that priceless trove of painfully acquired intelligence that gives a club member a leg up on visiting golfers. I learned, for instance, that hitting a ball into seventeen's left-front pot bunker was a major miscue. The bunker itself was unremarkable, but it was situated short and left of the greenside dune. "Eddie Hackett called for that bunker to be built so you'd have something to aim at from the tee," Eamon Mangan told me during one of our course walks. "He wanted to give the golfer a line." Fine idea, that, but if you were actually *in* the bunker, you were, to quote the Japanese golfer, *screwed*. You had to hit a totally blind twenty- or thirty-yard explosion shot, and you had to hit it high enough to clear the dune and land on the narrow shelf of green that tilted toward the chasm. If you took too much sand, your ball would plop on the dune and roll back into the bunker. If your ball flew farther, it could either bury itself in the duneface rough—leaving you an impossible downhill chip toward the cliff's edge—or bounce upon landing and race across the green and into the pit.

The one time I was in this bunker, during a club competition, I opened up the face of my pitching wedge and swung so hard that the strap on my cap went *twang*. The ball floated out of the fan of sand and disappeared over the dune, where, according to the testimony of sullen witnesses, it caught a lucky bounce and trickled onto the green, twenty feet from the hole. "You don't know how good that was," said Terry Swinson. He later e-mailed me a photograph he had taken on another Sunday. A golfer, laughing hysterically, rolled on the ground beside the seventeenth-hole bunker. A second golfer lay on his back, his legs dangling over the lip of the bunker, his arms stretched out. His sand wedge was at the other end of the trap. The photo was titled PJ MCHALE AIR SHOT IN 17TH BUNKER 2007.

If a ball in the bunker was bad, anything left of the bunker was calamitous. I learned that lesson one afternoon when I pull-hooked a 6 iron onto a blowout near the eleventh tee. My ball was high up the dune on a little ledge—sitting nicely but sitting, unfortunately, at the level of my belt. What's worse, there was no way to get above the ball, which was where I had to stand to hit a right-handed shot back toward the fairway. If Nick Faldo had been watching from the analyst's booth, he would have told me to declare my ball unplayable, take the penalty stroke, and look for the nearest point of relief. But there was no point of relief behind me, nothing but dark ravines and broken dunes. That left only one alternative: going back to the spot in the fairway where I had hit my last shot.

But that was 150 yards back toward the tee, and I didn't feel like retracing my steps.

So I decided to play the ball as it lay. Pulling my 9 iron, I scrambled up the bank. I gripped the club upside down—toe pointed down, clubface aimed to the right—and tried to address the ball left-handed. To do so, I had to choke down so far on the steel that the grip end of the club protruded about a foot beyond my right hip. That didn't work, so I tried gripping the shaft near the hosel. Then I tried holding the club off my *left* hip. Then I tried resting the grip end on my right shoulder. And then I fell off the dune.

It's a pity that Swinson wasn't there to snap a photo titled JS GARRITY BACKFLIP 2007. I went over backward, clawing the air with my hands, and landed well down the slope on my back and shoulders. I then slid another ten or twelve feet through sand and scrub before coming to rest with my feet in the air and my head in an aromatic patch of tall fescue.

I lay there for a moment or so, staring up at the puffs of white cloud drifting across the sky. I imagined myself in a hammock by a Hawaiian lagoon . . . or on a beach towel at Sanibel Island . . . or on a poolside chaise at the Hong Kong Marriott. I cautiously moved my arms and legs, checking for injury. I lifted my head for a look around and then let it fall back on the pillow of grass. Finally, with a sigh, I closed my eyes.

Thinking, *I'd better take the unplayable.*

Strategy sometimes reared its ugly head. I would write "5 WOOD/HYBRID 2" on the back of one of my business cards, expressing my intention to lay up off the tee and play seventeen as a par 5. This is known in golf circles as "the smart play."

My father was a firm believer in smart golf. It suited him, first of all; he was a consistent ball striker who could hit fairways and greens. On top of that, he was a brain-bound golfer. Jack Garrity saw the game as a repository of secrets that could be plumbed through trial and error or, better yet, by way of his other principal passion: reading. Dad's library of golf instructionals was extensive, and his very favorite was *A Round of Golf with Tommy Armour*. In that wonderful book, the former British Open and U.S. Open Champion coached a midhandicapper through nine holes, employing the Socratic method to get his pupil to save strokes through intelligent course management. "The brainless shot is the one unforgivable sin in golf," Armour wrote, "and a diabolical thing about it is that so many times it is made by men who, off a golf course, are mentally superior."

I was taught to play, therefore, by a man who was contemplative and measured in his own approach to the game, but who was, at the same time, dazzled by the raw power of younger golfers. Bragging about me to his golfing buddies, Dad would say, "Johnny can really bust it," as if three-hundred-yard drives were a bigger achievement than low scores. (In Tommy, of course, he had a son who was both a belter and a thinker.) Nevertheless, my own golf reading took me deep into the texts of Armour, Bobby Jones and Jack Nicklaus, all of whom put course management ahead of swing theory.

For further reminders that golf is played between the ears, I drew on my work with Rob Stanger, the teaching pro at the Mission Hills Golf Resort in Rancho Mirage, California. Stanger, a Johnny Miller disciple, was my West Coast swing guru when I was writing the *Mats Only* columns. In that capacity, he took me out for playing lessons on the Mission Hills courses, lessons that could have been torn from the pages of Armour's book. "You don't need your driver on this hole," Rob would tell me on a medium-length par 4. On another hole he'd say, "Take one club less and play to the front edge of the green," to discourage me from attacking a sucker pin. Rob used the Miller nomenclature of "red light," "yellow light" and "green light" to describe the risk/reward parameters of a shot, and before he'd let me putt he insisted that I describe how I visualized the ball going into the hole. ("Do you want the ball to topple in, or do you want it to hit the back of the cup?") One afternoon, when I was in Rancho Mirage on writing business, he coached me to a four-birdie, upper-seventies round on the Mission Hills Tournament Course—a performance so gratifying that I considered diving into the pond at eighteen.

So I was fully prepared to embrace one or more of the "various ways of playing the hole" that my brother had cited in his seventeenth-hole challenge. From the outset I knew that I shouldn't hit my driver when the wind was helping because the fairway shrank to the width of a skateboard about 275 yards out. But when I played the hole as a par 5, the choices multiplied. One afternoon I played it nine times using a 5 metal off the tee, my blueprint calling for a short drive to the widest part of the fairway followed by a 6 or 7 iron layup and a short pitch or chip to the green. My scores at the end of the trial were 5-5-6, 6-5-5, 6-5-5—48. A few days later, with a stiff wind quartering into me from the right, I played nine tee shots with my hybrid 2, a club that produces a lower, more penetrating trajectory (or as they say in baseball, "a hot grounder"). This time my scores were 6-5-5, 5-5-8, 5-5-5—49.

When I wasn't shuffling clubs, I fiddled with shot shapes. Gary Stanley had said that seventeen called for a fade off the tee and a draw into the green, so I waited for a day when the wind was blowing right to left and tried to hit nine left-to-right tee shots with my driver. (The countervailing wind was my insurance against a runaway slice.) I aimed toward the chasm on the left and tightened my grip to promote an open clubface at impact, and damned if it didn't work. My first three drives soared out toward the cliff's edge and then curved back into the fairway, coming to rest in a cluster around the 150-meter stone. I then made myself giddy by hitting three consecutive 6-iron shots with the intended draw, two of them leaving me birdie putts of less than twenty feet. The third, nuked, flew right over the flag and onto the upper tier of the green.

My exuberance was short-lived. The second set of tee shots produced an overcooked fade that landed in the high moguls, a high, screaming slice—or was that me screaming?—that crashed in the vicinity of Cross cemetery, and then a lost-my-nerve straight ball that sailed over the cliff on the left. My nine-ball line, which I labeled "Paradise Lost," was 4-4-5, 6-8-6, 5-6-4—48.

At night, in my quayside flat, I replayed the shots in my head and tried to work out the best strategy. Laying up off the tee was a clear winner in terms of percentage of fairways hit, and it resulted in more fives and fewer double- and triple-bogeys. If I wanted to shoot better scores at Carne, playing the seventeenth as a par 5 was the way to go.

"But I'm not trying to shoot better scores at Carne"—this was me arguing with myself—"I'm trying to shoot ninety on the seventeenth hole."

Taking another look at the numbers, I noticed that my eighteen-ball scores were actually *higher* using the layup strategy. That puzzled me, until I picked up on the fact that there were no fours on those cards. *No pars.* And I needed some fours to shoot ninety. (You do the math: 18 x 5 = 90.) Furthermore, laying up did not protect me from the occasional disaster hole. If I hit a wild tee shot with my 5 wood or hybrid 2, I wound up in trouble *short.* That put me in the awful position of needing two recovery shots to get within middle-iron range of the green.

With the driver, on the other hand, I usually hit the ball past the worst terrain and into trouble that could be escaped with a wedge or a short iron, leaving a manageable third to the green. (Touring pros call this the "bomb and gouge" strategy—*bomb* referring to the reckless blast off the tee and *gouge* to the brute-force wedge shot from the rough, a shot made possible by modern square-grooves technology. You'll also hear the term "spray it and play it," but this is a less manly description that conjures up a comedian's spit take.) Furthermore, when I did manage to find the short grass with my driver, I had a second shot of 140 to 165 yards from a relatively level lie. That meant I could fly my approach to the green, taking the pot bunker and the guarding mound on the left out of play. Par was possible.

So I rejected the layup strategies and committed to bomb and gouge. But I also gave up on the power fade off the tee, the perils of the right side outweighing my desire to hit more fairways. From late September on, I used the distant greenside bunker as an aiming point—wasn't that what Eddie Hackett wanted?—and tried to hit a draw over the mounds on the right.

If I was looking for confirmation that this was the right approach, I got it one afternoon in the form of a rainbow. I climbed onto the seventeenth tee, turned to look at the hole, and there it was: a watery band of primary and supernumerary arcs stretching from a distant dunetop to a point in the sky above the seventeenth green. The 'bow was still dangling from the clouds, fifteen minutes later, when I jotted down a line of 4-4-6. It was the first time I had recorded two pars in a set, and I would have made birdie on ball number two if my putt from eight feet had taken one more turn.

After putting out, I set my bag to the side and scrambled up the dune behind the green to get a better look at the sky. ("The work will wait while you show the child the rainbow," a wise man wrote, "but the rainbow won't wait while you do the work.") I sat in the tall grass and gazed across the dunetops at the distant clubhouse and the bay beyond.

There are three kinds of golf, I thought.

A ll right, the reader says with a sigh, *what are the three kinds of golf?*
"The first"—I raise a finger—"is companionable golf. That's the game you play with two, three or four partners, the kind that has you saying, "Hit it, Alice" or "That won't hurt you.""

The second is solitary golf. That's the calm, ruminative game that Thoreau would have played if some early-day Donald Trump had gotten development rights to Walden Pond.

The third is show golf. That's the version that is played in front of spectators.

Sitting on the dune, I thought of my dad in his retirement years. He'd get up at dawn on weekdays and drive out to Kansas City's Swope Memorial Golf Course, where the starter, with a wink and a nod, would let him go out by himself on the back nine. Dad would play two or three balls on every hole, waving to the maintenance guys on their gang mowers and stopping to chat with the greenkeeper as he cut new holes. I could count on Dad being home by noon.

That was solitary golf.

Sitting on the dune, I thought of my own predilection for solitary golf. In the years after Dad died, I'd drive out to Milburn Country Club, on the Kansas side of the state line, and spend the twilight hours playing holes at random. Sometimes I'd join another single, but just as often I'd pick up my ball and cut across two fairways to avoid an encroaching golfer. I told myself I needed to be alone to work on my game.

Sitting on the dune, I thought of my brother. He had played show golf, and perhaps for that reason he did not see the golf course as a place to escape from the noise and pressures of everyday life. He left tournament golf when he was still in his twenties, and he played infrequently after that. Offered a hundred years of solitude, Tommy would have spent it on a lake in a bass boat.

But I wondered: did he enjoy the show?

Because I would have.

It's autumn 2006, and I'm researching a Sports Illustrated *cover story about Tiger Woods. Hearing that I plan to fly to Hawaii for the PGA Grand Slam of Golf, one of* SI's *advertising sales executives calls me up with an interesting offer. "We have a few slots in the Grand Slam Pro-Am," he says. "Would you like to play?"*

"Sure," I gush, "that would be great." I don't disclose that I am a twelve-rounds-a-year golfer with no valid handicap and no experience playing in front of crowds.

"I'll see if I can pair you up with Tiger."

"Wow," I say. "That would really be something."

The next thing I know, I'm shaking hands with Tiger Woods on the sunny first tee at the Poipu Bay Golf Club and Resort. Spectators and palm trees line the fairway from tee to green. Press photographers scramble for position.

"Next on the tee," roars an amplified voice, "John Garrity!"

So what was Tiger like?" people ask me.

To which I reply, "I didn't notice."

I'm half-joking. My scramble partners and I had Tiger as our pro for six holes, or roughly an hour and a half. But I caught only glimpses of him. I was so absorbed in club selection, shotmaking and showboating that Tiger more or less vanished. He was this disembodied voice that followed me from hole to hole, a voice that murmured "Good swing there" when I pulled off a shot and said nothing when I didn't. My stock line is, *When you play golf with Tiger you don't learn much about him. But you learn a lot about yourself.*

The wind blew in hard gusts, bending the palms and shaking the live oak and mango trees. On the fourth hole, a 359-yard par 4, Team Tiger had a shot of about a hundred yards from the fairway to an elevated green, dead into the wind. Two of my scramble partners made solid contact, but their shots ballooned in the wind and drifted left, falling a good twenty yards short of the green. To do better, I knew I needed to take more club, grip down on the shaft, and spank a shot that would knife through the wind on a low trajectory. It's called a "knockdown shot," and it's one of the few specialty shots in my repertoire. My brother described it as "flighting the ball," and he had given me some knockdown pointers when we played at Carne. ("If I played this course every day," Tommy said, "I probably wouldn't hit a full iron shot more than once or twice a round.")

I was very conscious of Tiger and his caddie, Steve Williams, standing a few feet away, and I'd be lying if I said I wasn't aware of the big gallery. But I was not nervous in a crippling way. I choked down on my 8 iron, crouched over the ball . . . and I suddenly realized that I was channeling my brother's mannerisms, all his little shirtsleeve tugs, head tilts and hand gestures. I was *acting*. And maybe that's what you're supposed to do when you're performing in front of the world's greatest golfer and his adoring gallery. All I can tell you is, I set up to that shot pretending I was Tom Garrity in the third round of the 1960 West Palm Beach Open. I hit the shot with that same conviction, taking a short, smooth backswing, staying down through impact, and finishing with a waist-high follow-through.

The ball came off the club with a crisp click and rocketed toward the back right corner of the green, where just a tip of flagstick was showing.

"*Great* swing there!" It was the voice of Tiger.

"Am I long?" My shot was flighted so well that I feared it might carry the green.

"No, you're right there."

The ball drifted a foot or two to the right as it dropped, but a sweet patter of applause went around the green. I grinned and touched the bill of my cap.

The delusion that I belonged inside the ropes had been just as strong on the previous hole, a 183-yard par 3 with a hilltop tee and a way-down-there green ringed with white-sand bunkers and spectators. Tiger hit first, from the back tee, and stuck a long iron inside twenty feet. When it was my turn, I pulled a hybrid 4 and smacked a shot that felt "toesy" at impact but looked good in the air, drawing back toward the center of the green. I held my recoil position and watched the ball all the way down—I was *stylin'*—and when it plunged into the front bunker I indulged in a wry smile and a little shake of the head, the universal signal that either a bad yardage or a sudden gust of wind had spoiled an otherwise perfect shot. Minutes later, I holed my team's eight-footer for birdie, drawing loud yelps and another round of applause. I celebrated with a modest fist pump and an exchange of high-fives.

It was all bull, of course. The only pressure in a pro-am scramble is the pressure you put on yourself. You aren't keeping a personal score, you don't have to play your misses, and if you're paired with Tiger Woods or Sergio Garcia you're all but invisible to the crowd. It's the ultimate golf fantasy; no one notices you unless you hit a good shot. (Or wear a green golf glove. For the rest of the week, people would approach me on the course, saying, "Hey, you were the guy with the green glove! You played with Tiger!")

Three holes later, on the par-5 sixth, I hit my first good drive of the day, a rocket up the middle that rolled out to about 275 yards to another patter of applause. "Good swing there," said Tiger.

"Thanks," I said as we walked off the tee together. Thinking, *It doesn't get any better than this.* Thinking, *Wait'll I tell Tommy. . . .*

Until I remembered that I couldn't tell him.

A few days after my rainbow round at Carne, I birdied the seventeenth hole. Third ball, second set. Driver, 6 iron. The putt was an uphill twelve-footer from the edge of the green, and I knew it was good when it was halfway to the hole. *Plunk*, rattle. I looked around. No one was in sight. The only sound was the distant purr of a tractor.

Jotting down my scores, I noticed that I was four-under bogey with the first six balls of my round.

I walked back to the tee, stared at the ocean while a foursome played through, and then played a third set of three. This time my line was 5-5-5.

Out of curiosity, I went to my bag and rummaged through the top zipper pocket until I found the card from my previous round. Seeing that I had made two pars and nothing higher than a six on the last nine balls of that card, I did some hasty calculating and reached the shocking conclusion that I was three-under bogey for my last eighteen balls.

I had shot eighty-seven.

Not so fast, said a voice in my head. *You can't splice together rounds of golf to achieve an optimal score.*

I started to argue, but I knew the voice was right. Besides, it was exciting just to look at the two cards and see all those fours and fives—and a three! Until that moment, I had thought ninety was out of reach, a pipe dream. But clearly it wasn't. Furthermore, I was four-under bogey at the halfway point of my current round.

Get on with it, said the voice.

I pocketed both cards and lugged my bag back to the tee. This time, with a freshening wind at my back, I bounced two drives over the cliff and one of them led to a seven. But I saved bogey with the other and made a two-putt par with my third ball. I wrote 7-5-4 on the card. *Three-under bogey with six to play.*

There was a little daylight left, but dark clouds were gathering over the sea. The flagstick bent in the wind, and the flag crackled like a campfire. Tough conditions.

I also had to consider the possibility that darkness would fall while I was playing my final set. I might lose a ball or two in the gloaming and not shoot ninety.

And let's be honest, it was happening too fast. There was no chance of shooting ninety, and all of a sudden ninety was a couple of strolls to the tee and back. *Where's the drama? What will you do with the last month of your sabbatical?*

The first drops of rain stung my cheek, and that decided the matter. I shouldered my bag, popped my umbrella, and set off for the clubhouse at a brisk pace.

Play suspended at six-oh-five p.m.

CHAPTER 30

Across the blue water of the Bay the rowboats, filled with their living freight, swiftly glided, and upon the sands of the shore stood the remaining emigrants, while all around were visible the lofty rugged mountains of Mayo, their snow-clad heights glistening in the sunlight.

—from *The Irish Times*, March 31, 1883

Another evening, another parlor. A peat fire burning. Above the mantel, a gilt-framed painting of Jesus and a St. Bridget's cross made of straw. To the right, a painting of women doing stoop labor in a farm field. On the far wall, expensive-looking wedding photographs. A stack of VHS tapes, including *Titanic* and *Scooby Doo*. Martin Geraghty, the stonemason, sat with his wife, Ann, on a couch opposite the fire. Annie Geraghty, the matriarch, sat on a wooden chair.

Annie was a brilliant surprise. I had gone to the home of Martin and Ann Geraghty of Clogher on the recommendation of Ann Geraghty, the hairdresser, and they had cleverly sent for Annie, whom I recognized the minute I entered the room. Annie was the dear woman who had taken Pat and me behind her farmhouse in 1989 and pointed across the fields to the shore where my great-grandfather "took the little boat to get on the big boat for America." I had photographed Annie and her granddaughter Mary. Thirteen years later, on my first trip back to Belmullet, I had given some prints to George Geraghty. He had passed them on.

"That little girl is now a nurse in the Sligo hospital," Annie said. "And she remembers your visit. She always talked about the big man from America."

I smiled at that. It made me feel like John Wayne in *The Quiet Man*.

Annie had lost some mobility since our prior meeting. "She's had two hip surgeries," Martin explained. But she still had the curly brown hair, the spectacles, the lively eyes, and the mischievous smile. Not to mention the tangled bloodlines. "I'm a Geraghty both ways," she said. "I'm Annie Geraghty on my birth certificate, and I married a Geraghty."

While I tried to digest that fact, Annie explained that Martin was her "baby brother," and she was related to George the greenkeeper through his father, Martin Geraghty of Cross, whom I had met in eighty-nine. ("He was a tall man, like yourself," said the Martin of the moment, "six two or so.") John Geraghty, the builder and Belmullet Golf Club member, was a nephew. *His* father—one of Annie's eight siblings—was John "Jack" Geraghty, the beachcomber, who was now seventy and retired near Dundalk. Martin's son, Michael, lived just across the road in a house with a stone facade built by his dad. The facade, that is. Not the house.

"You're a builder?" I turned in my chair.

Martin nodded. "Walls and house fronts."

"If you told the truth," Ann said, "you're the only stonemason around here. There are plenty of block layers, but not many who can do stone anymore."

I mentioned that I had seen the name Geraghty on a charter boat at Saleen Harbour.

"That young man, he'd be a Jack Geraghty, as well," Annie said. "His father would be our first cousin."

"Another Jack," I said. "And so many Anns. Did I tell you that my brother, Tom, had a daughter named Anne?"

"Is that right?" Annie smiled like an indulgent granny. "You know, I was always sorry that I didn't put things together when you visited years ago.

When you were gone, I put my thinking cap on, and I realized that a lot of Geraghtys had come to look up the family tree, but their given names weren't at all in common with ours. We have the same names that keep appearing down through the years—John, Thomas, Martin, Michael, James. My dad had a brother Tom, and his uncle was named Tom, same as your family. But I thought of it too late. I said, 'That's one man I'll never see again.'" She laughed. "And I was so wrong!"

"Well, not so wrong." I felt guilty for not having stayed in touch. "I wouldn't have come back when I did if not for the golf course."

"I always wanted to know where you were," she said. "And how you were doing."

Ann got up and left the room while Annie talked, returning a minute later with some snapshots of Australian relatives. "That's Bridget," said Annie, holding a photo of an old lady. "She was eighty years in Australia without coming home." That triggered a memory of one Johnny Geraghty, who also went to Australia. Johnny died trying to save the lives of two swimmers at a Sydney beach. "He was a great swimmer and diver," Martin said. "He saved the first, but he hit his head on a rock trying to save the second."

Annie passed me another picture, a color portrait of twenty-six Irish-Aussies, toddlers to nonagenarians, gathered for a family reunion. "I was going to Australia when I was eighteen," she said, "but my partner wouldn't go with me. So that was that. But I always say, when this or that happens, 'If I'd gone to Australia . . .'" She chuckled. "My granddaughter Mary went there in 2005, and she had a picture taken of herself in front of the Sydney Opera House. She wanted the picture for me."

I told Annie that I had spent several months in Sydney in 1992, writing about golf and cricket for *Sports Illustrated Australia*. "Pat and I had an apartment on the Kiribili wharf, right across from the Opera House."

Annie's eyes widened. "Isn't that amazing? Australia used to be so far away."

That was my cue to ask again about my great-grandfather. "The day we met," I said to Annie, "you pointed out to the harbor where Michael Geraghty would have set sail for America. . . ."

"That's right," she said with a nod. "Barrack Point."

I tried not to show my surprise. "Where?"

Martin leaned in. "You know where you turned in off the main road? Just two hundred yards through the fields, on the shore there, that's where they went out on a little boat to board the American liner."

This was news to me. For eighteen years I had been telling people that my great-grandfather had departed Ireland from Saleen Harbour. George Geraghty had showed me the spot. Eamon Mangan had showed me the spot. Rita Nolan's book, *Within the Mullet*, identified Saleen as the embarkation point for generations of emigrants. What's more, the local council, following a suggestion made by my wife on an earlier visit, was planning to install an historical marker at Saleen Quay. But it struck me now that Annie had not named the port of embarkation back in eighty-nine; she had merely pointed toward Blacksod Bay.

"It's called Barrack Point because there was a barracks there," Martin continued. "It wasn't a real quay, just rocks about a meter high. You stepped onto the rocks, a little boat came along, and you went out to the liner."

Annie said, "My grandfather and grandmother went from Barrack Point."

Before I could comment, Martin returned to the small-world theme. "My son was coming back from America two years ago," he said. "He's sitting in the plane looking up at the video screen, and they're showing all these beautiful golf courses. And here comes Carne—number twelve in the ratings! It was a shock."

"I bet it was," I said, adding, "It's a world of surprises." I was thinking of Barrack Point.

Annie shifted on her chair to get comfortable. "All right, John," she said. "Tell us about your very interesting life and your wonderful family."

She waited expectantly, this sweet old great-grandma who was probably my fourth or fifth cousin, once removed. I looked over at Martin, who would also be a distant cousin, and at his wife, Ann, who was almost certainly my whatever-she-was-in-law. They, too, waited expectantly. It was as if I had been on a long journey and, home again, had to catch them up.

"I wish you could have met my father," I began, feeling the tide change.

———

I drove out to Carne the next afternoon, intending to play what I hoped would be the final six balls of the Seventeenth Hole Challenge. Instead, I joined a gray-haired gentleman from Dublin for a wind-blown nine holes. "It's very challenging in these conditions," he said with a big grin, having watched his drive on the ninth hole dive to the ground as if slapped by the hand of God.

The following afternoon I went out on my balcony to assess the conditions. Sunlight sparkled on the bay, but the yellow construction tapes on the work sites fluttered frantically, and the runty shrubs on the opposite shore swayed to a choppy rhythm. I decided that a day off from golf might be in order. "Goin' to McDonnells," I text-messaged my wife. "Call authorities if I'm not back by nine." I locked up the flat and stepped smartly across the street to the pub.

McDonnells' daytime clientele tended to be old guys with mussed hair and frayed sweaters. Two of them were reading newspapers at the bar, registering their interest in or disapproval of certain items with hums, clucks, snorts and guffaws. Perhaps a dozen more stood in the narrow corridor between the bar and a row of tables. An old fellow on a bench showed considerable facility with the button accordion, coaxing a melancholy waltz out of his squeeze box. Padraig Conroy was behind the bar. When he saw me walk in, he turned and took a bottle of 7-Up off the shelf.

Conroy, as I have mentioned, owned the pub and was co-owner, with his brother, of McDonnells Funeral Home, which was just up the street. The pub had opened in 1942 under the ownership of Padraig's grandparents, Michael and Elizabeth McDonnell. Padraig worked for them from the age of nineteen, but he went away to London in the early nineties to learn the funeral trade. ("I wanted to see the world," he said, his wry smile suggesting that he might have seen more had he picked another trade.) He returned to Belmullet in ninety-five, taking over the pub when his grandmother passed away. Now, at the tender age of thirty-four, he operated a traditional Irish pub that drew visitors from Mayo and beyond.

"What's the McDonnells mystique?" I asked over the reedy squawking of the accordion. "Why are you packed every night?"

"I can't say." He shoveled some ice into a half-pint glass and started pouring from the bottle. "As the man says, everyone is entitled to their opinion. But I have no idea." He let the foam bubble to the top and then put the bottle and glass in front of me.

"It can't be market forces," I said. "The pubs are drying up."

He nodded. "There used to be twenty-two pubs in Belmullet. Now there's only five or six left."

"Twenty-*two*?" I thought of my first visit, when the town had seemed dead at dusk. I didn't remember twenty-two lightbulbs in Belmullet, much less twenty-two pubs. "So why did you become a pub owner?"

"Just to keep the generations going. Someone was needed to run it."

"How about your parents?"

"They are teachers."

Padraig, I decided, would make a good witness in court. He gave direct answers to direct questions, but he volunteered little.

"You spent some time in England. Any of your ancestors migrate to America?"

He shook his head. "Australia. A century ago." Gathering momentum, he added, "But now people are coming back. There's more opportunity now."

It struck me that Padraig was an unusual guy in that he had found success both in a dying business (pubs) and in the dying business (funerals). "I've done some research in Wisconsin." I leaned across the bar so he could hear me. "I've studied church records. A hundred years ago, people were dying of apoplexy, consumption, dropsy, typhoid, cholera, alcoholism. They were burning to death in fires. There were drownings and . . . railroad accidents! There were lots of railroad deaths. But today we die from heart disease, cancer and diabetes, because it's a different world." I sipped my drink. "So now I'm looking at Belmullet, and it's not the place it was even ten years ago. So I'm wondering if you, as a funeral director, see a change in your business. Any death trends, that sort of thing?"

Padraig rubbed the bar with a towel as he gave my meandering question some thought. "A lot of young people are dying," he said at last. "Younger than years ago."

"Drugs? Car accidents? Fights?"

"No, no." He shook his head. "Cancer. Tumors. It's very prominent."

"Any idea why?"

"None." He gave me an apologetic shrug and turned to pour whiskeys for three men in flat caps who had started a round robin of darts in the back of the pub.

I finished my 7-Up and departed with a wave to Padraig and a nod to the squeeze box player, who was tapping his right foot to a sprightly reel.

CHAPTER 31

"You've got to do your own growing, no matter how tall your grandfather was."

—Irish Proverb

The next day I devoted to lazy pursuits. And the same the day after, when a dwindling wind failed to overcome my sense that the atmosphere was heavy in some respect. That took me to Sunday and the club competition, and it goes without saying that I didn't have the stamina to take on the seventeenth hole after a full morning with Terry and the boys. I joined Gary in the Spike Bar for a lunch of vegetable soup and brown bread, and afterward I drove around the banks and out past Corclough, a hamlet near the Atlantic cliffs and the Eagle Island lighthouse.

Seamus and Edith Geraghty lived in an ivy green cottage by a sheep pasture. Edith met me at the door, a big, vivacious woman with spectacles and dark hair that was tied back. "I'm a writer myself," she said, settling into an armchair in the corner of yet another cozy parlor. Edith was, in fact, a published poet and playwright, as well as the director of the local theater company, the Phoenix Theatre Works. "A lot of work, a lot of fun, and no money whatever," she said with a laugh. "Oh, here he is."

The man who walked in from the kitchen impressed me with his physical presence. Seamus had the big hands and thick chest of a farmer, but his salt-and-pepper beard and searching eyes suggested something more. A crucifix dangled from a chain around his neck.

After the ritual handshaking and offers of tea and biscuits, we talked about life on the Mullet and the possible connections between my Wisconsin forebears and the Geraghtys of Cross. "I've found very little on the American side," I said. "It's as if the Atlantic crossing scrubbed away our history."

"The people who left didn't want to talk about Ireland," Edith said. "They were living in exile, and there was an awful lot of survivor's guilt. They didn't know if the family they left behind had survived. As for the people who stayed behind, the emigrants were dead to them. They'd just as soon pretend they never existed."

"Those who became rich in America," Seamus added, "might have been ashamed of their poor relatives."

That aside, my new friends were willing to hazard a few guesses about the appearance, temperament and predilections of my great-grandfather, Michael Geraghty, even though they had never heard of him. "All the Geraghtys I know are very stubborn," Edith said. "And they have terrible tempers. They don't get angry often, but when they do, it's *bad*. And the Geraghtys are known for straight talking. A spade is a spade, it's not a digging implement."

Seamus nodded.

"When I came here," Edith continued, "I was told by neighbors that Geraghtys were different. They liked education. They read books. They were open to new ideas." She turned to Seamus. "Tell John the story about James and the artificial inseminator."

"Well, that would have been my grandfather, James Geraghty," Seamus said, leaning forward in his chair. "He was talking about artificial insemination way back in the thirties or forties. He said"—and here Seamus raised a finger—"he said, 'A day will come when a stallion in Ireland will be able to get a mare in New York in foal.'" He lowered his hand. "To which another farmer replied, 'Well, he'll have to have a pretty long tool!' " Seamus smiled, and Edith and I laughed. "The local fellows used to laugh at him a lot."

"Because he read," Edith said. "He would read books." I scribbled that fact in my notebook, mindful of my father's lifelong bibliomania and my own penchant for reading while eating or strolling.

"His son, my uncle Charlie, was also like that. He came in for a lot of ridicule—bullying, I suppose you'd call it. When he was in his thirties he was taken to work in Scotland—that was in 1962—and they tell a story that he was standing in the middle of a field with his newspaper while the other workers threw potatoes at him." Seamus chuckled. "Which I don't think is actually true."

Edith begged to differ. To her, the story rang true. "I mean, Seamus has lived here all his life, but *his* thinking is different. Otherwise, I wouldn't be married to him." Edith laughed and Seamus smiled.

Edith shifted her focus to me, saying, "You do have one Geraghty trait." Before I could guess, she said, "*Height*. The Geraghty men tend to be very tall."

"Really?" I had always assumed that my height, like my taste for short-bread, was a Stuart trait. My grandfather, Charles Stuart, measured well over six feet, and my mother was nearly as tall as my five-foot-ten-inch dad.

"But you said you were looking for stories of Geraghtys. Well, Seamus has them."

I was delighted to hear that, but first I had to ask if they were natives of the Mullet. Edith, it turned out, was not. She said she was born in Dublin to an engineer from County Cork, and she grew up in Zambia, of all places, where her father owned a construction company. It was in Cork that Edith, while in her teens, had met Seamus, who was down taking safety training. In the way of such stories, Seamus had won her heart and her hand and convinced her that she could be happy in some out-of-the-way village that nobody ever heard of.

"I never saw darkness until I got here," Edith said with surprising enthusiasm. "I thought I was coming to the end of the world. The houses were dark, and all you could see were these acres and acres of bog. I thought, My God, Seamus could kill me and bury me in the bog!"

Seamus gave a noncommittal shrug.

"As well, there was no running water. It was connected to tanks," Edith continued. "And there weren't many cars, and the phones didn't work. You felt cut off from the world. One time at the co-op I asked for lasagna sheets, and the clerk yelled, 'Have we got any Lazy Annies?'" She began to laugh. "And another clerk yelled, 'No, but I think they're coming in tomorrow!' " She smacked her forehead with an open hand.

"But getting back to the Geraghtys," she said, "I never even heard of the name Geraghty until I came here. There are some Geraghtys in Roscommon, but there aren't that many in the rest of Ireland."

Seamus, who had seemed content to let his poet wife speak for the clan, stirred and cleared his throat. "My grandfather's name was James Geraghty," he began in a sonorous voice, "and he was from Cross. He had two wives, and the first one died in the famous flu of either 1917 or 1918." He paused, giving the impression that he was a man who chose his words with care. "The first wife, Anne Toole, is a good story. She worked for the local landlord, Thomas Crampton. . . ."

Edith jumped in. "And she was the first woman in Erris to have a bicycle!"

A nd so began the story of Anne Toole.

"See that collapsed building?" Edith Geraghty had crossed the room and was pointing out the window.

From my parlor chair I scanned the surrounding farms and hills, which were leached of color by a slate gray sky. A half mile or so distant, in the direction of the Carne banks, there was an intersection of old stone walls. A ruin.

"That's where Thomas Crampton lived," Seamus said.

"Thomas Crampton," Edith explained, "was the landlord who owned all the land here. He wasn't one of the worst landlords. He treated his people well. He also had holdings down in Rossport, and when he came here to build his estate he brought most of his Rossport staff with him. And one of the members of his household staff was a woman called Anne Toole."

Another Anne, I thought.

"Anne Toole was very young and very capable," Edith continued in a lilting storyteller's voice, "and the people here were jealous of her relationship with Crampton because they could see that he favored her. So they started spreading rumors that there was something inappropriate happening between herself and Crampton. This put young Anne in an awkward position, living under the roof of a powerful, married man. So she went to Crampton and said, 'I have to leave your service. I want to be married, I want to have family and children, but if I stay with you much longer, no man will take me.'

"Crampton understood her position, he was a decent man. But he didn't want to give satisfaction to those who were spreading the rumors. So he said to her, 'If you stay with me for one year, I will build a house for you and provide a dowry. At the end of the year, you will have every man in the area queuing up to be your suitor.'

"So, just down the road"—Edith turned to her husband—"how many yards, Seamus?"

"A few." He shrugged. "A short walk."

"A short walk down the road, Crampton built Anne Toole a two-story house. Which was unheard of, at the time. And he furnished the house from top to bottom, every room. And he gave her a *bicycle*." Edith pointed at the wall behind me, which was covered with family photographs in attractive frames. "There's a photograph there of Anne Toole and the bicycle."

Seamus got up and moved a table to the side so I could get a better look at the sepia portrait, which showed a slender young woman in a buttoned-to-the-neck shirtwaist dress standing with her two-wheeler.

"He also signed over a farm of—" She looked to Seamus again.

"Oh . . . sixty acres."

"Sixty acres! And unusually for the time, he put the land in her name. It was *her* land, *her* house. So that part came true. And sure enough, at the end of the year there were suitors from all over Erris who came to win the hand of Anne Toole."

Seamus and I returned to our chairs while Edith gathered herself for the second act.

"One of the suitors was James Geraghty of Cross," she continued, "and James Geraghty was renowned for being something of an oddball. He *read*. He *wrote*. He discussed things that people had no understanding of. And he was a Geraghty man, in that he was tall and good looking, like yourself." Edith flashed a smile. "He was obviously a charming, erudite man, and he must have reminded Anne of what she was used to in Thomas Crampton, who was himself a man of education."

"Was there a serious rival for Anne's hand?" I asked, suspecting that there would be.

"Yes, a Keane man," Edith said, pronouncing it "Kane" with enough emphasis to suggest a road show villain with a waxed mustache. "When this Keane man heard about Anne Toole's property and land, he determined that he was going to get it for himself. He saw courting her as almost buying a prize cow or something."

"He had a very high opinion of himself," Seamus said, adding, "It's quite funny, actually. The person we're talking about was a man called Michael Keane, and he was my mother's uncle. Her name was Bridget Keane."

And the wife of John Geraghty of Aughleam, I surprised myself by remembering, was a Keane.

"Michael bitterly resented the fact that he had lost her hand," Edith said, "but as I said, the lads came from miles around to court Anne Toole and her considerable dowry. And along comes James Geraghty, a very tall, good looking man from Cross. And it was James she chose from all the suitors. James married Anne Toole and moved into her two-story house, and by all accounts they were very happy and very much in love. They had nine children, eight of whom survived."

"One little girl died of an infection at the age of nine," Seamus murmured.

"And then"—Edith looked toward the portrait on the wall—"Anne died tragically."

She paused again, letting the words sink in.

"She died in the famous flu pandemic of 1918," Seamus said, "the one that killed about fifty million people worldwide." I nodded, guessing that it was the same pandemic that had ravaged New York City, taking the life of one Mary Byrnes Garrity, a runaway mom.

"She actually died of complications after a stillbirth," Edith said, "but that won't be on her birth certificate. In any event, Seamus' grandfather lost all reason. He took to the drink in a bad way, and he smashed and wrecked the house. James never really came to terms with the fact that she was gone.

He did remarry shortly after, in about a year, but that was because—no disrespect to Seamus' grandmother—it was simply because in those days men were not allowed to raise their own children. They were seen as incapable of doing that. So Seamus' grandmother and James were a 'made match' as opposed to a 'love match.' But she was a lovely woman, Ellen Kilker, and she and James had three children together."

"Charlie, Mick, and my dad," Seamus said.

"There's a ghost story, too," Edith continued, "in that old Jimmy the Bridge and Martin—" She held up a hand, realizing that she had gotten ahead of herself. "As I said, Irish men were not seen to be able to raise their children. One of the sons, Martin, was taken to Cross to be raised, and James had three other sons—Jack, Anthony, and Jimmy the Bridge, who was called that because he lived by the old bridge to the Mullet. James was crazy with grief when Anne died, so he'd go to the pub at night and leave the older children alone in the house. It was a very dark place, as you can imagine—a country place with lots of noises, storms and things like that. So the boys would be very frightened. But they remembered this woman who came and tucked them in and sang them to sleep. They remembered this clearly and concretely, but there *was* no neighbor woman, nobody who admitted doing this." Now it was Edith who was leaning forward. "So they became convinced that it was the ghost of their mother who had come back to look after them in their distress. They couldn't remember her face, but they remembered her touch on their cheeks as she tucked them in and the sound of her voice as she sang them to sleep."

Edith fell silent, her sense of theatricality requiring a pause.

"What happened to James Geraghty?" I asked.

"He drank himself to death," she said, looking pleased that she had married into such a good story.

Seamus got to his feet and crossed the room to show me another framed photograph, a Geraghty family portrait from the 1920s. "This little fellow's my dad," he said, pointing out a boy at the far left of the grouping. "Everyone called him Pat."

I leaned in for a closer look. A tall, rugged-looking man in work clothes stood outside a farmhouse next to a tiny, weary-looking woman and four boys. The barefoot boy on the left, who might have been six or seven, had on short pants and a collarless tunic over a long-sleeved shirt. He had big ears and light brown hair combed into bangs. And he looked a lot like a little American boy who used to run around after his older brother and father as they hit plastic golf balls in a Kansas City park.

He looked a lot like me.

CHAPTER 32

My father didn't tell me how to live; he lived and let me watch him do it.
—Clarence Budington Kelland

Mary Walsh phoned me from the golf shop one morning. "I hope I didn't bother you," she said, "but there's a couple from New Richmond who just stopped by. They read about you in the New Richmond newspaper, and they're wondering if you're related to the Geraghtys in Ardowen."

I stopped loading the dishwasher and walked with my mobile to the glass doors overlooking the docks. The day was gray and blustery, and I had planned to spend it with my feet up on the couch. "Have they made the turn?" I asked. "What time do you think they'll finish?"

"Oh, they're not playing. They just came to the club on the chance that you might be around."

"They're there right now?" I hurried into the hallway and snatched my rain jacket off the hook. "Don't let them leave. Tell them I'll be there in five minutes."

Six minutes later, I pushed through the double doors of the Hackett Lounge and found Jim and Nancy Gleason having tea at a table by the windows. "Sorry," I said, "traffic held me up."

They were a fortyish couple, amiable, unhurried and dressed for practical tourism. They no longer lived in New Richmond, Jim explained, but twenty miles away in Baldwin, where the motto was "the Biggest Little Town in Wisconsin." But they still subscribed to the *New Richmond News*, and Jim's dad owned a New Richmond construction company. Their Geraghty connection was also solid. Nancy's mother was a Mary Agnes Geraghty, and her maternal grandfather was one Patrick Geraghty, who had sailed from Liverpool in 1904 on the steamship *Teutonic*. "He had twenty dollars in his pocket when he came into Ellis Island," Nancy said. Her grandfather had found his way to St. Paul, Minnesota, where he lost an eye in an accident.

"My uncle Mersh lost a leg in a train accident," I said, hoping that my remark didn't come off as one-upmanship.

"My uncle, Jack Garrity, was in the Battle of the Bulge," she continued. "He grew up on a farm outside Eden Prairie."

"My dad was a Jack Garrity, too!"

We went on in that vein for a few minutes, trading nuggets of family history without ever striking genealogical gold. My great-grandfather Michael had fled Ireland a good sixty-five years before her grandpa Patrick did, and there was no indication that their descendants had ever met. But I found her details no less interesting, especially when I learned that she had tracked her Geraghtys to Ardowen, which was no more than a good walk from Edith and Seamus' cottage in Gladree.

"I wanted to see where my grandparents came from," Nancy said. "So we went out to see the Termoncarra graveyard, and we were told there wouldn't be any tombstones. All they did back then was put a rock down."

"Well"—Jim snorted—"there's rocks all over!" And none of them, apparently, had the name Patrick Geraghty chiseled on them.

Still, they had gleaned enough to pass muster with Nancy's sister, who was a math teacher in Somerset, Wisconsin, the frog-legs capital of the upper Midwest. "She's a genealogy buff," Nancy said. "She has a book about the Geraghtys and a bunch of photos." Her eyes lit up. "Speaking of which . . . would you mind if we take your picture holding up the New Richmond paper?"

I did not mind, and Sharon, the barmaid, volunteered to take the snapshot. We stepped out onto the flagstone patio and stood against the railing with our backs to the sand hills. Linda, standing in the middle, held up her copy of the *New Richmond News*.

"Smile," said Sharon, peering through the viewfinder.

I spent the rest of the afternoon walking. I started on the docks and strolled up the Ballina Road, which runs along the water, until I reached the ninety-room Broadhaven Bay Hotel—which, second only to the Carne Golf Links, has opened up the Mullet to tourism. Retracing my steps, I walked back to the town square and took a left, which put me on Church Street. I passed the new municipal building, a modern structure of white stucco and glass that houses the council chambers, library, and arts center. I passed the firehouse. I passed an old stone church, boarded-up and forlorn at the back of a weedy lot. I passed the curbed entrances of new subdivisions, where town houses and condos with tile roofs and pick-from-the-catalog door treatments paid tribute to the American cul-de-sac lifestyle.

About a mile out, where the town melted away and the farms rolled gently down to the shore, I turned and looked back across a choppy Blacksod Bay toward the Mullet. Knowing what to look for, I had no trouble making out the bumpy profile of the Carne banks and the clubhouse nestled in its swells.

I stood there for some time. Thinking not of Belmullet, but of another town, another country. Remembering a house on Green Street. Shade trees out front, a garden in back, roses climbing white trellises. Remembering a water tower. Remembering a storefront law office with campaign posters taped to the windows. Remembering a Main Street bowling alley, where someone recognized Dad the minute we came in out of the hot sun. Remembering the summer of sixty-one.

Dad hasn't been home since 1940, when his aunt Jane died. His childhood friends have moved away. His brother Marshall has found a wife and a life in California. "They say you can't go home again," Dad says, driving past the old brick high school. "And I suppose they're right."

He has driven all night from Kansas City with me asleep on the back seat of the Buick. I'm fourteen and growing like a weed. I have to pull my knees up and sleep on my side.

Dad has talked for most of the trip. Talked about books. Talked about the golf swing. Talked about the New Richmond Irish. "Eccentric relatives? I can't think of any." He flicks his cigarette out the car window. It hits the pavement in a shower of sparks. "Oh, I think I know what Terry means. She means Bessie Casey, the spinster older daughter of my aunt Katy. There were two daughters on the Casey side, and they were both kind of nuts." He laughs. "Not nuts, exactly, but reclusive. Bessie Casey graduated from the University of Minnesota and came home, which is what everybody did in those years. She did some teaching. But I remember she got engaged to Gus Stenerud. And then her younger brother Marcus—Mark Casey—he was at the University of Wisconsin, but it was the start of World War I, and like everybody else he and Gus enlisted. Mark came home on leave as a second lieutenant, all set to go, and he was immediately shipped overseas. And he died in Russia. Two days later, Gus Stenerud died."

Dad pauses to light another cigarette with the dashboard lighter.

"Well, in those days, Johnny, women went into a decline when that sort of thing happened. Maybe they still do! But Bessie had a hell of a time. She didn't do anything for years, she was sort of a vegetable. She was very attractive, very quiet, very reserved. And her sister Catherine, that's Tody, came up the same way. It was quite a blow, of course, losing her brother. He was a handsome guy. They called him 'Snoot' Casey because he had a big nose. But they weren't crazy, Johnny. They were just completely withdrawn. They just gave up on life. Well, not Tody. She's been the librarian the last thirty-odd years."

Dad taps the high-beam switch with his toe in preparation for passing a truck. "There are a lot of peculiar people in small towns," he says. "It's normal. You get used to it."

It was a bittersweet journey. Tommy was entered in the St. Paul Open at Maplewood's Keller Golf Course, a parkland layout that my father had played many times. So Dad should have been beside himself with joy. But Tommy had let him know, through letters and long-distance phone calls, that he was not enjoying life as a nomadic golfer. There were money issues—nothing new there—and matters of the heart. Tommy was in love with a

Kansas City girl who, while mindful of his athletic potential, couldn't see herself caring for babies at home while her suntanned hubby played high-dollar skins games in Tucson or Tampa.

This, I hasten to add, was a rational point of view. Jack Nicklaus, the three-time U.S. Amateur champion, had recently turned pro, but only after carefully weighing his potential endorsement earnings against his certain-to-be-substantial income as an insurance broker. Other tour prospects said thanks, but no thanks. Prize money was meager. Only the top thirty and ties got paid, and thirtieth typically got you a handwritten check for fifty or sixty dollars. The other hundred or so players rolled out of town with nothing to show for a week's work but calluses and a bag of dirty laundry.

"Tommy's making noises about quitting the tour," Dad had told me in Kansas City, "and if that's what he wants, I'll support him a hundred percent. But I want to make sure he's considered all the angles. He's worked damned hard to get to where he is."

None of it made sense to me. I followed Dad around with a heavy heart, asking the same questions over and over again. "Is this Tommy's last tournament? . . . Is he going to be an amateur again? . . . Will he have to get a job?" Dad answered as best he could, but there wasn't the usual enthusiasm in his voice.

We stayed at the home of Jamie and Billie Hughes, an old frame house shaded by big trees. They were lawyers who practiced out of a red brick storefront on the other side of Main. Jamie Hughes was a force in the local Democratic Party, and Billie, according to Dad, had been the first woman to pass the Wisconsin bar exam; she later served the town as postmistress and president of the garden club. The walls of their home were lined with books, and Jamie quizzed me on literature. Afterward, I slept upstairs in a hot, pitch-black bedroom on a four-poster bed.

The next day, a Tuesday, was the Fourth of July. Dad wanted to play his old course, so we left at noon and took the short drive west on the highway, turning off at a sign that said NEW RICHMOND GOLF CLUB. Dad parked in a gravel lot by a small clapboard clubhouse. "This is new," he said. "The old clubhouse was . . ." He looked around in confusion. "Well, I don't know where the hell it was, Johnny. It's all turned around."

That was how it went for the next three hours. Dad and I played a nine-hole New Richmond course that he didn't recognize—a course that had somehow grown hillier, doubled in acreage and sprouted grass greens. There were trees—many of them planted by Billie Hughes, I would later learn—but they were just saplings. You could see from one corner of the golf course to the other.

There were lots of holiday golfers, so play was slow.

*D*ad *uses the time between shots to search for landmarks. Something that shows where an old fence used to hold back a cornfield. Something that says "A sand green was here." He finds nothing until we reach the back of the property, where railroad tracks run along a high berm.*

"There's the old Soo Line," Dad says, "so this must be . . ." A smile breaks out on his face. "Well, I'll be damned. Take a look at this, Johnny." He steps onto a patch of concrete that is overgrown with grass. "This would be the old third tee. The hole used to run that way"—he points—"right along the tracks."

*D*ad's discovery of the buried slab satisfied some inner need, and he was soon focusing again on his golf swing and praising mine whenever I hit a solid shot. Afterward, we stopped for a drink in the clubhouse—Schlitz for Dad, Pepsi for me. The Twins baseball game was on a TV behind the bar. A Hamm's beer sign, LAND OF SKY BLUE WATERS, buzzed and flickered on the wall.

We went back to the Hughes house to wash up, and then, at Jamie's suggestion, Dad drove me over to the New Richmond Armory for a picnic and fireworks display. We parked under a tree and walked across the drill field. The sight of families carrying blankets and ice chests got him reminiscing again.

"Everybody worked on Saturday in a small town," he said, "the farmers and everybody else. So Sunday was our only day off. We'd go to early Mass, and I think we were all on the golf course by about a quarter to seven. Well"—he chuckled—"Chuck Harrington and Mersh never played, but everybody else did, Miles McNally and the whole damn bunch. And we were out there for fourteen or fifteen hours, Johnny. We'd just go round and round the nine holes, and I don't remember anybody gambling or betting a nickel on it. You called everybody by their first name, the president of the bank, it didn't matter. Tom Doar, he was a very prominent attorney, and Miles McNally, they played with kids my age. There's that camaraderie in a small town."

Dad stopped and looked around, his voice trailing off.

It was an old-fashioned Fourth. A brass band played, children ran around waving sparklers. It smelled of hamburgers, watermelon and flash powder. But Dad didn't recognize anybody, so we didn't stay long.

Dreaming of (or remembering) my brother's final rounds as a pro. Dreaming of him on a tee, bouncing a ball off the face of his driver. Dreaming of him tugging at his sleeves before addressing the ball, his eyes on the target. Dreaming of his playing partner, Bob Charles—a player of promise who speaks with a New Zealand accent and plays left-handed. Dreaming of (or remembering) a fairway that doglegs right and then right again and then right again. . . .

It was on Thursday, I think, that Dad and I had lunch with Tommy and Dan Sikes in the Keller clubhouse. "Tommy belongs out here," said Sikes, a skinny Floridian who would go on to win six tour events and play for the U.S. in the 1969 Ryder Cup. "He's got the game. His only trouble is he keeps trying to perfect his swing while he's playing." He looked at Tommy, who was ready to concede the point, but couldn't because he had just taken a bite out of his hamburger. "You can't do that when the money's on the line," Sikes said. "You get it in the hole any way you can, even if it's not pretty."

Dad agreed with Dan. My father had no statistics to back it up—no GIRs, Sand Saves or Driving Distances—because no statistics were kept in those days. But Dad had Tommy's record of PGA finishes, which he wrote out in longhand after every tournament and kept in the middle drawer of his desk at the J. B. Garrity Scaffolding Company. At that point in his short career, Tommy had played in sixteen tournaments, finishing twenty-second in the West Palm Beach Open, twelfth at the Coral Gables Open, and thirteenth at the Sunshine Open in Miami Beach. He had also missed eight cuts and failed a number of times in Monday qualifying, the eighteen-hole mini-tournaments that were held for the "rabbits"—those players who had not made the cut the week before or finished high on the previous year's money list. Tommy had played his best golf, Dad pointed out, at the start—on the Florida swing, where he was so busy figuring out how to survive on $200 a week that he didn't have time for lengthy practice sessions.

"Now he's trying to be perfect, and he doesn't need to be," Dad said. "There's a hundred guys out here who'd pay a million bucks for the swing he's got right now."

"I'm one of 'em," Sikes said with a melancholy smile.

After lunch, Tommy went to the range to hit balls. Dad and I went for a drive. We stopped in quaint Stillwater, Minnesota, to look around and then drove along the tree-lined bluffs of the St. Croix River. Pleasure boats dotted the wide channel; children floated in inner tubes and dove off rafts. We crossed a bridge and drove into Wisconsin, where wooded hills gave way to farms that looked like those pictured in my Civics textbook—great swaths of corn and barley punctuated by farmhouses, windmills and silos.

Dad entertained me with his stories of small-town life and the formative years of American golf. The journey home had awakened so many memories for him: riding the blinds to Interlachen to watch George Duncan and Abe Mitchell play an exhibition against Willie Kidd and Jack Burke Sr.; following Bobby Jones at the Minikahda Country Club in Minneapolis as he won the 1927 U.S. Amateur; Jones again at Interlachen in 1930, the year of the Grand Slam. "Johnny, I saw, literally, every shot that he hit in all four rounds," Dad said, "including the famous Lily Pad Shot." The richest corner of Dad's life, next to his children, was reserved for those memories.

The sun was near the horizon when we knocked on Tommy's door at a motor court outside St. Paul. They began their discussion on a bench by the pool, paying no attention to me as I cannonballed off the diving board. They were still talking, two hours later, when I stretched out on one of the beds—the one closest to the air conditioner. I fell asleep to the familiar and comfortable drone of men talking golf.

I woke once or twice, troubled. Their voices were choked with emotion. Dad couldn't accept that Tommy was unhappy on the tour, that it had ceased to be an adventure for him and had become an ordeal. Tommy, for his part, didn't know how to express the paradox—that it was Dad's dependable love, support and pride that made him feel so wretched, that made him feel as if life offered no options beyond draw or fade, punch or lob, go or no-go. "I know how much this means to you," Tommy said, tears streaming down his face. "And it's killing me." It was a line of argument that I would employ with Dad myself, years later, about matters unrelated to golf, but with the same hot tears rolling down my face.

Tommy woke me when the blue light of dawn was showing between the curtains. Dad, not wanting to disturb me, had returned to New Richmond alone.

Friday was sunny and hot, and the galleries at Keller were larger than the day before. There were big names in the tournament, but Dad and I followed a young pro from Kansas City who was tall, graceful, and long off the tee. Dad's eyes devoured every move he made, every shot, as if trying to commit them to memory. "There's never been a better swing in golf," he murmured.

And I agreed. But when it was over, the scoreboard behind the eighteenth green said GARRITY +2. The cut was 145, or plus one.

I don't remember what Dad and I did on Saturday. Drove home, probably.

CHAPTER 33

Standing at the head of a course in the early light of a late-summer day, with the fog lifting and the sheep bleating, grass clippings sticking to the sides of your shoes and the air smelling of damp wool, the golf course is a sanctuary. You wonder: What's in store for me today? *There's hope in your voice, of course. Without hope, there is no golf.*
— from Michael Bamberger's *To the Linksland*

I knew my time in Belmullet was drawing to a close when Halloween decorations began appearing in shop windows and the aroma of peat fires filled the air. I sometimes stopped during a walk and inhaled deeply. Turf-smoke evoked the sweet plumes that rose from barrels of burning leaves in the Kansas City of my childhood.

"I've become addicted to the smell of peat," I told Chris Birrane.

"It's a unique smell," he said with a nod of agreement. "I remember coming home to Ireland, and one of the first smells you encounter getting off the plane is the peat fire. It's thousands of years old, that smell. The Druids would have smelt it when they were waiting for the moon to come out." He sniffed at the air. "I suppose it smells like barbecued grass. There's really no expression that describes it adequately."

It was also, I was sorry to hear, an endangered scent. The European Union, in an effort to enforce clean air standards and preserve boglands, had begun to limit turf exploitation. There would be no more sweet-smelling power stations like the one at Bellacorick, and the sight of farmers stacking the sods and covering them with sheets of plastic was already becoming quaint. "Peat cutting and burning is a thing that will actually die out," Chris said. "That's a bit sad. I would miss it big-time."

As pervasive as the smell of peat was this strange sense that my brother's spirit was in Belmullet. When I stopped at Casey's for a newspaper, I saw Tommy poring over the postcard racks, looking for a card with a castle on it to take back to his wife, Joanne. When I walked through the posh lobby of the Broadhaven Bay Hotel, I saw him grinning at the five clocks on the wall behind the front desk, clocks captioned TOKYO, NEW YORK, SYDNEY, PARIS and BELMULLET. When I played the seventeenth hole, I saw him at the edge of the blowout on the right, his head swiveling between the cavernous pit and the fairway in a pantomime of disbelief.

It struck me as odd—until I remembered that those were the last places I had seen Tommy out of a hospital bed.

Anything could trigger an association. Cleaning my Callaway irons with a wire brush one morning, I remembered the day in October, 2002, when the UPS man had delivered a long, brown box. Inside I found a set of MacGregor Wing MT irons, 1 iron through PW. A half century old, they looked as if they had been shipped straight from the factory.

"Dear Johnny," read the enclosed letter. "I realize that you have no idea what this is, but I will explain."

No explanation was necessary. A set of MT irons was the first full set that Dad had ever owned.

"I found this set in Dallas in 1995," Tommy's letter continued. "It had been sent back to MacGregor to be refinished. It has the original True Temper Dynamic shafts and is an absolutely pure grind. The leading edge is straight all the way past the scoring lines. The heads set up perfectly behind the ball. Pick the club up and you can feel the head. These are Bagger Vance clubs. They are special."

As a kid golfer, he reminded me, he had played with cut-down clubs: a brassie, a Walter Hagen 2 iron, a Wilson 5 iron and a 9 iron from some forgotten manufacturer. One of our neighbors had lent him a 7 iron, and it was with those five clubs and a putter that Tommy had won his first junior golf tournament. *The Kansas City Star* had run a photograph of the golf prodigy and his proud parents.

But it was Dad's MacGregor set of 1952, ordered from the pro shop at the Swope Park Number 1 Course, that made Tommy's pulse race. "I remember when they came in," the letter continued. "We unwrapped them and headed for the first tee. You might remember the old first hole. It was a long par 4 with a deep swale leading uphill to a smallish green on the flat. I remember clearly that my drive ended up on the right side of the fairway, short of the green. How far short I don't recall, but I do recall thinking that it was exactly a 7 iron to the hole. I walked across the fairway, picked out the club from Dad's bag, and walked over to the ball, the whole time thinking, 'I don't have to choke and cut a 5-iron. I can just hit this straightaway.' What a feeling!"

I had no trouble picturing the hole he was describing. When I took up golf again in my thirties, I played regularly at Swope Number 1, now known as Swope Memorial. Only by then the first hole, at 372 yards, was a *short* par 4.

"What you have in this box," he went on, "is that memory, that excitement, and, yes, that wonder—for it was a wonder to me."

Tommy's words made me feel warm and nostalgic—until I reached the paragraph that explained why he had sent the clubs:

"My doctors, being the lighthearted fellows they are, have suggested that I get things in order, just in case the chemo doesn't work out. I don't think it is going to go that way, but I don't want to get sick and have this set go out in some garage sale for $50. I want you to have them. They wouldn't mean anything to Jeff or Anne or even Terry, for that matter. You have to know golf clubs and be a real fan of this series."

I stared at the clubs in the long box as if they had suddenly turned to funeral lilies. My breathing shallowed out. I had trouble swallowing.

"As you can tell," I read, "they have never been hit since they were re-chromed. My aim was to wait until I retired. Then, some beautiful, clear, crisp fall day—with leaves swirling around and the whole bit, just like Dad and I experienced at the time—I would take them out and play a round with them."

I put down the letter and walked to the windows. An autumn sun filtered through the pin oaks and maples, laying patches of gold on the lawn. Across the street, a little boy in a ruby-colored helmet struggled to pedal a bike with training wheels. His big sister gave him assisting pushes with an open palm.

I may have cried.

The next day, another package arrived. This time it was a collector's display case lined with green felt. I hung the MT irons on a wall in our basement rec room. I give them a long look whenever I carry a basket of clothes to the laundry room, and sometimes I take a club down and give it a waggle or two. But I have never hit a golf ball with those irons, and I never will. I am not worthy.

Besides, I have the seventeenth at Carne. I thought of my brother every time I stepped onto the seventeenth tee, whether I was alone at sunset or part of a Sunday foursome. It happened off the course, as well. Asked to autograph a book, I complied by sketching a seventeenth-hole flagstick on the title page. ("It's symbolic.") Assigned by a Web editor to compile a list of favorite golf holes, I came up with the seventeenth at St. Andrews, the seventeenth at Cypress Point, the seventeenth at the TPC at Sawgrass, the seventeenth at Ballybunion, etc., etc., etc. The seventeenth was the *penultimate* hole; which made me wonder if Tommy's talk of shooting 80 on it wasn't an amiable dodge, a way to put off signing his card. He knew he was on his final hole, so to speak, so he fantasized about playing the next-to-last hole at Carne over and over and over again, always out of sight of the clubhouse, never climbing the steep path to the eighteenth tee.

Bellmullet, meanwhile, had begun to feel like home. "We only part to meet again," I told the butcher at the Centra supermarket—a theatrical line, but one that fit the circumstance. I expected the Carne Golf Links to be on my summer calendar for years to come. And if on some cold Missouri morning I wished to hear a familiar voice from Mayo—well, all I had to do was pick up the phone. "No need for an American wake," I told

Eamon Mangan and Frank Healy over dinner at the Phoenix Chinese Restaurant. To which Eamon replied, "Nor a Spanish one, either." (He was looking forward to his semiannual golf holiday on the Costa del Sol.) The Peking Duck, by the way, tasted the same in Belmullet as it did in Kansas City.

I had not yet read Thomas Friedman's *The World Is Flat*, but I had drawn my own conclusions about globalization after meeting Mayoites who had snorkeled on Australia's Great Barrier Reef or slalomed on the mall-enclosed slopes of Ski Dubai. The biggest change, I decided, wasn't that Mullet folk could go to those places—*leaving* was an Irish specialty—but that so many outsiders were suddenly on the Mullet's doorstep, undeterred by the forbidding cliffs and desolate bogs. *Golfers*, not the most adventurous people in the world, could read about the Carne Golf Links in *Sports Illustrated* and book a trip the same day. They could go online to schedule their tee times—and it didn't matter if they were in Tokyo, New York, Sydney, or Paris.

"The Internet has changed our life here," Edith Geraghty told me one night during a play rehearsal. "I get my CDs from Hong Kong, I get my books from Amazon, I get my costumes from New York, and I get my condiments from Harrods of London. Within a week I can have *anything* from *anywhere* delivered to my door."

I was slower to pick up on an aspect of globalization that was personally germane. My look down the golf branches of the family tree had been predicated on the likelihood that I would discover nothing of substance about my Geraghty and Stuart ancestors. Churches had burned, and ships had sunk. Diaries had rotted. The ink on letters had faded, and scorecards had turned to dust. I blamed the Atlantic Ocean, that great genealogical solvent; but the sad fact was, both my bloodlines had backed into the twentieth century with bunker rakes, erasing their footsteps so assiduously that I couldn't tell how many strokes they had taken, or even that they had played. But in the age of the World Wide Web, posterity would not be cheated. The digital family tree, searchable and replicable, would spread its limbs, but its reach would no longer exceed our grasp.

"Put simply," I told Pat in a video chat, "it's going to be hard to lose an ancestor."

Mine, of course, were not entirely lost. The Stuarts of Linlithgow Palace were claimable as progenitors of the golf gene. So, too, was Commander Stuart of Machrihanish, confidant of Old Tom Morris and star witness in the Haskell patent-infringement trial. Furthermore, only the willfully stubborn could fail to see the resemblance between your humble author and Lieutenant J. C. Stewart of the 72nd Highlanders. ("Pleasant legends cluster round his name," wrote Bernard Darwin in his account of an Autumn Medal at the Royal & Ancient. "How he disdained a tee and would throw his ball down on the teeing-ground with a noble gesture and drive it from where it lay; how he dared to play Allan Robertson on level terms and held his own; how Mr. Sutherland exclaimed in agonised tones that it was 'a shame of a man with such powers to go to India.'")

My Irish forebears were more elusive, but only in the sense that I could not nail down a certifiable link to anyone still living on the Mullet. It was suggestive that John Geraghty of Aughleam and George Geraghty of Cross were mainstays of the Belmullet Golf Club, as golfer and greenkeeper respectively. I was equally confident of my kinship with Annie Geraghty of Clogher, based on her astute analysis of given names and her treatment of me as a beloved grandson.

Or was I simply a sucker for a good yarn? Ann Geraghty's phantom-funeral story made my "for the grandkids" file, as did the legend of the Bellacorick musical bridge (told to me by a Kelly, but confirmed by a Geraghty) and Seamus Geraghty's tale of trembling brothers sung to sleep by their mother's ghost.

But it was the Anne Toole courtship story, with its whiff of balladry, that sang *me* to sleep. I felt a visceral connection to Seamus Geraghty's bookish grandfather James, described by Edith as "tall and good-looking, like yourself." The story of James reading a newspaper in the pasture while being pelted with potatoes—wasn't that my story? ("The only difference," I explained to Pat, "is that it's usually the *readers* who are throwing potatoes at me.") And there was that old photograph on the wall of the Geraghty cottage, the photo of a Mullet family with a boy who looked like me.

Edith Geraghty recognized the symptoms. "Irish-Americans are more Irish than the Irish," she told me that night at the rehearsal. "They have more Irish family traditions than we do. So they're disappointed that we have computers and wide-screen televisions. They expect us to be riding around on bicycles or herding sheep." She rolled her eyes. "What you'll find is, so many Irish here want to be American. There was a survey of Irish schoolchildren, and they asked them to sing the national anthem. And you had all these little children going, 'Oh say can you see . . . by the dawn's early light . . .' They could even do the Pledge of Allegiance with the hand on the heart, because they were watching so much American television." She looked up at the stage, where her husband Seamus was running through his lines with another actor. "But I suppose it's always that way when you're from a small country."

I nodded, hoping she didn't think *I* was one of those pathetic Yanks looking for Irish blessings, pennywhistles and golf genes.

But then, apropos of nothing, Edith surprised me with a question: "Did you ever read the P. G. Wodehouse golf stories?"

It turned out that she had. And that was another link.

My goodbyes did not float on tears, but I made the rounds. I squared my apartment and Internet accounts at the *Iorras Domhnann* office on the docks, thanking Geraldine Padden for her cheerful disposition of my endless entreaties. I popped into McDonnells for a 7-Up and to hear Padraig Conroy reprise "I'm the last man to comb your hair if you die." I drove out to the Eagle Inn, where the proprietor, my friend Paddy Lavelle, spoke proudly of his granddaughter Sarah. "She'll be thirteen tomorrow," he said, putting on spectacles to read a message on his mobile phone. "She lives in Castlebar and plays golf for her school, and she shot a sixty-five today." Still reading, he smiled. "She wants to tell me the story."

The farewells at Carne took an entire week, which may have diluted my expressions of gratitude to Mary, Martina and Caroline. I got a predictably voluble response from Chris Birrane when I told him that I had driven up to the Bellacorick Power Station and played a tune on the musical bridge. "I've watched people do it," he said, "and I've laughed so much that I couldn't summon the energy to try it myself. But either I'm absolutely tone deaf or it doesn't play for me. Maybe you have to be foreign to hear it." But mention of the power station reminded him of the time a foursome showed up at Carne, all abuzz over the enormous monolith they had seen while crossing the bog.

"Lovely guys," Chris said. "One of them wanted to know what it was, and I said, 'It's flats. There's a block of flats in there.' They didn't understand. 'Sorry,' I said. '*Apartments*. People live there.' The guy said, 'Really? In the tower?' I said, 'Yes, but they forgot to put windows in. It got too dark and people were getting sick, so they had to close it down.' The guy said, 'Could they not break windows out of it?' I said, 'No, they were afraid the whole thing would fall down. That's why you don't see any high rises around here. It didn't work out.'"

Chris took a puff on his cigar. "I walked away, but when I looked back I saw him talking to his mates, and I don't know if he was saying it was an apartment building up there or 'That's a *lunatic* on the tee.'" He gave his cigar a contemplative look. "But lovely guys."

The honorary secretary and his wife wanted to give me a proper send-off, so I drove down to the end of the peninsula one evening for dinner and star-gazing at their home by the sea. The Swinsons' little white cottage had two chimneys, an ancient tile roof, and a sandy beach so proximate that storm surges had left the previous owner's cattle in water up to their knees. "You can see what life must have been like a hundred years ago," Terry said, watching the setting sun drip honey on the looming profile of Achill Island. "God, it was grim."

Nicóla, a lithe and blithe spirit who still worked as a BBC news editor in Belfast—picture Holly Hunter ducking under the file drawer in *Broadcast News*—grilled some steaks while Terry showed me around the house. In a back room, where he fulfilled his golf-secretary duties, I noticed a music case leaning against the wall. "It's the old cello I used to play," he said with a dismissive shrug. "I gave up music when I took up golf."

After dinner, which ended with me practically groveling for a second slice of Nicóla's apple tart, Terry hauled out his refracting telescope and set it up in the front doorway, out of the wind. Nicóla turned off the room lights.

"There's a chance we might actually see a star," Terry said, aiming the big cylinder at a sky of broken clouds and a peekaboo moon. But after several minutes of peering into the viewfinder and making adjustments, he declared the atmosphere too unsettled for his five-hundred-magnification scope. "If you're an astronomer and a golfer in Ireland, you'll do better as a golfer," he joked. "You're only frustrated 90 percent of the time as a golfer.

"At least you can see the moon," he added, stepping aside to let me look. I bent over the eyepiece and got a bright eyeful of lunar magic, a landscape of craters, plains and arid seas that winked whenever an edge of cloud passed over. "All I'm showing you is eight magnification," he said by way of apology. "Nothing."

"No," I said, fixated on my great-grandfather's moon. "It's something."

The next morning, I skimmed the papers, paying special attention to WOMAN HAD NO DOG LICENSES and ENNISCRONE MAN SHOOK GARDA BY HIS UNIFORM. I then walked over to the tackle shop to top off my mobile phone. I stood in line behind a young American woman, a backpacker, who was asking about signal strength on Achill. "I have to take an important call tomorrow," she said. "I won't go if I can't use my phone." She sounded stressed.

After that, I drove out to the Termoncarra cemetery, on a hilltop above the sea. There were two parts to the cemetery. Behind a low wall was a modern graveyard with polished headstones and floral tributes. Farther up the hill was your basic boneyard. Ancient graves lay under collapsed walls and rubble. Clumpy grass and wildflowers filled the gaps. The stones in the boneyard bore no epitaphs; they spoke of a time when death outran memory.

The view was stunning, a panorama of sea, mountain, farm and bay. Cattle grazed in the ruins of the old Crampton estate, just down the hill. Beyond that, in a valley dotted with farm houses, I spotted the green cottage of Seamus and Edith Geraghty. Farther still was Annagh Head and the Eagle Island lighthouse.

It didn't take me long to find the Geraghty plot. There was a red granite headstone engraved with a haloed Jesus and the initials R.I.P.

IN LOVING MEMORY OF
ANNE GERAGHTY
TERMONCARRA

DIED 2ND FEB 1917 AGE 38
JAMES GERAGHTY
DIED 22ND NOV 1956 AGE 78
ERECTED BY THEIR LOVING
SON MARTIN AND FAMILY

I picked up a few bits of white gravel that had escaped the bed. Like a lazy golfer in a bunker, I smoothed the gravel with my foot.

The sound of a man yelping made me look up. Down the hill, a brawny farmer was driving about a dozen cows out a gate and onto the road, waving a rope to discourage any who would try to escape. Beyond the cattle, no more than a mile or two away, I noticed a rugged line of dunes, canyons, and sand-filled craters. *That,* I said to myself, *would make a great site for a golf course.* Then I realized: it was the ocean side of the Carne banks. If I squinted, I could just make out a ribbon of fairway tumbling down to the sea. The ribbon disappeared near a raised piece of ground that looked as if it had been flattened with a trowel—the twelfth green? That meant that the low-lying strip along the shore had to be the par-5 thirteenth. Which meant . . .

My eyes darted back to the green ribbon that had first caught my eye. It wasn't tumbling down to the sea. It was climbing *from* the sea, disappearing behind one of the tallest dunes.

The green ribbon was the seventeenth fairway at Carne.

CHAPTER 34

The seventeenth hole, from the MetLife blimp, is a polished ridge of green, bent like a boomerang, transversing the blistered terrain of the Carne banks. Deep pools of shadow surround islands of marron grass; pale craters wink like reflections of the moon. At the edge of the frame, a gradient of deep purple, blue, and violet melds into surging ranks of sea foam and yellow, shimmering sand. The blues flee as the camera tightens on a rectangular patch of green, where a solitary figure stands in rugged repose like stout Cortez, facing the dunes and destiny.

—Author's fantasy

That's how it was, give or take a blimp, on the afternoon of October 22, 2007. I stood on the seventeenth tee in the golden radiance of a five o'clock sun, feeling the breeze like a feather on the back of my neck. I smelled the pungent perfume of sea salt, cut grass and peat. I heard the lowing of cattle and the cry of a seagull.

"Three-under bogey," murmured the announcer in my head. "Six holes to play."

Thirteen days had passed since darkness had forced me to suspend the Seventeenth Hole Challenge in midround. I told myself that there was no meaning in the delay. Certain afternoons had been too windy. Others had been cloudy. (I wanted to wrap up my 90 on a seventeenth hole flooded with sunlight.) On a couple of occasions, I had driven out to the course with my clubs in the trunk, only to remember that I was out of Tesco brand shortbread or had forgotten to collect a packing carton at Mangan's Furniture.

But time was running out. If I delayed further, I might forfeit my choice of hour and setting.

So . . . this was the hour. This was the setting.

I teed up ball number one and smoked it down the left side and over the cliff.

I teed up ball number two and sliced it along the precipice and back into the fairway.

I teed up ball number three and drilled it down the middle.

"That last one was crushed," said the announcer in my head. "I don't think he'll have more than a seven iron into the green."

I shouldered my bag and set off down the path into the ravine, the sun warm on my back.

Why do we play? That's my question. I throw the ball, swing the club, make the tackle, plant the pole, and afterward all I can say is, "Because it's fun." Or if I'm a coach, "Because it teaches teamwork and builds character." Or if I'm a general: "Discipline!"

Christopher Lasch, the historian and social critic, had a better answer. "The essence of play," he wrote, "lies in taking seriously activities that have no purpose, serve no utilitarian ends. . . . Games simultaneously satisfy the need for free fantasy and the search for gratuitous difficulty."

You don't cite Christopher Lasch, of course, when you're standing over a sidehill four-footer for a double-bogey 6. I took a deep breath, gave the ball a tentative tap with my putter, and watched the putt slide and die a foot short of the hole. Disgusted, I tapped in for a 7.

Ball number two, which had started its journey in the fairway, now lay three feet from the hole in four. I looked at this putt from all sides, saw no break at all, and gave it a nice firm rap—so firm that the ball hit the right side of the hole and spun out.

I didn't make a sound, didn't move. I just stared at the hole, a great hairball of despair filling my gut.

Ball number three gave me reason for hope. Nine feet below the hole, it lay two after a 6-iron approach so good that I would have paid to have it preserved on film. "A birdie here will get him back to 2 under bogey," said the voice in my head, to which I added, sotto voce, "Just don't leave it short."

I didn't. With clenched teeth and a brain on cruise control, I hammered it through the break, four feet past the hole.

Every golfer knows the feeling. My chest tightened. My field of vision collapsed like a dying star. My ears burned. The voice in my head, no longer an announcer, began to race through the dodges: *These balls don't count, they were a warm-up. Tomorrow is the real deal.*

I straightened up and looked around. There were no witnesses. The surrounding dunes stood tall and mute, indifferent to my plight.

I looked at the ball, four feet above the hole. I walked toward it slowly, staring at *it* and not at the line of the putt. And yes, I may have bent from the waist as I passed the hole and reached down as if to pick something up. But I didn't. I brushed some invisible fluff off my pants and kept walking until I was ten feet or so behind the ball.

I turned. I crouched. I studied the line.

Then, with steady hands, I rolled the putt. The ball veered toward the pit, caught the low edge of the hole, and curled in.

My heart racing, I fished my business card and Marriott pen out of my pocket and jotted down the scores:

5) 7-6-4 (2 IN F, 1L/3PT, 6I/9' 2PT).

The dunes looked on, unimpressed.

On the walk back to the tee with my bag, I considered my options. One, I could postpone the final three balls for a day or two, during which time I could settle my nerves and read up on the great chokers in golf history. Two, I could hit a single tee shot and then, if I liked it, hit another. Three, I could walk too close to the edge of the fairway, lose my balance, and topple into the ravine. (I pictured the Japanese golfer looking down at my writhing body and saying, "Screwed!") Four, I could quit.

That was a pretty appealing option, quitting. After all, I hadn't *boasted* that I could shoot 90 on the seventeenth hole. It would cost me nothing to shrug at the end of my sabbatical and tell my Irish friends, "Couldn't do it. Tough hole."

But if admitting failure was so easy, why was I so afraid of actually failing? Assuming I played the final three balls as if nothing had happened (option five), there were only two possible outcomes: I would either shoot 90 or not shoot 90. Clearly, the only reasonable choice was the one that gave me the opportunity to succeed.

To give myself a little more time, I stood my bag up behind the markers on the seventeenth tee and scrambled up and around the dune overlooking sixteen's amphitheater green. There were no golfers in the grassy bowl, which was filling with shadow, or high up on the terraced tees on the opposite ridge. I spotted some movement in the dune slack below the fifteenth green—a red fox scampering up the slope, his bushy tail flaring in the sunlight.

I couldn't explain my nervousness. Less than a year before, I had walked with Tiger Woods up fairways lined with spectators. I had felt thousands of eyes on me. Could anything be more terrifying for a twelve-rounds-a-year dilettante with no tournament experience? And yet, I had stepped inside the ropes with minimal trepidation and played my usual game. *Three times*, I reminded myself, the great man had said, "Good swing there!"

My inner voice provided the obvious rejoinder: *That was a scramble. You had teammates. Your bad shots didn't count.*

I reached into my pocket and pulled out the *SI* business card. The corners were crimped from repeated handling. The printed side was red and white. The back was covered with handwritten numbers and glyphs. There was just enough room at the bottom for the judgment of posterity.

Pocketing the card, I walked back around the dune to the tee. I dropped three balls on the grass and turned to face the Atlantic. A distant freighter was outlined in the dazzling shimmer around Inishglora. The contrail of a high-flying jet pointed toward America, its white plume fluffing out like the fox's tail.

I needed more time. I walked behind the tee and started climbing the big dune. A few minutes on its peak, I thought, might reveal some deeper truth. It was on such summits, after all, that barefoot, wrinkled gurus sat cross-legged on their mats, ready to dispense The Meaning of Life. (A comedian's version, which my brother especially liked, had the wise man saying, "Wet Birds Fly at Night.")

I was atop the dune within seconds, and what I found there surprised me: a gleaming white golf ball. It was surprising because the peak wasn't much wider than a desktop. Padraig Harrington himself couldn't have gotten his ball to stop up there, assuming he hit it from two hundred yards away at the twelfth tee, the ball's only conceivable point of origin. But there it was, sitting on a flattened patch of marron grass like a pearl on a pillow.

I picked the ball up, half expecting the dune to start shaking and rocks to begin toppling, à la Indiana Jones. It was a shiny new Titleist NXT Tour ball, unblemished except for the owner's identifying mark: one green dot. Was it an offering to the golf gods, placed atop the dune by an Irish hand? Or had one of the ravens from Erris Head flown down from the cliffs, plucked it off a green and borne it through the sky?

Whatever its provenance, the ball spoke to me. It spoke to me in my brother's voice. *You know what I'd like to do?* it said. *I'd like to play the seventeenth at Carne with three balls in my pocket. I'd hit three tee shots, play all three balls into the green, and then hole them all out for a score. Then I'd go back to the tee and do it again. I'd play the hole six times with three balls until I'd played eighteen holes. I think 80 would be a great score.*

Eighty! Not 90. The ball was telling me that our worst fears wait at the threshold of success. The ball was telling me that we are doomed not by our actual shortcomings, but by our failure to seize the opportunities that come our way. Sometimes, in our pursuit of gratuitous difficulty, we fly too close to the sun.

There was no way, of course, that I could shoot 80 on the seventeenth hole at Carne. But I decided, at that moment, that 85 would be a great score.

Clutching the ball, I scrambled down the dune and pulled the driver from my bag. I went to the three balls I had dropped on the grass and swept them aside with my foot. For my first attempt, I teed up the Titleist with the green dot.

"He's got no shot at 85," murmured the announcer in my head. "But if he can bogey the last three holes he'll be the leader in the clubhouse at 89."

Stepping behind the ball, I bent down for a pinch of grass, tossed it in the air, and watched the blades spin and drift on the breeze, their sunny sides flashing like little bars of gold.

EPILOGUE

A six-year-old asks a lot of questions.

On the first green, for example, Jack looked up in surprise when his ball rattled in the cup.

"Do you like that sound?" I asked.

"I like it!" He took the ball out of the hole and dropped it back in, producing another rattle. He grinned. "How does it do that?"

I gave him a scientific explanation. "There's a hollow space at the bottom. It acts as a resonator, magnifies the sound."

A few holes later, when we stopped to let a fast-playing threesome through, my grandson stared in fascination as one of the young men kept a ball bouncing off the face of his wedge, à laTiger Woods. Jack turned to me again. "How does he do that?"

"Practice," I said. I thought of a certain touring pro who bounced a ball off the face of his driver at the 1961 St. Paul Open.

It was dinnertime in New Richmond—and six hours since we had left my dad's ashes in the parish cemetery—but there was still an hour of sunlight left. The yellow flags on the nine-hole Links course stirred to a lazy breeze, and bits of dandelion fluff floated by like specks in a snow globe. The domes of silos sparkled on distant hills.

Jack Olsen had hit a golf ball before—on the practice ground at Carne, during my sabbatical. But this was his first time playing golf. He had just the one club, an Accu-Length hybrid 4 with a black graphite shaft. "This is a very cool club," I told him in the first fairway. "As you get taller, you can add spacers to make the shaft longer. You won't have to use cut-down clubs."

He looked up. "What are cut-down clubs?"

My own clubs were strapped to the back of the electric cart. I wasn't going to play, but I thought I might drop a ball from time to time and hit a shot. Otherwise, I was Jack's caddie, swing coach, and audience. Mostly the latter, because Jack, with his wavy blond hair and endearing smile, was a very cute kid. He was dressed for golf (or tree climbing) in a green T-shirt, khaki pants and sneakers. He ran to his ball after every shot.

So he wouldn't be overwhelmed, I had Jack tee off from the fairways, fifty to a hundred yards from the greens. He whiffed his first tries, swinging so hard that he spun like a top. At my suggestion, he changed tactics, advancing the ball with little chip swings—*click, click, click*—until he was on the green. The same technique worked for putting; after six or seven tentative pokes he got to hear that sweet rattle.

When we got to the third hole, I dropped a ball in the fairway, pulled my 7 iron from the bag, and said, "Watch this, Junior."

"Junior?" He giggled. "My name is Jack!"

I choked up on the club and smacked a low punch shot that looked good in the air but landed short-right in a greenside bunker. That gave me the opportunity to teach bunker etiquette and raking, a lesson that Jack took to heart. On the very next hole he ran to the edge of a bunker and yelled, "Hey, I found some footprints! So I'm gonna rake 'em!"

While Jack raked, I leaned on a club and looked around. The New

Richmond Links, built in 1998 to provide a cheaper and less-challenging alternative to the eighteen-hole members' course, had the open aspect and gentle mounding of an Irish town course. The Links also bore a fortuitous resemblance to the sand-greens golf course my dad had helped build in the 1920s. The first hole ran due south with a rail fence and the County K highway on the left side. The south side of the course bordered a wider highway, Business 64. The fifth hole, a par 4, ran north again with a horse pasture hugging the left side. The seventh hole, also a par 4, stretched east along a dead-end stretch of farm road. I could almost hear my dad saying, "Here's the tee, and here's the fence and the cornfield, and nobody but an idiot is going to aim at the cornfield. . . ."

Funny thing, though. The Links, unlike the original New Richmond course, had an extra green and nine alternate tees. That made it reversible—that is, it could be played either clockwise or counterclockwise. Every Thursday, when the greenkeeper moved the tee markers, the first hole became the ninth, the second became the eighth, and so forth. I'm sure the course designer, Joel Goldstrand, got the idea from the Old Course at St. Andrews, Scotland, which was bidirectional until the 1870s, and which still allows backward play a few days per year. But he could just as easily have been designing for my dad, who would have seen reversibility as an ingenious solution to the everybody-slices paradigm of his youth.

"Hey, Papa!" Jack was waving to get my attention. "Watch this!" He took a swing and got one airborne, the ball landing in the right rough. "Hooray! It went up in the air!"

I paced off the distance to his ball. "Twenty-six yards. Not bad, Jack." The rough was thick, so I kicked his ball back to the fairway.

"Papa, is golf hard to learn?" He looked up at me with trusting eyes.

"Not really," I lied. "But it's hard to get really good at it."

"Was your father a good player? As good as you?"

"Oh, much better than me. I can hit it farther, but I never beat him."

"Was your brother really, really, *really* good?"

I nodded. "Yeah, Jack, he was."

I dropped a ball and hit an approach shot with my sand wedge. The ball covered the flag all the way and took one little hop upon landing, snuggling up close to the pin.

"Good one, Papa!" He ran over to give me a belt-high hug and then ran off again.

Smiling, I went to my bag, unzipped the top pouch and took out a divot-repair tool. Then, instead of zipping up the pouch, I slipped my fingers in again, felt around, and extracted a business card. The card's edges were frayed from handling, and it had a wilted look. I flipped the card over. The back was covered with weathered scribbles—tiny numbers, glyphs and a penciled date: OCT. 23, 2007. In the bottom-right corner, boldly circled, was the number 89.

I stared at the card for a moment, remembering. Then I slipped it back into the pouch and pulled the zipper.

We played on, my grandson and I, as the sun neared the horizon. Birdsong carried from the surrounding pastures, chirps and warbles that rang out like grace notes over the bowed tones of tires on pavement. At one point I asked Jack to look around. "Does it remind you of anyplace?"

"Yes," he said. "The golf course in Ireland."

On the sixth tee we let the threesome play through, and then Jack teed his ball up and hit a scorcher that flew thirty yards. Delighted with the shot, he ran to the end of the tee, picked up his ball, and brought it back for another try. His second attempt also flew thirty yards.

On the seventh hole I hit a knockdown 6 iron that released perfectly and rolled to a back-left hole location. "I see your ball," Jack sang, jumping up and down. "It's white. It's a white dot."

On the par-5 eighth I tried the knockdown shot again, only this time I pulled it badly. So I was up by the green, searching for my ball, when I looked back and saw Jack taking a swing from the fairway. He caught this one flush, and his ball flew high and long, carrying to the apron and bouncing onto the green.

"Papa! Did you see that?"

He started toward me, but I waved him back. "Stay there! I want to measure that." I hustled back down the fairway and then walked off Jack's shot as he trotted by my side. ". . . Thirteen, fourteen, fifteen. . . . Twenty-one, twenty-two . . . Thirty-three, thirty-four, thirty-five . . ." until I reached his ball with an exaggerated last step and a triumphant shout: "Forty-two!"

Jack beamed, but then his smile faded, as if he had some inherited understanding of golf's tenacious grip. "Papa," he said, "I'm starting to get good at golf. *Really* good."

At that very moment, a train whistle sounded in the distance. It came from beyond the wooded hill to our east, possibly from the spot where the Soo Line tracks skirted a stand of tall spruces at the corner of an old golf course.

I started to say something, but Jack had picked up his ball and was running toward the ninth tee.

ACKNOWLEDGMENTS

The inspiration for this most personal of books came from my literary agent, David McCormick, who thought I should write on one or two of the following topics: golf in Ireland, my golf-mad dad, sand-greens golf in Wisconsin, my tour player brother, Irish folktales, my life as a range rat, the Carne Golf Links, my six pro-am holes with Tiger Woods, and golf ghosts. He could not have anticipated that I would try to cram all of his good ideas into one book.

The book itself would not exist without the encouragement and support of Mark Chait, my editor at New American Library. Mark managed to crack the whip over this most sluggish of memoirists without ever causing offense—although he never explained to my satisfaction why I couldn't take two years to write a first draft and another year to check my facts and play golf in Ireland. Thanks also to NAL's Talia Platz, who guided me through the production maze, and to Edith Geraghty of Gladree, Mayo (and chapter 31), who graciously consented to check the manuscript for Erris errors, Mayo malapropisms and Gaelic gaffes.

No one will mistake this for a work of scholarship, but I did spend a few days with my elbows on a desk. My research on the golfing Stuarts got an early assist from Nancy Stulack, the librarian at the United States Golf Association Museum in Far Hills, New Jersey. For help with the

Wisconsin Garritys I turned to the Area Research Center at the University of Wisconsin–River Falls (thank you, Melissa Janz Barbey) and to Father James Brinkman and his staff at New Richmond's Immaculate Conception Church (thank you, Mike Bernd, for your help with the interment, and thank you, Patti Davis Leaf, for letting me examine nineteenth-century parish registers, including those scorched in fires). For New Richmond history I leaned heavily on the New Richmond Heritage Center and its tireless curator-author, Mary Sather.

The New Richmond Golf Club doesn't have (or need) an archivist, but I benefited from my father's unpublished writings and from the two or three hours of his oral history that I recorded in the eighties. Club member Tom Doar furnished me with a wealth of additional materials, including Don Reppe's thirty-page monograph "The New Richmond Golf Club: A History."

My Irish golf studies took me outdoors, but it was still research—even when I banged around the Carne banks with *Sports Illustrated* senior writer Gary Van Sickle or *Philadelphia Daily News* sportswriter Mike Kern. Both those guys visited Carne at my invitation, and both kept me laughing for the duration of their stays. I also owe a debt of gratitude to Geraldine Padden, Mary Niland and Mary Togher of *Iorras Domhnann*, who found me my dockside flat, hooked me up to telephone and broadband and answered all my questions when I dropped in unannounced at their offices in the old Angling Clubhouse.

A simple thanks won't do for Eamon Mangan and the staff at Carne, but I offer it anyway. Thank you, Mary Walsh, Martina Mills, Caroline Kilker, Chris Birrane, John Birrane, Gary Stanley and George Geraghty— for answering my unending questions and for letting me roam the course at will. Thank you, as well, to honorary secretary Terry Swinson, honorary treasurer Liam McAndrew, president Frank Brogan, Captain Sean Doherty, ladies' captain Geraldine Gallagher, and all the other members of the Belmullet Golf Club. I am proud to wear your cap and proud to have the four-swans medallion dangling from my golf bag. To paraphrase old Myles McNally, I executed some sort of jump during my time with you, sinking deep into the magic of the Carne banks. So now I say: *There, where my footprints are—there, no matter where I am, my heart will always be.*

(This page constitutes an extension of the copyright page:)

The author gratefully acknowledges permission to reprint the following copyrighted material:

One verse and one line of the chorus from the song "American Wake" by Brent Hoad, Eldorn Pub Music.

Lyrics from "Don't Let Me Come Home a Stranger." Words and Music by Robin Williams and Jerome Clark. Copyright © 1983 Songs of PolyGram International, Inc., and Brantford Music. International Copyright Secured. All Rights Reserved.

Photo by Fred Vuich/*Sports Illustrated*

John Garrity, a senior writer at *Sports Illustrated,* has covered more than 150 golf tournaments for the magazine since 1989. The Golf Writers Association of American Award winner is a regular contributor to publications such as *Golf Magazine* and *Travel + Leisure,* and he has authored and coauthored more than a dozen books, including *Tour Tempo* and *Tiger 2.0.* He lives in Kansas City, Missouri, with his wife, Pat, a church liturgist.